Practicing Positive CBT

Praise for *Practicing Positive CBT*

"*In reading Practicing Positive CBT there is a sense of being in the presence of a gifted, engaging, enthusiastic and inspiring therapist. The book practices what it preaches in supporting therapists to become more effective and successful, and I suspect enjoying their work along the way.*"

Professor Willem Kuyken
University of Exeter, UK

"*Practicing Positive CBT offers the best constructive vision to date of what CBT can look like when joined with positive psychology and solution focused brief therapy approaches. Bannink highlights positive therapy methods already embedded in CBT and offers a wealth of practical suggestions for how CBT therapists can become more positive in every aspect of therapy. Whether dipping into particular chapters for creative inspiration or studying this book cover to cover, therapists of all experience levels will find value on every page.*"

Christine A. Padesky, PhD
Center for Cognitive Therapy, California, USA
Co-Author, *Collaborative Case Conceptualization*

"*In this masterful and very accessible book Dr. Bannink captures the essential impor-tance of building on positive feelings, motives, imagery, memories and behaviors. The psychology of 'cultivation,' so much a focus in Buddhist approaches to human suffering, is brought to life in new ways with extensive knowledge of the research literature. Full of fascinating insights and practical applications, this is a book to change what we focus on and how we work in helping people change. A book to read many times.*"

Professor Paul Gilbert, PhD, FBPsS, OBE
Derbyshire Healthcare NHS Foundation Trust

"*This book describes Fredrike Bannink's synthesis of Cognitive Behavioral Therapy, Positive Psychology and Solution-Focused Brief Therapy. She names this Positive CBT. The emphasis is both on losing negative thoughts, emotions and behavior, and on enhancing positive experiences. As usual with her work, Fredrike has read very widely, including neuroscience, Appreciative Inquiry, Motivational Interviewing and many variations on the theme of CBT. In the text she demonstrates how to adapt Positive CBT to a number of the existing models and problems. The writing is clear and engag-ing. There are many illustrations with intriguing and apt stories about humans and other species. Case studies and exercises demonstrate how Positive CBT may be applied. Fredrike Bannink is also skilled in mediation and conflict management. Given the present ideological split between 'traditional' CBT, Positive Psychology and Solution-Focused Brief Therapy, this book may begin an interesting rapprochement between these therapies and their practitioners.*"

Dr. Alasdair J. MacDonald, MB, ChB, FRCPsych, DPM, DCH
Consultant Psychiatrist, UK

"*Positive Psychology is a research-based approach. Cognitive Behavioral Therapy (CBT) is often focused on cognitions and behavior that don't serve people well. Fredrike Bannink takes these two approaches, combines them with the best of solution-focused, strength-oriented clinical methods and blends them into a seamless combination that can help any therapist or coach be more effective. Like discovering the restaurant of a master chef who has invented a new fusion of different culinary traditions, Bannink's approach will leave you excited and satisfied.*"

Bill O'Hanlon
Psychotherapist and author of *Do One Thing Different* and
The Change Your Life Book, USA

Practicing Positive CBT

From Reducing Distress to Building Success

Fredrike Bannink

WILEY-BLACKWELL

A John Wiley & Sons, Ltd., Publication

Wiley-Blackwell is an imprint of John Wiley & Sons, formed by the merger of Wiley's global
Scientific, Technical and Medical business with Blackwell Publishing.

Registered Office
John Wiley & Sons Ltd, The Atrium, Southern Gate, Chichester, West Sussex, PO19 8SQ, UK

Editorial Offices
350 Main Street, Malden, MA 02148-5020, USA
9600 Garsington Road, Oxford, OX4 2DQ, UK
The Atrium, Southern Gate, Chichester, West Sussex, PO19 8SQ, UK

For details of our global editorial offices, for customer services, and for information about how to
apply for permission to reuse the copyright material in this book please see our website at www.
wiley.com/wiley-blackwell.

The right of Fredrike Bannink to be identified as the author of this work has been asserted in
accordance with the UK Copyright, Designs and Patents Act 1988.

Wiley also publishes its books in a variety of electronic formats. Some content that appears in print
may not be available in electronic books.

Designations used by companies to distinguish their products are often claimed as trademarks. All
brand names and product names used in this book are trade names, service marks, trademarks or
registered trademarks of their respective owners. The publisher is not associated with any product or
vendor mentioned in this book. This publication is designed to provide accurate and authoritative
information in regard to the subject matter covered. It is sold on the understanding that the
publisher is not engaged in rendering professional services. If professional advice or other expert
assistance is required, the services of a competent professional should be sought.

Library of Congress Cataloging-in-Publication Data

Bannink, Fredrike.
    Practicing positive CBT : from reducing distress to building success / Fredrike Bannink. – 1st ed.
        p. cm.
    Includes bibliographical references and index.
    ISBN 978-1-119-95270-1 (hardback) – ISBN 978-1-119-95269-5 (paper)   1. Cognitive therapy.
2. Positive psychology.   I. Title.
    RC489.C63B36 2012
    616.89'1425–dc23

                                                2012017715

A catalogue record for this book is available from the British Library.

Cover design by Simon Levy Associates.

Set in 9/11 pt Plantin by Toppan Best-set Premedia Limited
Printed in Singapore by Ho Printing Singapore Pte Ltd
1   2012

Contents

Contents

About the Author

Fredrike Bannink is a clinical psychologist and a child and youth psychologist. She currently has a therapy, training, coaching, and mediation practice in Amsterdam, the Netherlands. She is a trainer/supervisor with the Dutch Association for Behaviour and Cognitive therapy (VGCt) and cofounder and chair of the Association's Solution-Focused Cognitive Behavioural Therapy Section. She is a lecturer at various postgraduate institutes.

She teaches CBT, Solution-Focused Brief Therapy, and Positive Psychology to psychologists and psychiatrists, and solution-focused interviewing to medical professionals. She is a trainer of the Mental Health Team of Doctors Without Borders.

In addition, she provides numerous in-company training courses in solution-focused therapy at mental health care institutions; for companies, she organizes solution-focused coaching and solution-focused leadership trajectories.

Fredrike Bannink is also a Master of Dispute Resolution and a mediator for the Amsterdam District Court. She is the author of many international publications in the fields of solution-focused therapy, solution-focused interviewing, solution-focused mediation/conflict management, solution-focused leadership, and positive psychology. Since 2005 she has been writing and presenting worldwide on the topic of bridging traditional CBT, Solution-Focused Brief Therapy, and Positive Psychology. Not surprisingly her top strength (according to the VIA strengths test) is "curiosity and interest in the world."

Foreword

Cognitive-behavioral therapy has evolved to address a broad array of client presentations and an impressive body of evidence attests to its efficacy. Yet outcomes, and particularly longer-term outcomes, can leave a substantial margin for improvement. What would it take to help more clients benefit more substantively from therapy? What more can therapists do to support their clients in developing their longer-term resilience?

Many therapists are intrigued by the idea that identifying clients' strengths and explicitly working with clients' resilience might be an answer to these questions. But they feel ill equipped to work in this way. "It seems a good idea, but how do I do it in my practice?" *Practicing Positive CBT* is a wonderful addition to the CBT canon because it provides therapists with a well-structured, comprehensive, practical, and detailed manual for building their clients' strengths and resilience. Its core is the important work of assessment, engagement, case conceptualization, and treatment, but applied to strengths and resilience. *Positive CBT* provides therapists with ideas for working across the life span, with couples, with families, and in organizational settings. Dr. Bannink writes with sensitivity to issues of diversity, modeling how diversity can be framed as a strength and incorporated into treatment.

Practicing Positive CBT provides both the key background theory and the detailed clinical techniques therapists can use with clients to identify and work with client strengths and a framework for building clients' resilience. It is written in an engaging style that makes use of instructive stories, poems, and metaphors. A really potent tool in the book is the use of guided exercises that demonstrate experientially some of the key messages.

What Dr. Bannink is doing is radical, synthesizing CBT with the psychology of resilience in a grounded and pragmatic way. A key issue for the next decade will be to show that this integration enhances short and, most importantly, long-term client outcomes.

In reading *Practicing Positive CBT* there is a sense of being in the presence of a gifted, engaging, enthusiastic, and inspiring therapist. The book practices what it preaches in supporting therapists to become more effective and successful, and I suspect enjoying their work along the way.

Willem Kuyken
Professor of Clinical Psychology
University of Exeter
United Kingdom

Preface

Traditional CBT has been strongly influenced by the medical model of diagnosis and treatment. The structure of problem-solving – first determining the nature of the problem and then intervening – influences the content of the interaction between therapists and clients: they focus on pathology and on what is wrong with the client. I will use the term "client" instead of "patient" throughout the book, because I prefer not to use the medical model.

Traditional therapists tend to be preoccupied with client problems, limitations, and deficiencies. Client assessments by interdisciplinary teams are often negative and mention few or no client strengths and abilities. It is, however, not this negative way of thinking but the clients' strengths, abilities, and resources that are most important in helping to bring about change. The mission of the helping professions is to empower clients to live more productive and satisfying lives and to flourish. Empowering clients indicates the intention to, and the process of, assisting individuals, groups, families, and communities to discover and expend the resources and tools within and around them.

"If we want to flourish and if we want to have well-being, we must indeed minimise our misery; but in addition, we must have positive emotion, meaning, accomplishment, and positive relationships. The skills and exercises that build these are entirely different from the skills that minimise our suffering" (Seligman, 2011, p. 53). In other words: it's about time to shift the focus from reducing distress and merely "surviving" to building success and positively "thriving."

You don't have to be ill to get better

In the past 30 years there has been a development of competency-based, more collaborative approaches to working with clients. Positive Psychology and Solution-Focused Brief Therapy are amongst these approaches, which are predominantly directed toward clients' preferred futures and strengths instead of their past problems and deficits. In this book I will explore with you how traditional CBT becomes Positive CBT.

Mental health is more than the absence of mental illness. The focus of Positive CBT is no longer only on pathology, on what is wrong with the client and on repairing what is worst, but first and foremost on strengths, what is right with him and on creating what is best. The focus is no longer on merely reducing distress, but also on building success. In this quest, Positive CBT does not have to be constructed from the ground up, but it does involve a change of focus from reducing problems to a focus on building on clients' strengths and on what works. Positive CBT can be seen as being the other side of the "CBT coin." It is a competency-based model, which brings together the best elements of change-based and meaning-based psychotherapeutic approaches to offer a new perspective on psychotherapy and on traditional CBT.

Positive CBT is a new approach to the practice of CBT and this is the first book ever written on the subject. Mindfulness, ACT, and EMDR are considered to be the third wave in CBT, whereas Positive CBT may well become its fourth wave and will increase the repertoire of available interpretation schemes and create a broader range of therapeutic options when intervening with clients and their families. By increasing the intrinsic motivation of clients, a positive focus allows the practice of CBT to become shorter in time. It also generates more autonomy for clients, as well as more light-hearted conversations, which may in turn result in less stress, depression, and burnout among therapists.

This book is aimed at all professionals who would like to adopt a (more) positive approach to psychotherapy and CBT, or who would simply like to increase the range of techniques available to them. Cognitive behavioral therapists will discover a new approach to (or may become better at) significantly increasing client motivation, co-creating preferred outcomes and pathways to achieve them with their clients. Therapists trained in Positive Psychology and/or Solution-Focused Brief Therapy will find useful information on how to combine elements of CBT with their own therapeutic approach. The book is not intended for therapists who are satisfied with the current concepts and models in psychotherapy and CBT, but is meant for those therapists who reflect seriously enough on their profession and its possibilities to be dissatisfied with the current state of affairs. And it is meant for therapists who are interested in examining where the concept of Positive CBT may lead.

Are you curious to know how an elephant, a squid, a mule, dogs, monkeys, geese, a dragon, and a swarm of birds all contribute to Positive CBT? The answer will be revealed to you whilst reading this book. The format of the book has something of a workshop-like quality: 68 exercises, 41 cases (including 20 FAQ and answers), and 31 stories are introduced throughout the book to give you the opportunity to integrate the Positive CBT approach through action learning. Robert Frost (1874–1963) wrote a beautiful poem entitled "The Road Not Taken" in his collection *Mountain Interval* (1920) in which two roads diverged in a wood and he took the one less traveled by, which to him has made all the difference. Hopefully you have the courage and curiosity to take "the road less traveled"; it may make "all the difference" for your clients and for yourself! I invite you to share your comments via email at solutions@ fredrikebannink.com.

Story: The Hundredth Monkey

The Japanese monkey Macaca fuscata had been observed in the wild for a period of 30 years. In 1952, on the island of Koshima, scientists were providing monkeys with sweet potatoes dropped in the sand. The monkeys liked the taste of the raw sweet potatoes, but they found the dirt unpleasant. A young female found she could solve the problem by washing the potatoes in a nearby stream. She taught this trick to her mother. Her playmates also learned this new way and they taught their mothers too.

In a couple of years all the young monkeys learned to wash the sandy potatoes to make them more palatable. Only the adults who imitated their children learned this social improvement . . . other adults kept eating the dirty sweet potatoes.

Then something startling took place. In the autumn of 1958 a certain number of monkeys were washing potatoes – the exact number is not known. When the sun rose one morning there were 99 monkeys on Koshima Island who had learned to wash their potatoes. Suppose that later that evening the hundredth monkey learned to wash potatoes . . . by that evening almost everyone in the tribe was washing sweet potatoes before eating them. The added energy of this hundredth monkey somehow created an ideological breakthrough!

A surprising thing observed by the scientists was that the habit of washing sweet potatoes then jumped over the sea – colonies of monkeys on other islands and the mainland began washing their sweet potatoes. Thus, when a certain number achieves awareness, this new awareness may be communicated from mind to mind. Although the exact number may vary, the "Hundredth Monkey phenomenon" means that when a limited number of people know of a new way, it may remain the conscious property of just those people. But there is a point at which if only one more person tunes in to a new awareness, a field is strengthened so that this awareness is picked up by almost everyone!

Source: Unknown

How many monkeys do you think it will take before Positive CBT will flourish?

Acknowledgments

An author never writes a book alone. It is always a product of many people who work together and ultimately ensure that the name of the author appears on the cover.

I thank my husband, Hidde, and my daughters, Eva and Eline, for giving me the opportunity and encouragement to write my books. I thank my friends, colleagues, students, and above all my clients at home and abroad who have helped me discover, apply, and improve my work over the years.

I also thank my publisher Darren, who kindly invited me to write this book, my dear friends and translators Paula and Steve, and everyone else who has contributed to the realization of this book. Grazie also to my Italian cats for keeping me company during many pleasant hours of thinking and writing.

Part I
Theory

1

What is CBT?

Being happy doesn't mean that everything is perfect. It means that you've decided to look beyond the imperfections

Friedrich Nietzsche

Introduction

Cognitive behavioral therapy (CBT) is a psychotherapeutic approach, a talking therapy. The roots of CBT can be traced to the development of behavior therapy in the early 1920s, the development of cognitive therapy in the 1960s, and the subsequent merging of the two. It was during the period 1950 to 1970 that behavioral therapy became widely utilized, with researchers in the United States, the United Kingdom, and South Africa who were inspired by the behaviorist learning theory of Pavlov, Watson, and Hull.

Pioneered by Ellis and Beck, cognitive therapy assumes that maladaptive behaviors and disturbed mood or emotions are the result of inappropriate or irrational thinking patterns, called automatic thoughts. Instead of reacting to the reality of a situation, an individual reacts to his or her own distorted viewpoint of the situation. For example, a person may conclude that he is worthless simply because he failed an exam or did not get a date. Cognitive therapists attempt to make their clients aware of these distorted thinking patterns, or cognitive distortions, and change them (a process termed cognitive restructuring).

Behavioral therapy, or behavior modification, trains clients to replace undesirable behaviors with healthier behavioral patterns. Unlike psychodynamic therapies, it does not focus on uncovering or understanding the unconscious motivations that may be behind the maladaptive behavior.

CBT integrates the cognitive restructuring approach of cognitive therapy with the behavioral modification techniques of behavioral therapy. The goal of CBT is to help clients bring about desired changes in their lives. The objectives of CBT are to identify irrational or maladaptive thoughts, assumptions, and beliefs

Practicing Positive CBT: From Reducing Distress to Building Success, First Edition. Fredrike Bannink.
© 2012 John Wiley & Sons, Ltd. Published 2012 by John Wiley & Sons, Ltd.

that are related to debilitating negative emotions and to identify how they are dysfunctional, inaccurate, or not helpful. This is done in an effort to reject the distorted cognitions and to replace them with more realistic and self-helping alternatives. The client may also have certain fundamental core beliefs, called schemas, which are flawed and require modification. For example, a client suffering from depression may avoid social contact with others and suffer emotional distress because of his isolation. When questioned why, he reveals to his therapist that he is afraid of rejection, of what others may do or say to him. Upon further exploration with his therapist, they discover that his real fear is not rejection but the belief that he is uninteresting and unlovable. His therapist then tests the reality of that assertion by having the client name friends and family who love him and enjoy his company. By showing the client that others value him, the therapist both exposes the irrationality of the client's belief and provides him with a new model of thought to change his old behavior pattern. In this case, the client learns to think "I am an interesting and lovable person; therefore I should not have difficulty making new friends in social situations." If enough irrational cognitions are changed, he may experience considerable relief from his depression.

Initial treatment sessions are typically spent explaining the basic tenets of CBT to the client and establishing a positive working relationship. CBT is a collaborative, action-oriented therapy effort. As such, it empowers the client by giving him an active role in the therapy process and discourages any over-dependence on the therapist. Treatment is relatively short, usually lasting no longer than 16 weeks.

Both positive alliance – a positive bond between therapist and client – and empirically supported treatment methods enhance therapy outcome. There is evidence that positive therapy alliance potentiates the effectiveness of empirically supported methods (Raue and Goldfried, 1994) and there is also evidence that using effective methods leads to a more positive alliance (DeRubeis, Brotman, and Gibbons, 2005).

CBT Techniques

Different techniques may be employed in CBT to help clients uncover and examine their thoughts and change their behaviors. They include:

- Clients are asked to keep a diary recounting their thoughts, feelings, and actions when specific situations arise. The journal helps to make them aware of their maladaptive thoughts and to show their consequences on behavior. In later stages of therapy, it may serve to demonstrate and reinforce positive behaviors.
- Cognitive rehearsal. The clients imagine a difficult situation and the therapist guides them through the step-by-step process of facing and successfully dealing with it. The clients then work on rehearsing these steps mentally. When the situation arises in real life, the clients will draw on their rehearsed behavior to address it.

- Clients are asked to test the validity of the automatic thoughts and schemas they encounter. The therapist may ask the clients to defend or produce evidence that a schema is true. If clients are unable to meet the challenge, the faulty nature of the schema is exposed.
- Modeling. The therapist and client engage in role-playing exercises in which the therapist acts out appropriate behaviors or responses to situations.
- Conditioning. The therapist uses reinforcement to encourage a particular behavior. For example, a child gets a gold star every time he stays focused on tasks and accomplishes certain daily chores. The star reinforces and increases the desired behavior by identifying it with something positive. Reinforcement can also be used to extinguish unwanted behaviors by imposing negative consequences.
- Systematic desensitization. Clients imagine a situation they fear, while the therapist employs techniques to help the client relax, helping the person cope with his fear reaction and eventually eliminate the anxiety altogether. The imagery of the anxiety-producing situations gets progressively more intense until the therapist and client approach the anxiety-causing situation in real-life (graded exposure). Exposure may be increased to the point of flooding, providing maximum exposure to the real situation. By repeatedly pairing a desired response (relaxation) with a fear-producing situation (open, public spaces) the client becomes desensitized to the old response of fear and learns to react with feelings of relaxation.
- Relaxation, mindfulness, and distraction techniques are also commonly included.
- Cognitive behavioral therapy is often also used in conjunction with mood stabilizing medications to treat conditions like depression and bipolar disorder.
- Homework assignments. Cognitive-behavioral therapists frequently request that their clients complete homework assignments between therapy sessions. These may consist of real-life behavioral experiments where patients are encouraged to try out new responses to situations discussed in therapy sessions.

Empirical Evidence

There is empirical evidence that CBT is effective for the treatment of a variety of problems, including mood, anxiety, personality, eating, substance abuse, and psychotic disorders. Treatment is often manualized, with specific technique-driven brief, direct, and time-limited treatments for specific psychological disorders.

CBT is used in individual therapy as well as group settings, and the techniques are often adapted for self-help applications. Some clinicians and researchers are more cognitive oriented (e.g., cognitive restructuring), while others are more behaviorally oriented (e.g., *in vivo* exposure therapy). Other interventions combine both (e.g., imaginal exposure therapy). Many CBT treatment programs for specific disorders have been evaluated for efficacy; the health-care trend of evidence-based treatment, where specific treatments for symptom-based diagnoses are recommended, has favored CBT over other approaches such as psychodynamic treatments.

CBT may be seen as a class of treatments, which have the same features in common and also differ in important respects. It is problem-focused and structured towards the client; it requires honesty and openness between the client and therapist, as the therapist – being the expert – develops strategies for managing problems and guiding the client to a better life.

2

What is Positive CBT?

Treatment is not just fixing what is wrong; it is also building what is right

Martin Seligman

Introduction

Suppose you are hungry and decide to eat in a restaurant. After having waited for some time, you are invited to take a seat and the manager introduces himself. He asks you questions regarding your hunger: "How hungry are you? For how long have you been preoccupied with this feeling? Were you hungry in the past? What role did hunger play at home with your family or with other relatives? What disadvantages and possibly advantages does hunger have for you?" After this, having become even hungrier, you ask if you can now eat. But in addition the manager wants you to complete some questionnaires about hunger (and perhaps about other issues that the manager finds important). Once everything is finished, a meal is served to you that you did not order, but that the manager claims is good for you and has helped other hungry people. What are the chances of you leaving the restaurant feeling satisfied?

According to the traditional cause-effect model (also called the "medical model" or the "problem-focused model"), one must first find out exactly what the matter is in order to assert a correct diagnosis before a remedy can be provided. In our western thinking, the cause-effect model is the pre-eminent model to make the world understandable. The model is useful if one is dealing with relatively straightforward problems that can, in actual fact, be reduced to simple and unambiguous causes, as is the case with medical or mechanical problems. When you have a toothache, the first question you ask is: what is wrong with my teeth? When your vacuum cleaner breaks down, the first question you ask is: what is wrong with my vacuum cleaner? The medical model consists of: diagnosis + prescribed treatment = symptom reduction. As far as psychotherapy is concerned, however, this model has a major disadvantage, that is, that it is heavily problem-focused. If the problem and its possible causes are studied in depth, a vicious circle may develop with ever-growing problems. The atmosphere becomes

Practicing Positive CBT: From Reducing Distress to Building Success, First Edition. Fredrike Bannink.
© 2012 John Wiley & Sons, Ltd. Published 2012 by John Wiley & Sons, Ltd.

laden with problems, which poses the risk that solutions recede ever further from view and also that the hope of improvement dwindles. In this vein psychology became a victimology and psychologists and psychiatrists became pathologizers. Exploring or analyzing the factors that cause or perpetuate a problem does not automatically result in an improvement of the problem. Einstein (1954) stated that we cannot solve problems by using the same kind of thinking we used when we created them. Duncan (2010) also states that psychotherapy is not a medical endeavor, it is first and foremost a relational one. Yet, the medical model is the predominant description of what we do. "My account of psychotherapy lies outside of the language of diagnosis, prescriptive treatment, and cure and seeks to reflect the interpersonal nature of the work, as well as the consumer's perspective of therapeutic process, the benefit and fit of the services." (p. 184)

The British Psychological Society in their DSM-5 response (2011) state that they are concerned that clients and the general public are negatively affected by the continued and continuous medicalization of their natural and normal responses to their experiences – responses which undoubtedly have distressing consequences which demand helping responses but which do not reflect illnesses so much as normal individual variation.

Furthermore, research shows that among professionals using the problem-solving model there is a high percentage of stress, depression, suicide, burnout, and secondary traumatization. I shall explore these shortcomings further in the next paragraph.

Shortcomings of the Problem–Solving Paradigm

The problem-solving paradigm has become very popular in business, government, and in coaching, psychotherapy, and conflict management. In traditional forms of psychotherapy – and also in CBT – the focus is on pathology. The diagnosis of the problem is the first step. The next step is finding the causes of the problem, using the cause-effect model (the so-called "medical model" or "mechanical model") as previously mentioned.

This is a very common way: something has gone wrong and we have to put it right. In medicine and psychotherapy problems are called a "deviation" from the normal: health is normal, sickness is a deviation and has to be removed.

The problem-solving model is very straightforward: identify the cause and remove it. And indeed analyze the problem, find the cause, put it right is a simple and attractive idiom. It makes sense and it is action-oriented. But unfortunately is it inadequate for a number of reasons:

- In a complex interactive situation we may never be able to isolate one cause;
- There is a danger in fastening on to a particular cause, because it is easy to identify, ignoring the rest of the situation;
- We may identify the cause but cannot remove it;
- The sometimes false notion that once the cause is removed the problem will be solved and things will be back to normal, or should it be: which is usually not the case;
- If we define the goal and decide how to get there, how precise does our definition of the destination have to be.

Problem-solving certainly has a place in psychotherapy and other areas. The main limitation is that we may put much too definite a view on what we believe the solution should be before we have really done our thinking about the matter. As soon as we say "this is the problem" we have defined the sort of solution we expect.

In *designing a positive outcome* – instead of problem solving – in Positive CBT we set out to design something, there is an output, there is something to achieve. It is not just a matter of removing a problem; there is a designed something that was not there before. In this design the focus shifts from problem analysis to outcome analysis or goal analysis.

"With design there is a sense of purpose and a sense of fit. Problem analysis is always looking back at what is already there; design is always looking forward at what might be created. We need to design outcomes. I do not even like saying design 'solutions' because this implies that there is a problem. Even when we cannot find a cause, or, after finding it, cannot remove it, we can always attempt to design an outcome. The main point about the design idiom is that it is open ended. We set out to achieve an outcome. At the beginning we do not know exactly what the outcome is going to be, though there is yet a strong sense of purpose" (De Bono, 1985, p. 42).

There is growing dissatisfaction among clients and professionals with the use of problem-focused models of therapy. Studying problems in depth often leads to the premature discontinuation of sessions, because nothing changes and the client loses hope of improvement. The good news about psychotherapy is that the average treated client is better off than 80% of the untreated sample. It facilitates the remission of symptoms and improves functioning. It also often provides additional coping strategies and methods for dealing with future problems (Lambert and Ogles, 2004).

The bad news, however, is that there has been no improvement in psychotherapy outcomes in more than 30 years, that the drop-out rates are very high (47–50%), and that there is a lack of consumer confidence in therapy outcome. There is a continued emphasis on the medical model and there are continued claims of superiority amongst models despite the absence of evidence. Wampold (2001, p. 204) states: "Research designs that are able to isolate and establish the relationship between specific ingredients and outcomes . . . have failed to find a scintilla of evidence that any specific ingredient is necessary for therapeutic change." So let's see if we can find an answer to the bad news mentioned previously.

Exercise 2.1

Consider a typical problematic situation. Write down the typical questions you ask yourself or others about it. Examine these questions closely. Does asking them help you feel better or worse? Does asking them help move you forward to where you want to be or merely give you an explanation for why you are stuck or can't change? If your questions are not helping you, find some more helpful questions.

Story 2.1: How to Not Be Unhappy

The ancient Greeks already faced the choice between "how not to be unhappy" or "how to be happy." The Stoics (third century BC: *Zeno, and later Seneca and Epictetus) practiced discomfort and difficulty; their aim was not to be unhappy. Today the word "stoic" commonly refers to someone indifferent to pain, pleasure, grief, or joy.*

Epicurus was another ancient Greek philosopher (second century BC*) and the founder of the school of philosophy called Epicureanism. For the Epicurists the objective was to attain a happy, tranquil life, surrounded by friends and living self-sufficiently. Their aim was to be happy.*

As we face the same dilemma today, we can also let our clients decide what they would prefer: how to not be unhappy or how to be happy. In Chapter 6, I will elaborate further on these so-called approach goals (to be happy) or avoidance goals (to not be unhappy).

Towards a Strengths and Solutions Paradigm

As stated before, traditional therapists tend to be preoccupied with client problems, limitations, and deficiencies. Client assessments by interdisciplinary teams are often negative and mention few or no client abilities. It is, however, the clients' abilities, strengths, and resources that are most important in helping to bring about change.

A "strengths-based approach" with its roots in Positive Psychology may be the answer to the bad news, mentioned earlier. It is a meta-view, an overarching philosophical perspective in which people are seen as capable and as having abilities and resources within themselves and their social systems. When activated and integrated with new experiences, understandings, and skills, strengths offer pathways to reduce pain and suffering, resolve concerns and conflicts, and more effectively cope with life stressors. The outcome is an improved sense of well-being and quality of life and higher degrees of interpersonal and social functioning. Strengths-based Positive Psychologists and other practitioners promote change through respectful educational, therapeutic, and operational processes that encourage and empower others.

Saleebey (2007) calls this the "strengths perspective" with the following basic assumptions:

- Despite life's struggles, all persons possess strengths that can be marshaled to improve the qualities of their lives. Therapists should respect these strengths and the directions in which clients wish to apply them;
- Client motivation is increased by a consistent emphasis on strengths as the client defines them;

- Discovering strengths requires a process of cooperative exploration between clients and therapists; expert therapists do not have the last word on what clients need to improve in their lives;
- Focusing on strengths turns therapists away from the temptation to judge or blame clients for their difficulties and toward discovering how clients have managed to survive, even in the most difficult circumstances;
- All environments – even the most bleak – contain resources.

Furthermore, a solutions-based approach, focusing on "what works" for this client, in this context, and in this moment, with its roots in Solution-Focused Brief Therapy may add to the well-being and flourishing of clients by inviting them to define their preferred future (instead of their problems) and finding solutions to reach their goal. Biologists Histed, Pasupathy, and Miller (2009) found that monkeys learn more from their successes (e.g., what has successfully worked before) than from their failures and states that the same is probably true for human beings. This book brings together the best of these two approaches, which are at the basis of Positive CBT. Chapter 4 will provide a detailed description and a short comparison of both.

Exercise 2.2

Sit comfortably, close your eyes and repeat the following sentence ten times: "I have a big problem!" Observe closely what you are experiencing physically and emotionally. Notice carefully the effect that this sentence has on your body and on your emotions.

Stretch a little, get up and do the exercise again. Set yourself comfortably again, close your eyes, and then repeat the following sentence ten times: "I have a great opportunity!" Once again, observe the effects that this sentence has on your physical and emotional state.

CBT therapists Kuyken, Padesky, and Dudley (2009, p. 114) state: "Therapists often consider amelioration of client distress the most important therapy outcome. It is an outcome that CBT therapists generally view as primary; they assume that their clients share this view. However, a recent large survey of people receiving mental health services revealed the most important outcomes for clients are: attaining positive mental health qualities such as optimism and self-confidence; a return to one's usual, normal self; a return to usual level of functioning; and relief from symptoms (Zimmerman *et al.*, 2006)."

Kuyken, Padesky, and Dudley state that although identified strengths can be incorporated at each stage of case conceptualization, this has not typically been demonstrated in the CBT literature. There has been a much greater emphasis on identifying precipitating, predisposing and perpetuating factors for problems. They advocate the inclusion of strengths whenever possible during case conceptualization. These strengths can be personal or cultural values or both. Resilience is a broad concept that refers to how people negotiate adversity to maintain their well-being. The term describes the psychological processes through which people draw on their strengths to adapt to challenges. Research done by Masten (2001) shows an important distinction between strengths and resilience. Strengths refer to attributes about a person such as good coping abilities or protective circumstances such as a supportive partner. Resilience refers to the processes whereby these strengths enable adaptation during times of challenge. Thus, once therapists help clients identify strengths, these strengths can be incorporated into conceptualizations to help understand client resilience.

When therapists focus on problems, on what their clients do not want, on disadvantages, failures, deficits, and the dreaded future, there will be less resilience, whereas when therapists focus on what their clients want instead of their problems, on exceptions to the problems, advantages, successes, strengths, and their preferred future, there will be more resilience.

What a client (and his therapist) focuses his attention on tends to increase and expand in both his awareness and his life. When someone is having problems, it is usually because he is attending to the same thing over and over again. The statement: "Insanity is doing the same thing over and over again and expecting different results" is generally attributed to Einstein. In Positive CBT clients and therapists are invited to shift their attention from analysis, explanations, and problems, to thoughts, actions, and feelings that can help clients flourish. Positive CBT therapists always listen for openings in problem-focused conversations. These openings can be about what clients want different in their lives, openings about exceptions, openings about competences and resources, openings about who and what might be helpful in taking the next step.

Improvement is often realized by redirecting attention from dissatisfaction about a status quo to a positive goal and to start taking steps in the direction of that goal. This process of shifting attention often uses three steps:

1. Acknowledge the problem of the client ("This must be hard for you")
2. Suggest a desire for change ("So I guess you would like things to be different?")
3. Ask about the desired outcome ("How would you like things to be different?")

According to Positive Psychology, getting rid of unhappiness is not the same thing as achieving happiness. Getting rid of fear, anger, and depression will not automatically fill you with peace, love, and joy. Getting rid of weaknesses will not automatically maximize your strengths (see Table 2.1). In traditional CBT book titles you find the same problem-focused way of thinking: "Overcoming depression," "Coping with obsessive-compulsive disorder," or "Your route out of perfectionism."

Happiness and unhappiness are not on the same continuum. Strategies to minimize fear, anger, or depression are not identical to strategies to maximize peace, joy, strength, or meaning. Subjective well-being is a function of three different factors: high positive affect, low negative affect, and high life satisfaction, whereby positive and negative affect are on different continua. Fredrickson (2009) argues that a key to emotional flourishing is having a high positive-to-negative emotion ratio. We can improve our state, either by increasing positive emotions or by decreasing negative emotions (or both), and these are different processes with different metrics (see Chapter 9).

It is important that Positive Psychologists don't make the same mistakes that traditional psychologists have. While many traditional psychologists seem to think that taking away negatives will automatically create positives, Positive Psychologists need to avoid the trap of thinking that creating positives will automatically take away the negatives. Because the positive and the negative are on two separate (albeit related) continua, it is crucial that attention is paid both to processes for building the positive and to processes for reducing the negative. In this view, traditional interventions and positive interventions are both important and that is why I think Positive CBT may be an important contribution to the ever-changing field of – so far – traditional CBT, where the emphasis lies predominantly in reducing the negative.

Exercise 2.3

What percentage of time in your intakes and/or treatment do you spend asking your clients about their strengths, their successes, and what works in their life? Is it 10%? Is it 20%? Is it 50% or maybe even 0%? Suppose you were the client yourself, how would you like your therapist to spend his time during your intake and/or treatment? Would you like to be invited to talk about your strengths and resources? You probably would! So why not raise the percentage of time you normally use by just 10% (if you use 10%, make it 20%) and notice what difference this makes both for your clients and for yourself!

Exercise 2.4

This is an exercise I often use to explain the difference between problem-focused and solution-focused interviewing. I invite the participants on my training courses to look around them and find five objects that are beige. If they have found five beige objects, I want someone, before he begins to list them, to quickly say, which blue objects he saw. He probably did not see any blue objects and he has to focus again to find blue objects.

This exercise makes clear how clients see their negative situation. They will describe it as always beige: they don't want beige, and they suffer from it. By asking clients what they want instead of beige (e.g., blue, or their own favorite color), they can begin to focus on blue, as a better alternative to beige. What will a blue life look like? When are or were there already pieces of blue (exceptions)? On a scale where 10 means a totally blue life and 0 means a totally beige life, where are you right now?

You can carry out this exercise with your clients too, if they describe the problems as always present or when you want to clarify your approach as a Positive CBT therapist.

One last question to all participants is: what do you as a professional have to know about beige to be able to look with your clients at (more) blue? The answer to this question is – often to their own amazement – "nothing."

Table 2.1 Differences between traditional CBT and Positive CBT.

Traditional CBT	Positive CBT
Interventions meant to increase well-being by diminishing that which impedes or destroys human flourishing	Interventions meant to increase well-being by enhancing that which causes or constitutes human flourishing
Avoidance goals: away from what clients do not want (problems or complaints)	Approach goals: towards what clients do want (preferred future, what clients want to have instead of their problems or complaints)
Goals (sometimes) defined by the therapist	Goals always defined by the client
Past or present oriented: cause-effect medical model	Future oriented, letting go of cause-effect medical model
Analyzing problems is important	Designing positive outcomes and analyzing exceptions is important
Focus on problems and weaknesses	Focus on solutions and strengths
Conversations about what clients do not want: positive reinforcement of "problem-talk"	Conversations about what clients do want instead of their problems: positive reinforcement of "solutions-talk"
Conversations about the same and impossibilities	Conversations about differences and possibilities
Conversations for insight and working through	Conversations about accountabilty and action
Clients' view sometimes is not validated	Clients' view is validated (which makes letting go of a point of view easier)
Clients are (sometimes) seen as incompetent (deficit model)	Clients are always seen as competent (strengths and resources model)
FBA's of problem behavior	FBA's of exceptions of problem behavior or of behavior in the preferred future
Clients are (sometimes) seen as not motivated (resistance)	Clients are always seen as motivated (although their goal may not be the goal of the therapist)

Traditional CBT	Positive CBT
Therapist gives advice	Therapist asks questions to elicit clients' expertise
Therapist is the expert	Therapist adopts a stance of "not knowing"; client is co-expert
Resources must be acquired, new skills must be learned	Resources are already present. Clients may want to become better at some skills
Therapist confronts	Therapist accepts the clients' view and asks: "In what way does that help?"
Therapist persuades clients	Therapist lets himself be persuaded by clients
Big changes are needed	A small change is often enough
The problem is always present	The problem is never always present: there are always exceptions
Insight or understanding is a precondition for change	Insight or understanding comes during or after the change
Therapists' theory of change	Clients' theory of change; therapist asks: "How will this help you?"
Feedback at the end of therapy	Feedback to and from clients at the end of every session in therapy
Therapist indicates end of the therapy	Client indicates end of the therapy
Success is defined as the solving of the problem	Success is defined as reaching the preferred outcome, which may be different from (or better than) solving the problem
Higher percentage of depression, burnout, and secondary traumatization among therapists	Lower percentage of depression, burnout, and secondary traumatization among therapists

© Fredrike Bannink

Notes on Learning Theory

In Positive CBT there is a different focus from that of traditional CBT. The focus is on clients' adaptive, operant behavior, rather than on passive, respondent behavior.

By operant behavior clients can approach, escape, or avoid stimuli that influence their personal state and well-being. For optimal functioning everyone should have a stable repertoire of operant behaviors, not only to diminish negative situations, but first and foremost to obtain social inclusion. Personal strength grows when individuals feel themselves socially significant and worthwhile.

In an operant procedure clients use the possibilities which are offered by the situation they are in, or in other words, to get a grip on their existence and take control of their own life. Operant conditioning, therefore, is of great value for the improvement of well-being. With operant behavior individuals are able to manage their own situation by controlling and directing the stimuli. In this way they can adopt an active role in contributing to an improvement in their mood and situation. This is a big advantage over the passive role adopted in respondent conditioning procedures.

The majority of techniques in traditional CBT cling to the respondent conditioning process, especially in the undoing of "damage" from earlier unfavorable experiences; as if it were more important to remove the dents from the bodywork of the car than to teach clients better driving skills (Bruins, 2008).

Story 2.2: I Can Choose

Groucho Marx once said: "Each morning when I open my eyes I say to myself: 'I, not events, have the power to make me happy or unhappy today. I can choose which it shall be. Yesterday is dead; tomorrow hasn't arrived yet. I have just one day, today, and I am going to be happy in it.'"

Changing Role of the Therapist

In Positive CBT the role of the therapist is also changing. From being, as in traditional forms of psychotherapy and CBT, the only expert in the room, who explores and analyzes the problem and then gives advice to clients on how to solve their problems, the role changes to one where the therapist does not need to push or pull. Rather, he is always one step behind the clients and looks in the same direction as they do (towards their preferred future). The Positive CBT therapist poses questions in order to direct the clients' attention and thereby helps them look at something from a different angle. This stance is also called the stance of "leading from one step behind."

Clients are seen as co-experts and the therapist invites them – by asking questions (Bannink, 2009a; 2010a) – to share their knowledge and expertise to reach their preferred future. After 30 years of clinical practice it is my conviction that the solutions are always in the room!

The therapist also changes his focus of attention in using, wherever and whenever possible, the positive reinforcement of "solution-talk" (conversations about goals, exceptions, possibilities, strengths, and resources) and negative punishment of "problem-talk" (conversations about problems, causes, impossibilities, weaknesses). This does not mean that the client is not allowed to talk about his problems or that Positive CBT is "problem-phobic." The difference is that the Positive CBT therapist does not seek any details about the presented problem, thus not reinforcing "problem-talk." He does, however, ask for many details about goals, solutions, exceptions, strengths, and competences, thus reinforcing "solutions-talk." In Chapter 12 I return to the changing role of the therapist in more detail.

Differences Between Traditional CBT and Positive CBT – An Overview

Here you will find a detailed overview of the differences between traditional CBT and Positive CBT.

Exercise 2.5

Think back to a period in your life when you had a problem. How did you get over these difficulties then? Think of at least three things that you did that were helpful.

If you currently have a problem: which of those former ways could you apply again (or are you already applying) to the current problem? And what do you know about the ways in which other people got over a similar problem? This exercise can also be used in group therapy, where all participants anonymously write on a slip of paper three coping strategies which proved successful in their own lives. The slips of paper are laid out on a table and everyone chooses from them a strategy, which is either new to him or may be repeated in a behavioral experiment to ameliorate his present problem.

Story 2.3: Looking for Problems?

During the French Revolution an attorney, a physician, and an engineer were sentenced to death. When the day of their execution arrived, the attorney was first onto the platform that supported the guillotine. "Blindfold or no blindfold?" asked the executioner. The attorney, not wanting to be seen as fearful or cowardly in the face of death, held his head high and answered "No blindfold." "Head up or head down?" continued the executioner. "Head up" said the attorney proudly. The executioner swung his axe, severing the rope that held the razor-sharp blade

(continued)

at the top of the scaffold. The blade dropped swiftly between the shafts and stopped just half an inch above the attorney's neck. "I am sorry" said the executioner. "I checked it just this morning. This should not have happened."

The attorney seized on the opportunity. "I think" he addressed the executioner, "if you check The Procedural Manual For Execution By Guillotine, you will find there is a clause that states that if the guillotine malfunctions, the condemned is permitted to walk free." The executioner checked his manual, found the attorney to be correct, and set him free.

The doctor was the next to be led to the platform. "Blindfold or no blindfold?" asked the executioner. "No blindfold" said the doctor as proudly as the attorney. "Head up or head down?" asked the executioner. "Head up" said the doctor standing tall and defiant. The executioner swung his axe, cutting the rope cleanly. Once again the blade stopped just half an inch above the doctor's neck. "I can't believe this" exclaimed the executioner. "Twice in a row! I checked it out thoroughly this morning, but rules are rules and I have to abide by them. Like the attorney, your life has been spared and you may go."

The engineer was the third to mount the stand. By this time, the executioner had double-checked the guillotine and everything looked operational. "Blindfold or no blindfold?" he asked the engineer. "No blindfold" came the reply. "Head up or head down?" asked the executioner. "Head up" said the engineer. For the third time, the executioner swung back his axe to slash the rope. Just as he was about to bring the blow forward and sever the line, the engineer called out "Stop! I think I see the problem."

Source: Anonymous

3

Possibilities of Positive CBT

You cannot discover new oceans unless you have the courage to lose sight of the shore
André Gide, 1869–1951

Introduction

If there is a "Positive CBT," is there also a "negative" CBT, you may wonder. I personally do not believe that there is a negative form of CBT, since all forms of psychotherapy – including traditional CBT – have as their main goal to help clients bring about desired changes in their lives. The good news is that Positive CBT does not have to be built from the ground up. Here we may ask some solution-focused questions: What is already positive in traditional CBT? And what are the possibilities of an even more positive CBT?

This summary of CBT interventions which already – albeit partly – focus on positive emotions, thoughts, images, and behavior is by no means extensive or inclusive – please forgive me for that – but it will hopefully give you a pretty good idea of the ongoing change in focus in CBT from negative to positive and the shift from reducing distress to building success. I will conclude this chapter with my preferred future of Positive CBT in which more clients will hopefully profit from CBT and in which CBT will be kinder to its therapists.

It is not only humans who think that building success is important but also some animals who consider it to be "the most important subject of all." In Winnie-the-Pooh on Success, the wise Stranger tells the animals how they can become successful:

"What does the success formula taste like?" "It's not that kind of formula, Silly Bear," said The Stranger. He took a sheet of paper out of his case and began writing on it. When he finished, he turned it around and showed it to his friends. This is what he had written:

Select a Dream
Use your dreams to set a Goal

Practicing Positive CBT: From Reducing Distress to Building Success, First Edition. Fredrike Bannink.
© 2012 John Wiley & Sons, Ltd. Published 2012 by John Wiley & Sons, Ltd.

Create a Plan
Consider Resources
Enhance Skills and Abilities
Spend time Wisely
Start! Get Organized and Go

"It spells Suchness!" shouted Piglet.
"Close, Piglet," said The Stranger. "It spells Success."

(Allen and Allen, 1997, p. 17)

What is Positive in Traditional CBT?

Building hope

Positive CBT does not have to be built from the ground up. Since the 1950s, physicians and psychologists have pointed to the role of hope in health and well-being. In his 1959 address to the American Psychiatric Association, psychiatrist Menninger suggested that the power of hope was an untapped source of strength and healing for patients. He defined hope as "a positive expectancy of goal attainment" and "an adventure, a going forward, a confident search" (p. 484). Menninger stated that hope is an indispensable factor in psychiatric treatment and in psychiatric education.

The interest in hope in psychotherapy was initially aimed at reducing despair rather than increasing hopeful thoughts. Given the link between despair and suicide, Beck, Weissman, Lester, and Trexles (1974) focused on combating hopelessness. Their definition of hopelessness was: "A system of cognitive schemas whose common denomination is negative expectations about the future" (p. 864). Reducing hopelessness, however, is not the same as increasing hope. Frank (1974) described the "restoration of morale," for the first time using a positive formulation.

Bakker, Bannink, and Macdonald (2010) state that a positive focus also proves very useful in crisis interventions. The available time does not usually lend itself to an elaborate diagnosis and, further to this, clients in crisis benefit from regaining confidence in their personal competences and a future-oriented approach. Think for example of questions such as: "How do you manage to carry on? What has helped you in the past weeks, even if only slightly?" Commonly, in a crisis situation the client relinquishes competences to the therapist (You tell me what I should do) – a pitfall that can be avoided with Positive CBT. More on the importance of building hope and research on "hope theory" can be found in Chapter 5.

Focus on strengths

Hawton *et al.* (1995) already stated that discussion of the client's assets, skills, and strengths is important (environmental features like a supportive spouse, a satisfying job), skills which may facilitate change (like self-esteem), and strengths such as a sense of humor, persistence, interpersonal warmth, which make it more likely that treatment suggestions will be carried through.

In her latest book Beck (2011) also emphasizes the positive. She states that most clients, especially those with depression, tend to focus unduly on the negative. Their difficulty in processing positive data leads them to develop a distorted sense of reality. To counteract this feature of depression, therapists should continually help clients to attend to the positive. These positive interventions are:

- Eliciting clients' strengths (What are some of your strengths and positive qualities?) at the evaluation of the therapy (In my opinion a bit late!);
- Asking, from the first session on, for positive data from the preceding week (What positive things happened since I saw you last?);
- Using the therapeutic alliance to demonstrate that the therapist sees the client as a valuable human being;
- Asking clients for data that are contrary to their negative automatic thoughts and beliefs (What is the positive evidence on the other side, that perhaps your automatic thought isn't true?);
- Pointing out positive data to the clients and asking what this data means about them (What does this say about you?);
- Being alert for and noting aloud instances of positive coping (What a good idea to ask your friend to help you);
- Collaboratively setting homework assignments to facilitate their experiencing a sense of pleasure and achievement.

Focus on helpful cognitions and beliefs

Bennett-Levy *et al.* (2004) mention two major strategies in cognitive therapy, the first being a problem-focused one and the second being a strengths- and solutions-focused one:

1. To assist clients to identify and reality-test unhelpful cognitions which underlie repeated negative patterns of emotion and behavior;
2. To develop and test new, more adaptive cognitions that can give rise to a more positive experience of the self, others, and the world.

Positive CBT, as this book will describe, chooses the second strategy, predominantly focusing on helpful cognitions, beliefs, and behavior, not so much for developing and testing new adaptive cognitions, beliefs, and behaviors, but in order to search for and build on the adaptive and helpful ones which every client already possesses.

Collaborative case conceptualization

Kuyken, Padesky and Dudley (2009, p. 3) define CBT case conceptualization as follows: "Case conceptualization is a process whereby therapist and client work collaboratively to describe and then to explain the issues a client presents in therapy. Its primary function is to guide therapy in order to relieve client distress and build client resilience." Case conceptualization evolves over the course of CBT, progressing from descriptive to increasingly explanatory levels.

Furthermore, it not only incorporates client problems but also client strengths and resilience. They propose that therapy has two overarching goals:

1. To alleviate clients' distress;
2. To build resilience.

Conceptualization actively identifies and incorporates clients' strengths in order to apply existing client resources to presenting issues and to strengthen client awareness and use of strengths over time (e.g., building resilience). "Most current CBT approaches are concerned either exclusively or largely with a client's problems, vulnerabilities, and history of adversity. We advocate for therapists to identify and work with client strengths at every stage of conceptualization. A strengths focus is often more engaging for clients and offers the advantages of harnessing client strengths in the change process to pave a way to lasting recovery."

Use of imagery

The use of imagery in psychotherapy has a long history and there is evidence of the significance of imagery in a number of psychological disorders. Since its inception, cognitive therapy has emphasized the role of mental imagery (Beck, 1967). Contending that mental activity may take the form of words and phrases or images, Beck observed that affective distress can be directly linked to visual cognitions – as well as to verbal cognitions – and that modifying upsetting visual cognitions can lead to significant cognitive and emotional shifts. Imagery plays an important role in CBT interventions like systematic desensitisation (SD) and flooding.

Imagery can be either positive or negative. From a problem-focused perspective negative imagery can be removed or transformed, whereas from a solution-focused perspective positive imagery can be created or enhanced. Until recently imagery in CBT was based on the problem-focused paradigm, but lately more positive forms of imagery are being developed.

For example, research done by Vasquez and Buehler (2007) shows that imagining future success (positive imagery) enhances people's motivation to achieve it. Research shows that a positive image of oneself in the future motivates action by helping people to articulate their goals clearly and develop behaviors that will allow them to fulfill those goals. The very act of imagining future events not only makes those events seem more likely but also helps to bring them about.

Intrusive images are very common in psychological disorders and are therefore an obvious target for imagery-based interventions. Additionally, clients often experience an absence of positive, adaptive imagery. For example, happy, predictive images of the future are often lacking in depression and generalized anxiety disorder (Hackmann, Bennett-Levy, and Holmes, 2011). A sound body of theory suggests the potential value of positive imagery interventions and a growing empirical base derived from neuroscience, cognitive science, and sports psychology. For example, generating positive images has a powerful and positive impact on emotion and enhances goal setting and skill development.

Hackmann, Bennett-Levy, and Holmes (2011, p. 171) states: "Positive imagery is one of the main psychological interventions in sports psychology, with an evidence base over several decades of research. Currently, there is little overlap between the sports psychology and CBT imagery literature. In contrast to the CBT literature, imagery research in sports psychology has focused on positive imagery and paid little attention to negative imagery. The impression within the sports psychology literature is that negative imagery is an irritant to be circumvented; in contrast, until recently CBT has paid little attention to the deliberate construction of positive images." Maybe the reason for this difference is that sports psychology, in attempting to help athletes build better perform-ances, never adopted a medical model from the outset.

Imagery rescripting (ImRs) is a problem-focused imagery technique in which a distressing image is modified in some way to change associated negative thoughts, feelings, and/or behaviors. The use of imagery rescripting to treat psychological problems such as nightmares, posttraumatic stress disorder (PTSD), bereavement, intrusive images, and eating disorders has been described by Arntz and Weertman (1999).

One set of instructions for imagery rescripting in the treatment of nightmares is as follows: choose a nightmare and modify it in *a positive way*, rehearse the modified nightmare for at least several minutes daily, and modify additional nightmares as necessary every 3 to 7 days, rehearsing no more than one or two new dreams per week. Imagery rescripting is not only used to overcome problems but to enable clients with a *positive* view of themselves (see compassion focused imagery) and of their strengths in order to empower them to overcome other difficulties and to promote their self-determination and well-being.

Competitive Memory Training

In this section, I will describe two CBT interventions, which already employ positive imagery: Competitive Memory Training (COMET) and Compassion Focused Therapy (CFT).

Brewin (2006) states that vulnerability to emotional disorders is thought to lie in memory representations (e.g., negative self-schemas) that are activated by triggering events and maintain negative mood. There has been considerable uncertainty about how the influence of these representations can be altered, prompted in part by the development of new metacognitive therapies. His research suggests that there are multiple memories involving the self that compete to be retrieved. Brewin suggests that CBT does not directly modify negative information in memory but produces changes in the relative activation of positive and negative representations such that the positive ones are assisted to win the retrieval competition. This is related to the treatment of common symptoms typical of emotional disorders, such as phobic reactions, rumination, and intru-sive images and memories. It is shown to provide a parsimonious set of principles that have the potential to unify traditional and more modern variants of CBT. The most important benefit a retrieval competition account offers, however, is to assist therapists to think more creatively about their practice and to respond more flexibly to clients who fail to respond to the standard techniques of CBT. It may thus be unnecessary for negative thinking to be corrected, only disengaged from. Methods such as rescripting of intrusive memories or images, use of compassionate imagery, mindfulness-based cognitive therapy, acceptance and commitment therapy (ACT), and now Positive CBT open up new possibilities for exploiting what it has to offer.

COMET targets *positive instances* of self-worth after negative self-opinions have been identified. COMET for low self-esteem is a short (6–9 sessions) CBT technique that can be applied individually as well as in groups. Personalized experiences where positive characteristics are manifest are made more emotionally salient and competitive with the aid of imagining, body posture, facial expression, and music. The enhanced positive self-opinions are associated with triggers that have always been connected with low self-esteem by using counter-conditioning techniques. COMET was initially used for clients with low self-esteem but is now also used as a transdiagnostic approach for eating disorders, personality disorders, and depression (Korrelboom *et al.*, 2009).

Compassion Focused Therapy

"Stimulated by Martin Seligman's concept of Positive Psychology on strengths and virtues, clinicians have become more aware that we need to help people, not just by working with their threats and problematic behaviours, but also by helping them develop well-being. This positive approach is increasingly being integrated into various therapies" (Gilbert, 2010, p. 197).

Developing compassion for self and others, as a way to enhance well-being, has been central to Buddhist practice for the enhancement of well-being for thousands of years. Feeling cared for, accepted, and having a sense of belonging and affiliation with others is fundamental to our physiological maturation and well-being (Siegel, 2001). These are linked to particular types of *positive affect* that are associated with well-being and a neuro-hormonal profile of increased endorphins and oxytocin (Panksepp, 1998). They can be seen as part of the 24 character strengths (humanity and temperance), as described in Chapter 4.

Compassion Focused Therapy (CFT) progressed from doing CBT and emotion work with a compassion (kindness) focus and – as the evidence for the model developed and more specific exercises proved helpful – on to CFT. CFT was originally developed with people with high shame and self-criticism. These people can find experiencing positive, affiliative emotions (accepting compassion from others and being self-compassionate) difficult. It is process- rather than disorder-focused, because shame and self-criticism are transdiagnostic processes that have been linked to a range of psychological disorders. CFT aims to develop care and affiliative-focused motivation, attention, emotion, behavior, and thinking. Key skills include the use of compassion-focused imagery, building the compassionate self, and using the sense of a compassionate self to engage with areas of personal difficulty. As an example of this "compassionate rescripting" the client who is trained in the compassionate self can approach a difficult memory holding the compassionate position as he watches the scene unfolding. Then gradually, with the compassionate self he might bring new things into the scene (e.g., helpers) and begin to decide on new endings. The compassionate self can offer any support to the self that he sees in his memory and they can make up the most fantastic endings (Brewin *et al.*, 2009).

Compassion-focused exercises can be oriented in four ways:

1. Developing the inner compassionate self;
2. Compassion flowing out from you to others;
3. Compassion flowing into you;
4. Compassion to yourself.

Gilbert (2010, p. 11) states: "There is increasing evidence that the kind of 'self' we try to become will influence our well-being and social relationships, and compassionate rather than self-focused self-identities are associated with the better outcomes."

Fredrickson (2009), one of the researchers in the field of Positive Psychology, mentions another compassion-focused intervention, called "loving-kindness meditation." It aims directly to evoke *positive emotions*, especially within the context of relationships. It is a technique used to increase feelings of warmth and caring for self and others. Like mindfulness, loving-kindness evolved from ancient Buddhist mind-training practices. In a guided imagery exercise the client first directs these warm and tender feelings to himself and then to an ever-widening circle of others (nice people he knows, then to strangers, and finally even to people with whom he has a negative relationship).

Exercise 3.1

Here is a solution-focused intervention, widely used in the treatment of post-traumatic stress disorder. Write a letter from your future self to your current self from X years from now (six months, one year, five years, or maybe ten years, whichever is for you a relevant period of time). Describe that you are doing fine, where you are, what you are doing, what you have gone through to get there, and so on. Tell yourself the crucial things you realized or did to get there. Finally give your present self some sage and compassionate advice from the future.

Mindfulness-Based Cognitive Therapy

Mindfulness practices for cultivating *well-being* and transforming suffering have a long lineage dating back at least 2000 years. Kabat-Zinn (1994) began teaching mindfulness systematically to people with chronic health problems in medical and psychiatric settings in the 1970s. He called his work Mindfulness-Based Stress Reduction (MBSR). His definition of mindfulness is: paying attention in a particular way: on purpose, in the present moment, and nonjudgmentally.

Mindfulness-Based Cognitive Therapy (MBCT) has been developed as an approach that combines the mindfulness mediation rooted in Buddhist thought and the western tradition of CBT approaches. It is considered to be part of the so-called "third wave" in CBT. It is an intervention that helps increase a wide, open awareness as well as focused attention and reduces automatic responding. The power of mindfulness is that it can literally sever the link between negative thoughts and negative emotions.

Siegel (2010, p. 86): "Mindfulness is a form of mental activity that trains the mind to become aware of awareness itself and to pay attention to one's own intention. As researchers have defined it, mindfulness requires paying attention to the present moment from a stance that is non-judgemental and non-reactive. It teaches self-observation; practitioners are able to describe with words the internal seascape of the mind. At the heart of this process, I believe, is a form of internal 'tuning in' to oneself that enables people to become 'their own best friend'. And just as our attunement to our children promotes a healthy, secure attachment, tuning in to the self also promotes a foundation for resilience and flexibility." Research shows that among clients with recurrent depression MBCT halves the rate of relapse compared with usual care and it is equivalent to staying on antidepressant long term. It has also proved useful in the treatment of children and adolescents with ADHD.

The important element to remember is that mindfulness involves paying attention to our changing moment-to-moment experience, whether it be pleasant, unpleasant, or neutral. To do this, we employ the character strengths of self-regulation (of our attention) and curiosity (being open to the present moment). Mindfulness can be practiced *formally*, through regular sitting/walking/ eating meditation, or *informally*, through bringing deliberate focus to what we are doing (e.g., feeling the softness of the cloth as we make our bed; listening to the sound of the food hit the ceramic bowl as we feed our cat).

Applied relaxation

Applied Relaxation (AR) takes progressive relaxation as its starting point, but since this takes too long in a natural anxiety situation, it has been reduced from 15 minutes to only 20–30 seconds. The treatment takes about 10–12 sessions with the following six steps. Progressive relaxation tension-release, progressive relaxation tension-only, cue-controlled relaxation, differential relaxation, rapid relaxation, and finally application training, during which the client practices how to apply rapid relaxation in natural anxiety-arousing situations in order to prevent the initial anxiety reactions to escalate into full-blown panic attacks. AR is used in the treatment of generalized anxiety disorders, panic disorders, and several phobias.

Dialectical Behavior Therapy

Dialectical Behavior Therapy (DBT) (Linehan, 1993) is a treatment for suicidal behaviors, borderline personality disorder, and other disorders of high emotion dysregulation. DBT focuses on increasing emotion regulation and includes four sets of basic behavior skills: mindfulness, distress tolerance, interpersonal effectiveness, and emotion regulation. Just to name a few interventions within these four skills: increasing positive emotional events; use positive actions that are enjoyable; help out others or the community; provoke a sense of humor; improve the moment by relaxing or thinking what went well; skills to maintain self-respect and to maintain a healthy body.

Part of DBT consists of increasing "self-soothing skills" in which the client behaves in a comforting, nurturing, kind and gentle way to himself by doing something that is soothing to him. It can be used in moments of distress or agitation. Obviously, this is comparable to compassion-focused therapy and to loving-kindness meditation.

The therapists' skill of normalizing is used to depathologize clients' concerns and present them instead as normal life difficulties. It helps people to calm down about their problem. It helps them to realize they're not abnormal for having this problem. Thinking it's not normal to have a problem causes a further problem. People are more compassionate with themselves and experience lower negative affect when they see that others have the same problems they have.

Well-being therapy

The concept of psychological well-being has received increasing attention in clinical psychology. Recent investigations have documented the complex relationship among well-being, distress, and personality traits, both in clinical and nonclinical populations (Ruini and Fava, 2004). The findings show that psychological well-being cannot be equated with the absence of symptomatology, nor with personality traits. It is thus particularly important to analyze the concept of well-being in clinical settings, with emphasis on changes in well-being occurring during psychotherapy.

Well-Being Therapy (WBT) is a short term, well-being-enhancing psychotherapeutic intervention, encompassing environmental mastery, personal growth, purpose in life, autonomy, self-acceptance, and positive relations with others. It may be applied as a relapse-preventive strategy in the residual phase of affective (mood and anxiety) disorders, as an additional ingredient of CBT treatment, in patients with affective disorders who failed to respond to standard pharmacological and psychotherapeutic treatments, in body image disorders, and in psychosomatic medicine. The first validation studies appeared to be promising. The author's, Ruini and Fava, hope that WBT may herald a new trend of psychotherapy research and practice in the current symptom-oriented settings.

Motivational Interviewing

Motivational Interviewing (MI) refers to a therapeutic approach developed by Miller and Rollnick (2002). It is a semi-directive method of engaging intrinsic motivation to change behavior by developing discrepancy and exploring and resolving ambivalence within the client.

Motivational interviewing recognizes and accepts the fact that clients who need to make changes in their lives approach therapy at different levels of readiness to change their behavior. If the therapy is mandated, they may never have thought of changing the behavior in question. Some may have thought about it but not taken steps to change it. Others, especially those voluntarily seeking counseling, may be actively trying to change their behavior and may have been doing so unsuccessfully for years. In Solution-Focused Brief Therapy these working relationships between the therapist and the client are defined as a visitor-, a complainant-, or a customer-relationship (see Chapter 5 for further explanation).

Motivational interviewing is nonjudgmental, nonconfrontational, and non-adversarial. The approach combines problem-focused and solution-focused interventions. It attempts to increase the client's awareness of the potential problems caused, consequences experienced, and risks faced as a result of the behavior in question. Alternatively, therapists help clients envisage a better future and become increasingly motivated to achieve it. Either way, the strategy seeks to help clients think differently about their behavior and ultimately to consider what might be gained through change.

Motivational interviewing is based upon four principles:

1. Express empathy, guides therapists to share with clients their understanding of the clients' perspective;
2. Develop discrepancy, guides therapists to help clients appreciate the value of change by exploring the discrepancy between how clients want their lives to be vs. how they currently are (or between their deeply-held values and their day-to-day behavior);
3. Roll with resistance, guides therapists to accept client reluctance to change as natural rather than pathological;
4. Support self-efficacy, guides therapists to explicitly embrace client autonomy (even when clients choose to not change) and help clients move toward change successfully and with confidence.

The main goals of motivational interviewing are to establish rapport, elicit change talk, and establish commitment language from the client. The "change talk" in MI is derived from Solution-Focused Brief Therapy. Some of these solution-focused questions are: How would you like to see things differently? What would be the positive consequences of this change? How would you like your life to be in five years' time? What makes you think you can change this? Where do you find the courage to change if you want to? How did you make positive changes before? Which personal strengths do you have that can help you make these changes? Bannink (2010a) lists more than 1000 solution-focused questions for general use and for use in specific situations.

Acceptance and Commitment Therapy

Acceptance and Commitment Therapy (ACT) differs from CBT in that rather than trying to teach people to better control their thoughts, feelings, sensations, memories, and other private events, ACT teaches them to "just notice," accept, and embrace their private events, especially previously unwanted ones. ACT was developed by Hayes, Strosahl, and Wilson (2003) and is also considered to be part of the so-called "third wave" of CBT.

ACT helps the individual get in contact with a transcendent sense of self known as 'self-as-context' – the you that is always there observing and experiencing and yet distinct from one's thoughts, feelings, sensations, and memories. ACT aims to help the individual clarify their personal values and to take action on them, bringing more vitality and meaning to their life in the process, increasing their psychological flexibility.

The core conception of ACT is that psychological suffering is usually caused by experiential avoidance, cognitive entanglement, and resulting psychological rigidity that leads to a failure to take needed behavioral steps in accord with core values. As a simple way to summarize the model, ACT views the core of many problems to be due to the concepts represented in the acronym, **FEAR**: **F**usion with your thoughts; **E**valuation of experience; **A**voidance of your experience; **R**eason-giving for your behavior. The healthy alternative is to **ACT**: **A**ccept your reactions and be present; **C**hoose a valued direction; **T**ake action.

ACT has shown preliminary research evidence of effectiveness in randomized trials for a variety of problems including chronic pain, depression, anxiety, psychosis, and eating disorders. ACT has more recently been applied to children and adolescents with good results.

Eye movement desensitization and reprocessing

Eye movement desensitization and reprocessing (EMDR) is a form of psychotherapy that was developed by Shapiro (2001) to resolve the development of trauma-related disorders caused by exposure to distressing events such as rape or military combat. According to Shapiro's theory, when a traumatic or distressing experience occurs, it may overwhelm usual cognitive and neurological coping mechanisms. The memory and associated stimuli of the event are inadequately processed and are dysfunctionally stored in an isolated memory network. The goal of EMDR is to process these distressing memories, reducing their lingering influence and allowing clients to develop more adaptive coping mechanisms.

EMDR uses a structured eight-phase approach to address the past, present, and future aspects of a traumatic or distressing memory that has been dysfunctionally stored. During the processing phases of EMDR, the client focuses on disturbing memory in multiple brief sets of about 15–30 seconds. Simultaneously, the client focuses on the dual attention stimulus. Following each set of such dual attention, the client is asked what associative information was elicited during the procedure. This new material usually becomes the focus of the next set. This process of alternating dual attention and personal association is repeated many times during the session. EMDR is established as an evidence-based treatment for PTSD. In several phases *positive interventions* are used, such as creating a safe place – an image or memory that elicits comfortable feelings and a positive sense of self. This safe place can be used later to bring closure to an incomplete session or to help a client tolerate a particularly upsetting session. Apart from a negative statement about the self, a positive cognition is also identified – a positive self-statement that is preferable to the negative cognition. In the debriefing phase the therapist gives appropriate information and support.

Schema Therapy

Schema Therapy (ST) is based on a theory that childhood and adolescent traumas are the most likely causes of borderline personality disorder and other personality disorders. Young, Klosko and Beck (1994) use the concept of schemas or core beliefs, which they call "lifetraps," as it is defined in Cognitive Psychology, and as such, schemas can be either healthy or maladaptive. Schema Therapy ultimately seeks to replace maladaptive schemas by more healthy schemas and thus repair early negative experiences. Maladaptive schemas are defined as and relate mainly to the lack of basic emotional needs met in childhood and a lack of appropriate relationships, bonds, and behaviors of the parents, caretakers, and others involved in the life of a growing child. The basic philosophy of Schema Therapy is that if basic safety, care, guidance, and affection are not met in childhood then these schemas begin to develop and often lead to unhealthy/unstable relationships, poor social skills, unhealthy lifestyle choices, self-destructiveness, and overall poor functionality.

By building caring bonds and enforcing self-examination, Schema Therapy aims to help a person to gain the self-confidence needed in order to achieve their ultimate goals.

Kuyken, Padesky, and Dudley (2009), however, not only focus on negative core beliefs but also on *positive client values*. These values can be understood as beliefs about what is most important in life. These beliefs typically are relatively enduring across situations and shape clients' choices and behaviors. Incorporating values into conceptualizations as part of a client's belief system enables the therapist to better understand clients' reactions across different situations. An example of such a positive value is: It is important to show love to my children. Besides personal values also positive cultural values may play an important role and can be a source of power in the clients' life (e.g., dignity, faith).

"Strengths can be incorporated at each stage of therapy. Goals can be stated as increasing strengths or positive values (e.g., be more considerate) as well as reducing distress (e.g., feel less anxious). Therapists can routinely ask about positive goals and aspirations in early sessions and add these to the client's list of presenting issues. Discussions of positive areas of a client's life often reveal alternative coping strategies to those used in problem areas. These often more adaptive coping strategies can be identified as part of the same process that identifies triggers and maintenance factors for problems. When it is time for behavioral experiments to alter maintenance cycles, the client can practice alternative coping responses drawn from more successful areas of life. Later in therapy, positive assumptions and core beliefs prove just as important as negative ones when forming longitudinal case conceptualizations (p. 101)." In this form of Schema Therapy there is a close collaboration with the client, the therapeutic alliance is used to encourage and motivate clients, Socratic methods are used to help construct new belief systems rather than to test out the old, behavioral experiments are used for the construction of new behavior patterns, and the focus is on building clients' resilience.

De Boer and Bannink (article forthcoming) conducted a pilot study, using a solution-focused form of ST. In Solution-Focused ST (SFST) the preferred future is the starting point and the focus of therapy. Then the pitfalls or "lifetraps" on the road to the goal are identified. This is similar to the "fantasy realization theory" described by Oettingen and Stephens (2009) (see Chapter 6). Already existing strengths and competences of the clients are used to form a new schema, which will help in reaching their goals: a so-called "helpful schema."

The focus is also on the strengths and competences themselves, which are often highlighted in SFST group therapy, where each client is a supporter for the others (see also Chapter 13). Positive self-affirmations are sought and strengthened and these are linked to the positive schema. This is similar to Kuyken *et al.* in the sense that therapists no longer only focus on reducing maladaptive schemas but help to build healthy schemas instead.

In this vein, Positive CBT does not use the – not very respectful – terms "difficult" or "complicated" clients, as is so often the case when referring to clients with personality disorders. These terms could also easily undermine the therapist's hope and optimism. The therapeutic alliance with these clients, or indeed their problems, may be seen as "difficult" or "complicated" but not the clients themselves.

Combination of CBT and Solution Focus

Green, Oades, and Grant (2006) combine CBT and Solution-Focused Brief Therapy in their life coaching group program. They examined the effects of a 10-week cognitive-behavioral, solution-focused program. Participants were randomly allocated to a life coaching group program or a waiting list control group. Participation in the life coaching group program was associated with significant increases in goal-striving, well-being, and hope, with gains maintained up to 30 weeks later on some variables.

These results are consistent with hope theory that suggests the articulation of goals stimulates hope (Snyder, Michael, and Cheavens, 1999). Hope theory may also be useful in explaining enhanced well-being. Hope theory states that the unimpeded pursuit of one's desired goals results in positive emotions and well-being (Snyder, Rand, and Sigmon, 2005). In the life coaching program a cognitive behavioral component was employed to encourage examination of self-talk that may hinder or help the goal striving process. Participants were encouraged to increase their agentic thoughts using this technique.

The use of solution-focused techniques in the life-coaching program was utilized to help participants determine possible routes to their goal and thereby increase "pathways thinking" (see Chapter 5). Green, Oades, and Grant (2006) conclude: "It seems therefore a cognitive-behavioural, solution-focused coaching intervention, such as the one utilized in this study may be a hope-enhancing intervention" (p. 148). Life coaching programs that utilize evidence-based techniques may provide a framework for further research on psychological processes that occur in nonclinical populations who wish to make purposeful change and enhance their positive psychological functioning.

Possibilities of Positive CBT

So what are the possibilities of an even more positive CBT than described in the interventions mentioned previously? In Solution-Focused Brief Therapy the client is invited to define his preferred future. If you invite me to define mine, I see in my mind's eye a Positive CBT where:

- the 60–70 percent of clients now profiting from traditional CBT will go up to maybe 80–90 percent, with more people benefiting from CBT;
- there will be better and/or faster results within the 60–70% group when using Positive CBT;
- according to the "least burden principle" therapists will impose the least demanding interventions on their clients. As an example it may not always be necessary to go through exposure procedures during the treatment of posttraumatic stress disorder, when a focus on posttraumatic success (resilience) sometimes may be sufficient (Tedeschi and Calhoun, 2004; Bannink, 2008b);
- there will be an increase in self-efficacy and self-esteem, because Positive CBT focuses on character strengths, positive values, competences, and resources, ensuring more sustainability of the changes made in therapy;
- there will be an increase in behavior maintenance. In other – more negative terms – there will be a decrease in relapse;
- the average number of sessions will be shorter, as in Solution-Focused Brief Therapy, where the average number is 3–4 sessions, with the same follow-up results as in problem-focused psychotherapies (Stams *et al.*, 2006);
- CBT will therefore be more cost-effective;
- Positive CBT will be used in the prevention of problems, such as depression by training clients to be more optimistic (see the exercise in Chapter 7); or preventing suicide (Seligman, 2011);
- Positive CBT will work (better) for "therapy veterans": clients with chronic and severe mental illness (see later);
- Positive CBT can be used as a form of "e-therapy," commonly called Online Therapy. This refers to mental health services delivered by email, chat, and/or webcam. Clients seeking help with their psychological problems and concerns can often, from the comfort of their own home, speak to an online psychologist. E-therapy allows for individuals to seek help confidentially, conveniently, and if desired, anonymously. The protocols used in Positive CBT (see Appendices 1 and 3 for the protocols of the first and subsequent sessions) are a very good fit for e-therapy;
- last but not least Positive CBT will be more kind to its therapists: there will be less stress, less depression, less suicide, less burnout, and less secondary traumatization amongst CBT therapists. In this way, the "least burden principle" applies not only to our clients but also to ourselves as therapists.

Chronic and severe mental illness

Is Positive CBT only useful in cases of light to moderate symptomatology or can it also be applied in cases of chronic and severe mental illness? The answer is that also in these cases there is always a person beyond and outside the chronic and/or severe mental illness who can, as much as possible, reclaim his life and his identity from the illness. O'Hanlon and Rowan (2003, p. ix) state: "Over time, we have become increasingly convinced that traditional pathological language, labels, belief systems, and treatment methods can inhibit positive change. In fact, a hopeless situation can be engendered with unintentional and unfortunate cues from treatment milieus, therapists, family members, and oneself. Iatrogenic discouragement – that which is inadvertently induced by treatment – is often the result of such an unfortunate view of human perception and behaviour. The impact of inpatient psychiatric treatment and a pathological view increases the probability of iatrogenic illness and discouragement through stigmatization, self-depreciation, and chronicity. Our approach seeks to avoid iatrogenic harm and, instead, to create iatrogenic health and healing."

They offer an approach to therapy that emphasizes health, competence, and possibilities, instead of the traditional emphasis on pathology, deficits, and limitations. People have fluctuations in their biochemical and neurological states, and these fluctuations can influence the severity and course of their problems; various external and internal elements can influence state changes. It is this fluctuation in a positive and helpful direction that gives us hope (exceptions to the problem). Their approach is to help clients (and others) to notice and use the best of what works to lessen the symptoms or cope with them in the best way, thereby triggering better biochemical, psychological, and emotional states. Some useful questions are:

- When did you not have this problem, even when you expected you would? (finding exceptions);
- What happens when the problem ends or starts to end?
- How come the problem is not worse?
- What do you do when you don't listen to the voices? (in the case of psychosis);
- Tell me about some times when you haven't believed the lies these voices try to tell you (exceptions);
- When paranoia whispers in your ear, do you always listen? (technique of "externalization" – see Chapter 7);
- What happens when you overcome the urge to cut yourself? (in the case of automutilation) (finding exceptions);
- When you look back at the last 14 days, when was there a day you automutilated less, even just a little bit? What was different then? (finding exceptions);
- How long has anorexia had you in its grip? (externalization);
- What strengths do you think you possess to stand up to depression?
- What can you tell me about your past that would help me understand how you have been able to stand up to these symptoms so well?
- Which other people, who have known you when you were not ill, could remind you of your strengths, your accomplishments, and that your life is worth living?

In Chapter 16 I will return to the possibilities mentioned previously and describe what this means for further research and the training of CBT therapists.

On a scale where 10 stands for my preferred future and 0 stands for the worst situation possible, I think CBT is at this moment at a 3–4. What is already present in this 3–4 is described earlier in this chapter. However, I am confident that the number will and can increase in the coming years. Hopefully the writing of this book will be one of the steps in the right direction towards Positive CBT.

4

Two Positive Sources

It is never too late to be who you might have been

George Eliot

Introduction

In this chapter I will present two positive sources of Positive CBT: Positive Psychology and Solution-Focused Brief Therapy.

Positive Psychology is an umbrella term that includes a basic academic discipline principally concerned with understanding positive human thought, feeling, and behavior; an empirical pursuit of systematically understanding psychological phenomena; and finally an applied discipline in which certain interventions are created and employed.

Solution-Focused Brief Therapy is the pragmatic application of a set of principles and tools, probably best described as finding the direct route to "what works." The nature of Solution-Focused Brief Therapy is nonacademic; the pursuit is finding what works for this client at this moment in this context. The emphasis is on constructing solutions as a counterweight to the traditional emphasis on the analysis of problems. "Interventions can initiate change without the therapist's first understanding, in any detail, what has been going on" (De Shazer, 1985, p. 119). It is an approach to change, which invites conversations about what is wanted, what is working, and what might constitute progress.

I will conclude this chapter with a short comparison between the two: their research and how recent findings from neuroscience underline their effectiveness. Although Positive Psychology and Solution Focus are different enterprises, the conclusion is that both are aiming to help clients to have a better future and to flourish.

Practicing Positive CBT: From Reducing Distress to Building Success, First Edition. Fredrike Bannink.
© 2012 John Wiley & Sons, Ltd. Published 2012 by John Wiley & Sons, Ltd.

Source 1: Positive Psychology

Positive Psychology is the study of what makes life worth living and what enables individuals and communities to thrive. It is also the study of the conditions and processes that lead to optimal functioning in individuals, in relations, and in work.

The notion of a Positive Psychology movement began at a moment in time after Seligman had been elected president of the American Psychological Association (1997). While he was weeding his garden, his five-year-old daughter Nikki was throwing weeds into the air and dancing around. He yelled at her, Nikki walked away, came back, and said: "Daddy, I want to talk to you. Do you remember before my fifth birthday? From the time I was three to the time I was five, I was a whiner, I whined every day. When I turned five, I decided not to whine any more. That was the hardest thing I've ever done. And if I can stop whining, you can stop being such a grouch."

Seligman learned from Nikki something about raising kids, about himself, and about his profession. He realized that raising children is more than fixing what is wrong with them. It is about identifying and nurturing their strongest qualities, what they own and are best at, and helping them find niches in which they can best live out these positive qualities. He realized about himself that he was a grouch and decided to change. The broadest implication, however, was about the science and practice of psychology. After World War II psychologists discovered that they could make a living treating mental illness and academics found out that they could get grants if their research was about pathology. This has brought many benefits: at least 14 disorders can now be cured or considerably relieved. But the downside was that making the lives of all people more productive and fulfilling and identifying and nurturing high talent were forgotten. Psychology became a victimology and psychologists became pathologizers. Psychology's empirical focus shifted to assessing and curing individual suffering. There has been an explosion in research on psychological disorders and the negative effects of environmental stressors such as parental divorce, death, and physical and sexual abuse. Practitioners went about treating mental illness within the disease-patient framework of repairing damage.

In 2005, Seligman, one of the founders of Positive Psychology, wrote: "The message of the positive psychology movement is to remind our field that it has been deformed. Psychology is not just the study of disease, weakness, and damage; it also is the study of strength and virtue. Treatment is not just fixing what is wrong; it also is building what is right. Psychology is not just about illness or health; it also is about work, education, insight, love, growth, and play. And in this quest for what is best, Positive Psychology does not rely on wishful thinking, self-deception, or hand waving; instead, it tries to adapt what is best in the scientific method to the unique problems that human behaviour presents in all its complexity" (p. 4).

The focus on (mental) health did, however, not start with Seligman and his daughter Nikki. Already in 1937 a philanthropist, Grant, met with a director of a university health service and together they decided that medical research was too weighted in the direction of disease. They agreed that large endowments had been given for the study of the mentally and physically ill, but very few had thought it pertinent to make a systematic inquiry into the kinds of people who are well and do well. As a result they selected a healthy sample of several consecutive college classes (268 Harvard graduates from the classes of 1939–1944) for intensive medical and psychological study: the now famous "Grant study" was born. The Grant study is the longest longitudinal study of adult development ever conducted. For 68 years, men have been studied (they forgot to include women!) from adolescence into late life to identify the predictors of healthy aging (Vaillant, 1995).

The original Positive Psychology theory was that happiness could be analyzed into three different elements: positive emotion, engagement, and meaning. The first is positive emotion: what we feel: pleasure, serenity, ecstasy, warmth, comfort, and so on, called the "pleasant life." The second element is engagement: this is about flow, being one with the music, time stopping, and the loss of self-consciousness during an absorbing activity, called the "engaged life." The third element is meaning: this consists in belonging to and serving something that is bigger than the self: religion, nature, family, political party, called the "meaningful life."

In his latest book Seligman (2011) changed the topic of Positive Psychology from happiness to well-being. The goal of Positive Psychology is to increase flourishing by increasing positive emotion (P), engagement (E), positive relationships (R), meaning (M), and accomplishment (A). A handy mnemonic is PERMA.

His recent well-being theory (former happiness theory) adds "positive relationships" and "accomplishment" to the three previous elements. The element of positive relationships is added because other people are the best antidote to the downs of life and the single most reliable up. Doing a kindness to another person produces the single most reliable momentary increase in well-being of any exercise tested in Positive Psychology research. Happiness and life satisfaction are all aspects of positive relationships.

The fifth element is accomplishment: people pursue success, accomplishment, winning, achievement, and mastery for their own sakes, even when it brings no positive emotion, no meaning, and no positive relationships. The addition of the "achieving life" also emphasizes that the task of Positive Psychology is to describe, rather than prescribe, what people actually do to get well-being.

In authentic happiness theory, the strengths and virtues are the support only for engagement. You go into flow when your highest strengths are deployed to meet the highest challenges that come your way. In well-being theory, the 24 strengths underpin all five elements, not just engagement. Deploying your highest strengths leads to more positive emotion, to more meaning, to more accomplishment, and to better relationships.

Exercise 4.1

Each morning, after waking up, note to yourself at least 20 things for which you are grateful. This may seem daunting, but once you get into the habit and find the right frame of mind, it may become easier. Here are some examples of things you could note and appreciate: That I have hot and cold running water, that I have a roof over my head, that I have clean clothes, that I am alive, that I have friends, and so on.

Experiment to discover what works best for you; writing down the appreciations, saying them out loud to your spouse, a family member, writing them on a piece of paper, or silently noting them to yourself. Try this activity for a week and notice what difference it makes. Then decide whether you would like to continue this habit or not.

The label of Positive Psychology represents those efforts of professionals to help people optimize human functioning by acknowledging strengths as well as deficiencies, and environmental resources in addition to stressors. The study of mental health is distinct from and complementary to the long-standing interest in mental illness, its prevalence, and its remedies (Keyes and Lopez, 2005, p. 55). "This new approach would recognize that health is not merely the absence of illness symptoms but also the presence of symptoms of well-being. To achieve the goal of genuine or complete mental health, we must begin to diagnose and study the aetiology and treatments associated with mental health, and we must develop a science of mental health. The data clearly show that mental illness and mental health are correlated but distinct dimensions."

In Positive Psychology the question is not: "What is wrong with you?" but: "What is right with you?" What amazes me is that many practitioners working within Positive Psychology still use the problem-focused pathology model of psychotherapy, as does traditional CBT. Seligman for example (2011) describes how he uses traditional problem-focused CBT techniques in building mental toughness in the US army. In one part of his training the theme is: learning the skills of resilience. They start out with Ellis's ABC model: C (the emotional consequences) do not stem directly from A (the adversity), but from B (beliefs about the adversity). Then the focus shifts to so-called "thinking-traps," like overgeneralizing, followed by identifying and questioning "icebergs" (core beliefs) and minimizing and challenging catastrophic beliefs.

This is all very much based on the pathology model and is problem-focused: reducing distress by using the problem-solving medical model. In my opinion a more positive approach would be to build on successes, using the solution-focused model. The focus is no longer on which cognitions are wrong and should be replaced with more realistic cognitions, but on finding which cognitions are already "right" and can be repeated.

Peterson (2006) developed the Values in Action Signature Strengths (VIA) test (available on the Authentic Happiness website at www.authentichappiness. org). This survey has been developed to reliably classify people on the basis of 24 character strengths, ranging from honesty, loyalty, perseverance, creativity, kindness, wisdom, courage, to fairness, and 16 others. Together with Seligman, Peterson surveyed diverse world cultures to create a comprehensive index of character strengths and virtues.

The taxonomy of strengths and virtues is meant as a positive alternative to the DSM-IV-TR taxonomy of psychiatric disorders (and can also be used in combination with the DSM-IV-TR). Every person can register at this website and take all the tests for free. The website is intended as a public service (more than 2 million people have already registered at the website and taken the tests, among them the VIA test). Tests include emotion questionnaires, engagement questionnaires (among which is the Brief Strengths Test, measuring the 24 Character Strengths, see Table 4.1), meaning questionnaires, and life satisfaction questionnaires.

Assessment in Positive CBT may take the form of inviting clients to take the test online at home and bring the printed outcome with them to the next session. The therapist and client then pay attention to the rank order of the strengths of each client. Then clients are asked to list their five highest strengths and are invited to provide some examples of how they used these strengths lately (or in the past). Not surprisingly the atmosphere in the session becomes more positive when clients are invited to talk about their successes and strengths.

The key to extracting more than a temporary high out of listing these strengths, however, is to invite clients to reshape their lives in such a way that they are able to apply their strengths more often. Seligman, Steen, Park, and Peterson (2005) discovered that the boost in positivity that comes from learning about one's strengths is significant, but temporary. By contrast, the boost in positivity that comes from finding new ways to apply these strengths is significant and lasting.

Table 4.1 Organization of the 24 character strengths.

Wisdom and knowledge. These are the five strengths that involve the acquisition and use of knowledge: creativity, curiosity, open-mindedness, love of learning, perspective and wisdom
Courage. These are the four strengths that allow one to accomplish goals in the face of opposition: bravery, persistence, integrity, and vitality
Humanity. These are the three strengths of tending and befriending others: love, kindness, and social intelligence
Justice. These are the three strengths that build a healthy community: social responsibility and loyalty, fairness, and leadership
Temperance. These are the four strengths that protect against excess: forgiveness and mercy, humility, prudence, self-regulation and self-control
Transcendence. These are the five strengths that forge connections to the larger universe and provide meaning: appreciation of beauty, gratitude, hope, humor and playfulness, and spirituality

Source: Adapted from Flourish, 2011.

Exercise 4.2

This "defining moments" exercise builds on research of the "you at your best" exercise (see Chapter 9). The purpose of this exercise is to facilitate exploration of your character strengths, to build a bridge between past critical experiences and future possibilities, and to link positive identity formation with character strengths. There are three steps:

1. *Name the defining moment; tell the story (e.g., passing an important exam);*
2. *List the character strengths involved in your story;*
3. *Reflect on how this story has shaped how you are (your identity); how has it impacted you to the present day.*

Exercise 4.3

After you (and you may also invite your client to do so) have completed the VIA test (or have taken a look at Table 4.1), create a designated time in your schedule when you will exercise one or more of your signature strengths in a new way, either at work or at home or in leisure. Just make sure that you create a clearly defined opportunity to use it. For example if one of your strengths is creativity, you may begin working on writing a book or play. How did you feel before, during, and after engaging in the activity? Was the activity challenging or easy? Did time pass quickly? Do you plan to repeat the exercise?

Exercise 4.4

The key to building a new habit is to practice the behavior, over and over. This works for your character strengths as well. Find ways that are comfortable for you to practice using them. Here are a few ways that resonate for many people:

Conversation: *talk with others about your strengths; tell stories about how your strengths have helped you and were at play when you were at your best. Use your strengths while you are in conversation, for example; if you want to build upon your curiosity, ask questions with a sense of genuine interest.*

Journaling: *write about your strengths; explore them in this intra-personal way. For example, if you want to build upon your prudence, consider a situation you are conflicted about, and write about the costs and benefits of both sides.*

Self-monitoring: *set up a tracking system to monitor your experiences throughout the day. Track one or more of the strengths you are using hour by hour; you might need an alarm or another external cue to remind yourself to closely track the use of your strengths. This strategy involves using your strength of self-regulation.*

Positive Psychology is an umbrella term for the research and application of many different constructs. The so-called "Positive Psychology Family" consists of family members such as optimism, hope, self-efficacy, self-esteem, positive emotions, flow, happiness, gratitude, and so on. In the last decade much research has taken place and many books have been published on Positive Psychology (Snyder and Lopez, 2005; Fredrickson, 2009; Bannink, 2009a, 2011; Seligman, 2011).

One of the researchers in the Positive Psychology field is Fredrickson (2009). She developed the "broaden-and-build theory of positive emotions," introducing 10 forms of positivity: joy, gratitude, serenity, interest, hope, pride, amusement, inspiration, awe, and love. These forms are targets of a growing amount of scientific research and they color people's day-to-day lives the most. Positive emotions have a broadening effect: they open us, broaden our minds and expand our range of vision. They broaden people's attention, and enhance creativity and empathy. Scientific experiments confirm that people who come to the negotiation table with a cooperative and friendly spirit, strike the best business deals (Kopelman, Rosette, and Thompson, 2006).

Fredrickson (2009) found that the connection between the "positivity ratio" and flourishing is evident at three very different levels of human experience. Whether you are one person, two partners, or a team, this so-called positivity ratio is worth attention. The positivity ratio is the amount of heartfelt positivity relative to the amount of heart-wrenching negativity. Stated formally, the positivity ratio is the frequency of positivity over any given time span, divided by the frequency of negativity over that same time span (P/N). Below a certain ratio, people get pulled into a downward spiral fueled by negativity. Yet above this same ratio, people are drawn along an upward spiral energized by positivity. Fredrickson (2009, p. 16) states: "Downward spiral or upward spiral. As I see it, that's your choice."

Research has shown that when individuals flourish, with a positivity ratio of 3:1 or more, health, productivity, and peace follow. And the good news is that happiness, in the long run, turns out to be more contagious than depression (Fowler and Christakis, 2008), so an upward spiral of positivity will occur.

Exercise 4.5

Here are three questions for a happy life and for well-being:

1. *What did I do today that I found satisfying?*
2. *What did someone else do that I found satisfying? Did I react in a way so this person might do this again?*
3. *What else do I see, hear, feel, smell, or taste for which I am grateful?*

Story 4.1: The Power of Positive Emotions

Scientists examined the ways physicians make medical diagnoses by having them think aloud while they solved the case of a patient with liver disease. Astonishingly, this research team found that when they gave physicians a small gift – simply a bag of candy – those physicians were better at integrating case information and less likely to become fixated on their initial ideas, coming to premature closure in their diagnosis.

Source: Adapted from Isen, Rosenzweig, and Young (1991)

Exercise 4.6

In this exercise there are listed 5 × 10 = 50 positive things to find happiness and well-being. It is great fun to talk about these 50 things with your partner, children, or colleagues. Don't forget to ask them about their 50 positive things:

1. *Name 10 positive personal traits;*
2. *Name 10 successes in your life;*
3. *Name 10 ways in which you are kind to others;*
4. *Name 10 windfalls in your life;*
5. *Name 10 ways in which others support you.*

Source 2: Solution-Focused Brief Therapy

Solution-Focused Brief Therapy (SFBT) is an approach to psychotherapy based on solution-building rather than problem-solving. It explores current resources and future hopes rather than present problems and past causes and typically involves only 3–5 sessions. It has great value as a preliminary and often sufficient intervention and can be used safely as an adjunct to other treatments. It is a structured process for understanding how to capitalize on change, whereby problems are acknowledged but not analyzed. SFBT is about a useful interaction that leaves the client changed; with more hope, more creative ideas, a feeling of competence, and a clearer view of possibilities.

The solution-focused model in psychotherapy was developed during the 1980s by De Shazer, Berg, and colleagues at the Brief Family Therapy Center in Milwaukee, USA. They expanded upon the findings of Watzlawick, Weakland, and Fisch (1974), who found that the attempted solution would sometimes perpetuate the problem and that an understanding of the origins of the problem was not always necessary. Propositions of De Shazer (1985) are:

- The development of a solution is not necessarily related to the problem. An analysis of the problem itself is not useful in finding solutions, whereas an analysis of exceptions to the problem is;
- The clients are the experts. They are the ones who determine the goal and the road to achieving this;
- If it is not broken, do not fix it. Leave alone what is positive in the perception of the clients;
- If something works (better), continue with it. Even though it may be something completely different from what was expected;
- If something does not work, do something else. More of the same leads nowhere.

Story 4.2: Do Something Different for a Change

According to a Japanese legend, a coastal village was once threatened by a tidal wave, but the wave was sighted in advance, far out on the horizon, by a lone farmer in the rice fields on the hillside above the village. There was no use in shouting and there was no time to go home to warn his people. At once he set fire to the field, and the villagers who came swarming up to save their crops were saved from flood.

Asking questions is an important technique in Solution-focused Brief Therapy. The four basic solution-focused questions, developed by Bannink, (2009e, 2010a, 2010b) are as follows:

1. What are your best hopes?
2. What difference will that make?
3. What is already working?
4. What will be the next step/next sign of progress?

Solution-focused questions differ from the problem-focused questions used in "Socratic questioning," a widely used technique in traditional CBT. The purpose of Socratic questioning is to help uncover the assumptions and evidence that underpin people's thoughts with respect to problems. Some Socratic questions to deal with automatic thoughts that distress the patient are about: revealing the issue ("What evidence supports this idea?"); conceiving reasonable alternatives ("What might be another explanation or viewpoint of the situation?"); examining various potential consequences ("What are the worst, best, bearable, and most realistic outcomes?"); evaluate those consequences ("What's the effect of thinking or believing this?"); and distancing ("Imagine a specific friend/family member in the same situation or if they viewed the situation this way, what would I tell them?").

The *first basic solution-focused question* is: What are your best hopes? Hope is one of the major constructs of Positive Psychology. *Hope theory* states that hope is like a journey: a destination (goal), a road map (pathway thinking), and a means of transport (agency thinking) are needed. Research on the subject of hope (Snyder, 2002) has shown that it is important to have a goal and ways to reach that goal. Hopeful people have a clearer goal (destination) than nonhopeful people. They also have a clearer image of the route via which they can reach their goal: they have a mental map. In addition they believe that they themselves can do something to get closer to their goal (they are their own means of transport). And should the route to the goal be blocked, high-hope persons will think of an alternative more easily and will continue to feel better than low-hope persons. Therefore the first question in SFBT, after establishing rapport, is: "What are your best hopes?" Or: "What is your hoped for outcome of this therapy?" In a systems- or group therapy the therapist makes sure he invites all participants to think and talk about their hopes for a better future.

Offering a vision that change is possible and that there are new and better ways to deal with the situation, is important in therapy. SFBT fits well with this value, because solution building is about the development of a well-formed goal through asking about client's best hopes and what differences those would make. Those questions encourage clients to develop a detailed vision of what their lives might be like when their problems are over. The emphasis is on inviting clients to create the vision by drawing on their own frames of reference by listening for openings in sometimes problem-focused conversations. It relies less on therapists' suggestions than do problem-solving approaches. It fosters hope and motivation in clients and promotes self-determination. SFBT also counters any tendency to raise false hope in clients. They define their own visions for change and, as experts about their situation, clarify what parts of the preferred future can and cannot happen. They think and explain what is realistic and what is not.

Questions about hope are different from questions about expectations. The question: "What do you expect from this therapy?" invites clients to look at the therapist for the solution of their problem. The risk might be that they see you (the therapist) as the only means of transport to reach their goal instead of themselves.

The *second basic solution-focused question* is: "What difference will that make?" Asking this question invites clients to describe their preferred future in positive, concrete, and realistic terms. Many will say that they will feel relieved, at rest, relaxed, or happy, when they describe their preferred future. How will they react and how will they interact? What will their day look like? What will they be doing differently, so others will know that the clients have reached their preferred future? Questions about differences are always asked in the future tense, since hope can only ever be about the future. Mostly this preferred future will be described without the problem that brought them to therapy, although some clients describe their preferred future with the problem still present, but without it bothering them so much anymore.

De Shazer (1991) states that it is difference itself that is an important tool for professionals and clients. In and of themselves, differences are just differences, they do not work spontaneously. Only when recognized, can they be put to work to make a difference. "In the language game of therapy, the client's story makes the therapist see things one way: the therapist's revision (a difference) makes the client see things another way" (p. 156). The therapist needs to find a point or element in the client's story that allows for a difference being put to work. There are many possible points where a distinction can be marked, places where a difference can be pointed to. Any of these differences might be put to work toward making a difference so that the client can say that his life is more satisfactory.

Change is happening all the time and the role of the therapist is to find useful change and amplify it. Since SFBT is about change and helping clients to make a better future, questions about positive differences are considered very important. What difference will it make when your best hopes become reality? How will your future look? What will you be doing differently? How will your relationship with the other person(s) differ? What will they be doing differently (Bannink, 2010a, 2010c).

Asking about exceptions to the problem in the present or in the past is another way of asking about differences. When the problem is/was there to a lesser extent, what is/was different then? What are/were you doing differently, what are/were other persons doing differently? How is/was your relationship different back then? Questions about exceptions can be very useful, since they may reveal what is/was working in better times. Some things that were helpful in the past may be used anew to improve the life of the client. Also scaling questions (see later) may help to find "differences that make a difference." Scaling questions can be asked about progress but also about pretreatment change, hope, motivation, and confidence that the client can reach his goal.

Exercise 4.7

Think of something you would like to change. Ask yourself: Suppose things could change, what difference will that make? What else will be different? What else? See how you will probably come up with more things than you imagined you would (this is called the "upward arrow technique," described in more detail in Chapter 7).

Exercise 4.8

This is an exercise for "positive blame." When we ask for exceptions to the problem, past successes, or present solutions, we are using a form of "positive blame." "How were you able to do that?" "How did you come up with that fine idea?" The hidden message behind this question is that the client has achieved a degree of capability and – if appropriate – this success may be repeated.

Case 4.1

The therapist says to the client: Here is a different kind of question, called a "scaling question," one which puts things on a scale from 10 to 0. Let's say that 10 equals how your life will be when all is going very well and 0 equals how bad things were when you made the appointment to see me. Where are you on that scale today? And where would you like to be at the end of this therapy? What will be different in your life then?

Case 4.2

A client says she might feel happy if she lost 50 pounds. The therapist asks her: What difference will it make in your life when you have lost the first 1 or 2 pounds? The woman replies that she might feel slightly better and that she would cautiously begin to believe that losing more weight was possible. The therapist then asks her what difference that slightly better feeling and that bit of hope would make in her life. She says that she would go outside more and would also be a bit nicer to her children and her husband, because her mood would improve. The client's vision of her preferred future is further magnified, which increases the chance that she will take the first step.

The *third basic solution-focused question* is: What is already working?

The therapist may start by asking for pretreatment change (see Chapter 6). Most clients have tried other ideas before seeing a therapist. The therapist can inform whether changes already occurred before the first session. It still is a common assumption that clients begin to change when the therapist starts to help them with their problem. But change is happening in all clients' lives. When asked, two thirds of clients in psychotherapy report positive change between the moment they made the appointment and the first session (Weiner-Davis *et al.*, 1987).

Shining a spotlight on change illuminates already existing clients' strengths and resources and allows their enlistment. Of special interest is what clients have done to bring about this change. The therapist may ask: "Many clients notice that, between the time they call for an appointment and the first session, things already seem different. What have you noticed about your situation?"

Exploration of pretreatment change can reveal new and useful information. When clients report that some things are already better, even just a little bit, the therapist may ask competence questions like: How did you do that? How did you decide to do that? Where did you get this good idea?

When asked about what is already working, exception-finding questions are frequently used. Those questions are new to many clients, who are more accustomed to problem-focused questions. When asked about exceptions, which are the keys to solutions, they may start noticing them for the first time. Solutions are often built from formerly unrecognized differences. Wittgenstein (1968) states that exceptions lie already on the surface, you don't have to dig for them. The aspects of things that are most important for us are hidden because of their simplicity and familiarity. We are unable to notice something, because it is always before one's eyes.

The therapist, having heard and explored these exceptions, then compliments the clients for all the things they have already done. Exploration of exceptions is similar to other aspects of SFBT in that it respects the client's frame of reference.

A "scaling question" can be used: "On a scale where 10 equals you have reached your preferred future and 0 equals the worst situation you can imagine, where would you say you are right now?" By means of scaling questions, the therapist can help clients to express complex, intuitive observations about their past experiences and estimates of future possibilities. Scaling questions invite clients to put their observations, impressions, and predictions on a scale from 10 to 0. For example, you may ask your client: "On a scale from 10 to 0, where 10 means you are confident that you can reach your goal and 0 means you are not confident at all, where would you say you are now?"

Scaling questions can function as the starting point for successive approximation, also known as "shaping." This is a form of operant conditioning, in which the increasingly accurate approximations of a desired response are reinforced.

The *fourth and last basic solution-focused question* is either: What will be your next step? or: What will be a next sign of progress? By asking: What will be *your* next step, the therapist invites each client to – maybe for the first time – actually think about what they themselves can do to ameliorate the situation instead of waiting for other(s) or the therapist to do something.

This question is only asked when clients want or need to go up further on the scale of progress. When the current state is the best possible state at that moment, then the conversation can continue by asking clients how they can maintain the status quo.

The question about the next sign of progress is open as to who should do what and when. A sign of progress may also be something that could happen without the clients taking action.

These four basic solution-focused questions can be seen as *skeleton keys*: keys that fit in many different locks. You don't have to explore and analyze each lock (e.g., each problem) before you can use these keys. The keys can be used for all Axis I and Axis II disorders (DSM IV-TR). Research done by Grant and

O'Connor (2010) shows that problem-focused questions reduce negative affect and increase self-efficacy, but do not increase understanding of the nature of the problem or enhance positive affect. Solution-focused questions increase positive affect, decrease negative affect, increase self-efficacy as well as increase participants' insight and understanding of the nature of the problem.

When is the client able to see glimpses of the future he desires? If these positive exceptions have manifested themselves, the therapist can solicit more information about them. If they have not yet appeared, but a goal can be formulated at this point, the therapist can inquire about that. If that is not the case, the problem can be analyzed. It is only necessary to shift to problem analysis if no improvement has occurred before the first session, if no exceptions can be found, and if no goal can be formulated in behavioral terms by means of, say, the miracle question (described later in this book) or other goal-formulation questions. In most cases, one can immediately begin working toward a solution without elaborately mapping the problem first (De Shazer, 1985).

Is it possible to solve problems without even talking about them? The answer is "yes." The question is: "Suppose there is a solution, . . ." and then ask your clients to think about:

- . . . what difference will that make in their own lives and in the lives of important others;
- . . . who will be the first to notice;
- . . . what will be the first small sign that a solution is underway;
- . . . what else will be better.

Most of our clients – and colleagues – still think the only therapy-game is the "problem-focused game," whereby it is necessary to explore and analyze the problem before solutions can be found and administered. In the new "strengths and solutions-focused game," the problem does not have to be explored and analyzed (again). The new game is about what clients want to be different in their lives and how to make that happen: exploration and analysis is about the clients' goal, at the same time acknowledging their suffering. This may be done without knowing or understanding the problem in great detail, making psychotherapy more positive and more cost-effective.

The Dutch Association of Behavioural and Cognitive Therapy (VGCt) founded in 2006 the successful Solution-Focused Cognitive Behaviour Therapy Section. By way of result, one out of ten Dutch CBT therapists are now already working in a positive and solution-focused way and their number is still growing. SFBT can be seen as a form of CBT, which is explained in more detail by Bannink (2005, 2006a, 2008a, 2010a).

Selekman (1993) gives a number of pragmatic solution-focused assumptions. They offer therapists a *new lens* for looking at their clients.

1. *The term resistance is not useful.* It suggests that the client is not willing to change and that the professional is detached from the treatment system (De Shazer, 1984). Therefore resistance is not a useful concept. It is preferable to approach each client in a cooperative manner rather than from a position of

resistance, power, and control. The professional uses the client's strong points and resources, his words and opinions, and asks competence questions.

2. *Change is a continuous process; stability is an illusion.* The question is not whether but when change will occur. The client can be helped in making *positive self-fulfilling prophecies.* A direct relation appears to exist between talking about change and the actual result. It is helpful to talk about successes in the past, present, and future. Collecting information about past and present failures, however, often leads to negative outcomes.

    As soon as the client is invited to notice and value small changes (the exceptions), he will begin to expect other changes to take place and will start believing in the snowball effect. Often the beginnings of a solution already lie in the client but remain unnoticed. These are the exceptions to the problem (hidden successes). Inquiring into the exceptions gives insight into which positive actions could happen to a larger extent or more often; inquiring into hypothetical solutions also gives insight into the direction of the search. Because the client is the expert and finds the solutions himself, they suit him and are compatible with his situation, are found quickly, and will endure. Solution-focused therapists maintain a nonpathological view of people. Generally people have, or have had, one or more difficulties in their life. These may have become chronic, depending on the way in which the client or those around him (including therapists) react. The client possesses resources and competences that can be drawn on. As a result, hope and self-confidence can be rebuilt.

3. *No problem is always there to the same extent: there are always fluctuations.*

4. *Not a great deal about the problem needs to be known in order to solve it.* The professional may investigate what the client is doing differently when the problem is not there or there to a lesser extent, or what is different about those times when there ceases to be a problem for a while.

5. *The client defines the goal for treatment.* It is important to receive from the client a very precise and detailed *description* of what his life will look like once his goal is reached.

6. *Our theories determine what we observe.* Reality is observer-defined and the professional participates in co-creating the system's reality. A psychoanalytical therapist will probably see unsolved conflicts and psychological deficits. It is impossible for professionals to not have a theory. Solution-focused therapists are co-authors who help the clients rewrite their problem-saturated story. De Shazer (1984) sees professional and client as tennis players on the same side of the net; the professional is not an observer on the sidelines.

7. *There exist no definitive explanations or descriptions of reality.* There are many ways to look at a situation, all equally correct. Therapists should not be too attached to their own preference models: nothing is more dangerous than an idea, if that is the only one you have!

Finally, traditional forms of psychotherapy engage in an "A" (present) to "B" (preferred future) planning, whereas SFBT engages in a "B" to "A" planning. Through application of detailing a preferred future, scaling, identifying what is already working and specifying signs of progress, the whole strategic planning process is literally turned on its head, as can be seen in the following story.

Story 4.3: Working from the Future Back

An English psychiatrist, named MacAdam, told this story: "A young girl I was working with had experienced abuse. She walked into my office . . . a very large girl with shaved hair, tattoos on her head and I don't think she'd showered in a week. I'd been asked to see her because she was so angry. She clearly didn't want to come and see a shrink. She'd been to a bunch of therapists before, social workers, psychologists, and school counselors. I just said, "You've talked to everybody about your past; let's talk about your dreams for the future." And her whole face just lit up when she said her dream was to become a princess.

In my mind, I couldn't think of two more opposite visions, but I took it very seriously. I asked her about what the concept of princess meant to her. She started talking about being a people's princess who would do things for others, who would be caring and generous and a beautiful ambassador. And she described the princess as slender and well dressed. Over the next few months, we started talking about what this princess would be doing. I discovered that while this girl was 14, she hadn't been attending school for two to three years. She'd refused to go.

The princess she described was a social worker. So I said, "Okay, it's now ten years' time and you've trained as a social worker. What university did you go to?" She mentioned one to the North of England and I asked, "What books did you read . . . what did you study there?" She said, "I don't know, Psychology and Sociology and a few other things like that." Then I said, "Remember when you were 14? You've been out of school for two or three years. Remember how you got back in school."

She said, "I had this psychiatrist who helped me." And then I asked the important question: "How did she help you?" And she started talking about how she made a phone call to the school and I followed-up: "Who spoke? Did you or she?"

She replied, "The psychiatrist spoke, but she arranged a meeting for us to go to the school." "Do you remember how you shook hands with that teacher when you went in? And how you looked and what you wore?" We went into these minute details about what that particular meeting was like, looking from the future back. She was able to describe the conversations they'd had, how confident she had been, and how well she had spoken.

About a month after this conversation, she said to me, "I think it's about time we went to school, don't you? Can you ring and make an appointment?" I asked her if she needed to talk about it anymore and she said, "No." She knew how to behave. When we went to the school, she was just brilliant.

I first met that girl about 10 years ago. Now she's a qualified social worker. She fulfilled her dream, even though she attended a university different from the one she envisioned."

Source: Adapted from MacAdam.

Short Comparison Between Positive Psychology and Solution-Focused Brief Therapy

Bannink and Jackson (2011) compared Positive Psychology (PP) and Solution Focus (SF). Here is a summary of their comparison. The main similarities between PP and SF are:

- Both are part of a wave of positive approaches to change;
- In medical contexts both share a "health focus" instead of an "illness focus";
- The focus is not to get away from what the client does not want but towards what the client does want;
- Both investigate people's strengths and resources;
- Both share the goal of learning and promoting how individuals, families, and communities thrive;
- Both look at the past to find workable solutions and previous successes;
- Both do not seek or create pathology;
- Both do not use extensive diagnosis of problems;
- Both have as their philosophical roots a constructivist tradition;
- Both are still relatively unknown to each other.

The main differences between PP and SF are:

- The nature of Positive Psychology is academic, it is the scientific understanding of effective interventions to build thriving individuals, families, and communities; the nature of SF is finding what works for this client at this moment in this context;
- PP talks of strengths: there is an interest in the constructs of "personality"; SF has no interest or belief in universal strengths. SF picks out salient aspects of a particular situation, finding resources of exceptions within contexts;
- PP asks: where are you now and where do you want to go (from A to B); SF begins with the end in mind and works backwards (from B to A);
- PP wants to find out what is generally true and produces theories that can be tested; SF has a not-knowing stance: every case is different;
- PP's attitude is "leading" (if you are depressed try this gratitude exercise); SF's attitude is "leading from one step behind": asking questions in order to draw out clients' expertise;
- PP's focus is mainly individual: what happens in the head; SF's focus is more interactional: the action is in the interaction. The mental is manifest in our way of action. Lately PP adopts the view that strengths are not fixed traits across settings and time, therefore the view of PP and SF about strengths might begin to converge.

Empirical Evidence

Both Positive Psychology and Solution-Focused Brief Therapy are evidence-based forms of psychotherapy. For more information on the evidence-based practice of Positive Psychology see Fredrickson (2009) and Seligman (2011). Research in Positive Psychology uses the same scientific methods as in traditional research but for the most part refocuses on the measurement, understanding, and building of those characteristics that make life most worth living.

For more information on the evidence-based practice of Solution-Focused Brief Therapy (SFBT) see Macdonald (2011) and Franklin, Trepper, Gingerich, and McCollum (2012). Meta-analytic reviews of the outcome research show SFBT to have a small to moderate positive outcome for a broad range of topics and populations. When SFBT has been compared with established treatments in recent, well-designed studies, it has been shown to be equivalent to other evidence-based approaches, producing results in substantially less time and at less cost.

Neuroscience

Neuroscience, the study of all aspects of the nervous system, is surging forward on the crest of a wave due to the availability of ever faster and more advanced computers. Neuroscientists employ many different perspectives, from molecular to total systems, in their approach to studying the brain. Positive Psychology and Solution-Focused Brief Therapy seek to use the findings of neuroscience in order to test hypotheses about positive emotions with relevance to the functioning of the brain, immune system, the role of hormones, transmitters, and the role of antidepressant drugs. In this section I describe a short summary of the research, in which it was proven that positive emotions have a clear impact on the neurobiological field. These findings support my plea for the application of Positive CBT.

The brain

"Positivity alters the brain and changes the way people interact with the world" (Fredrickson, 2009, p. 59). One of the consequences of positivity is enhanced creativity. This fact was demonstrated by Rowe, Hirsh, and Anderson (2007), who "injected" volunteers with positivity, negativity, or utter neutrality, using music to induce emotions and then tested them on two different tasks. One task measured the scope of visual attention by tracking the influence of peripherally presented information. The other task measured verbal creativity, by asking volunteers to come up with a single word that related to three given words (for instance: mower, atomic, and foreign > power, using the Remote Associates Test). When people felt positive, their performance on the two tasks changed in tandem: the broader the scope of their visual attention, the more creative they became on the verbal task. This is an important linkage because it documents that positivity broadens minds in multiple, interrelated ways.

Recent insights in the field of neurobiology and knowledge about the functioning of both cerebral hemispheres (Siegel, 1999) show that the right hemisphere deals principally with processing nonverbal aspects of communication, such as seeing images and feeling primary emotions. The right hemisphere is involved in the understanding of metaphors, paradoxes, and humor. Reading fiction and poetry activates the right hemisphere whereas the reading of scientific texts essentially activates the left hemisphere. There the processes relating to the verbal meaning of words, also called "digital representations," take place. The left hemisphere is occupied with logical analyses (cause-effect relations). Linear processes occurring are reading the words in this sentence, aspects of attention, and discovering order in the events of a story. The left hemisphere thus dominates our language-based communication. Some authors are of the opinion that the right hemisphere sees the world more as it is and has a better overview of the context, whereas the left hemisphere tends to departmentalize the information received. The left hemisphere sees the trees, the right hemisphere the forest.

Exercise 4.9

Try listening to a favorite piece of music through headphones, first with your left ear, then with your right; what differences do you experience? Several studies show that most (right-handed) people prefer to listen to music with their left ear (connected to the right hemisphere), rather than with their right ear (connected to the left hemisphere). If one listens to music with the left ear, this gives a more holistic sensation, a "floating with the flow of the music," whereas the experience is different if one listens with the right ear. This tendency is reversed in professional musicians. An explanation for this is that they listen to music in a more analytical way than "the casual listener."

Brain plasticity

Neuroscientists have discovered that the mature adult human brain does not remain stable but changes throughout a lifetime. New connections are made and some areas of the brain can even generate new cells, a process called neurogenesis. Recent research suggests that physical exercise and cognitive stimulation enhance such "brain plasticity" and enhance the brain's information processing capacity.

Brewin (2006) suggests that CBT does not directly modify negative information involving the self in memory but produces changes in the relative activation of positive and negative representations such that the positive ones are assisted to win the retrieval competition. From a retrieval competition perspective, the behaviors that therapists have their clients perform, are creating additional detailed representations of encounters with the fear-eliciting situation. The new representations differ, however, in that they incorporate a positive context involving, for example, free choice, comparative safety, or a belief in at least partial self-efficacy, rather than a negative context involving compulsion, fear, or helplessness. Rehearsal will increase the level of activation of these new representations, deliberate self-exposure will help to make them distinctive, and the reduction in experienced anxiety will give them a positive valence.

The interventions used in Competitive Memory Training (COMET) are based on this retrieval competition account. COMET has been described in more detail in Chapter 3. It was initially used for clients with low self-esteem but is now also used as a transdiagnostic approach for eating disorders, personality disorders, and depression (Korrelboom *et al.*, 2009).

Mindsight

Science has also documented that mindfulness training leaves a lasting mark on the brain. It alters the basic metabolisms in brain circuits known to underlie emotional responding, reducing activity in circuits linked with negativity and increasing activity in circuits linked with positivity (Davidson and Kabat-Zinn, 2003).

Siegel (2010) states that experience creates the repeated neural firing that can lead to gene expression, protein production, and changes in both the genetic regulation of neurons and the structural connections in the brain. By harnessing the power of awareness to strategically stimulate the brain's firing, "mindsight" (focused attention that allows us to see the internal workings of our own minds) enables us to voluntarily change a firing pattern that was laid down involuntarily. When we focus our attention, we create neural firing patterns that permit previously separated areas to become linked and integrated. The synaptic linkages are strengthened, the brain becomes more interconnected, and the mind becomes more adaptive.

Optimism bias

The belief that the future will be much better than the past and present is known as the "optimism bias." A growing body of scientific evidence points to the conclusion that optimism may be hard-wired by evolution into the human brain. The science of optimism opens a new window on the workings of human consciousness. Our brains aren't just stamped by the past. They are constantly being shaped by the future as well. To think positively about our prospects, we must be able to imagine ourselves in the future. Optimism starts with what may be the most extraordinary of human talents: mental time travel, the ability to move back and forth through time and space in one's mind, which is critical to our survival.

To make progress, we need to be able to imagine alternative realities – better ones – and we need to believe that we can achieve them. Such faith helps motivate us to pursue our goals. Optimists work longer hours and tend to earn more. Economists found that optimists even save more. And although they are not less likely to divorce, they are more likely to remarry.

And even if that better future is often an illusion, optimism has clear benefits in the present. Hope keeps our minds at ease, lowers stress, and improves physical health. Researchers studying heart-disease patients found that optimists were more likely than nonoptimistic patients to take vitamins, eat low-fat diets, and exercise, thereby reducing their overall coronary risk. A study of cancer patients revealed that pessimistic patients under the age of 60 were more likely to die within eight months than nonpessimistic patients of the same initial health, status, and age. Should something unpleasant happen to us, we soon see the cloud's silver lining and we rapidly return to our former level of happiness. This phenomenon is called "impact bias" whereby we overestimate the negative effect that an unpleasant incident could have on our well-being.

This capacity to envision the future relies partly on the hippocampus, a part of our brain crucial to memory. Patients with damage to their hippocampus are unable to recollect the past, but they are also unable to construct detailed images of future scenarios. They appear to be stuck in time. Research shows that most of us spend less time mulling over negative outcomes than we do over positive ones. Positive expectations enhance the odds of survival (Sharot, 2011).

"Amygdala whisperers"

We as therapists are "amydala whisperers." We want our clients to be able to be conscious of their amygdala activation and say: "Don't worry, everything will be fine." Amygdala activation takes place if constitutional features, traumatic experiences or negative attachments have produced maladaptive emotion regulation, restricting people in their ability to achieve emotional resilience and behavioral flexibility. Addressing the neocortex can override these responses and bring the deeper structures of the amygdala into a more tolerable level of arousal. This can be done by a number of "self-talk" strategies in which imagery or internal dialog is activated. Over time and with continued practice, the frequency and intensity of these responses can be significantly decreased, and the speed of recovery can be enhanced. Siegel (1999) describes a client with a fear of dogs, after having been mauled by one, losing part of his left ear, and sustaining deep wounds to his arms and chest. Teaching him about the nature of the fear response and the neural circuits underlying it was relieving for him, and relaxation techniques and guided imagery with exposure to self-generated images of dogs were provided. Nevertheless, he still had an initial startle response to dogs, so a "cognitive override" strategy was then tried. The client learned to acknowledge the relevance of his amygdala's response to the present dog and the past trauma (the initial arousal mechanism). He then would say to himself: "I know that you (the amygdala) are trying to protect me, and that you think this is a dangerous thing" (the specific appraisal stage). What he would say next was what eventually allowed him to buy his children a (small) dog: "I do not need to see this sense of panic as something to fear or get agitated about." He would then imagine his amygdala sighing with relief, having discharged its duties to warn, and the sense of doom would dissipate. After several weeks of performing these internal override discussions, he felt ready to proceed with the purchase of the pet. Six months later, he and his family were doing well with the new addition to their household.

Wanting or liking

The limbic system in the brain is linked to feelings, motivation, and memory. There are two subsystems to distinguish – "wanting" and "liking." Wanting ensures that we want things. Wanting inclines us to doing things where reward ensues. Liking indicates if we shall become happy or fortunate in what we do and in what happens to us. If it works out then these two systems can correlate and learn from each other. However, sometimes we want to do things which do not make us happy at all, like becoming addicted or having bad habits or avoiding difficult social situations, which we had every intention of confronting. Therefore the question, "what do I want?" is not a very useful question for our clients or ourselves, because then we focus only on wanting. It would be better if we pose the question: "what makes me/you happy?" For that considering previous experiences is important: "What made me/you happy in the past?" Then liking/wanting make a better match: you want and do more of the things, which make you happy (Litt, 2010).

Story 4.4: The Drip System

In changing the brain repetition is key. Rock (2009) uses the metaphor of the brain as a garden. In this garden it is sunny all the time and it rains naturally once in a while. If you want to grow some nice tomatoes, you first plant seedlings, which need careful daily watering. Once the plants are a bit hardy, to keep them growing, you should water them regularly. How often is the right amount? If you water once a year, it will probably wash everything away. Once a quarter won't do much. Once a month will help, maybe. Once a week does make a difference to some plants, but watering twice a week seems to make a sustainable and noticeable difference. It seems that the best technique for growing plants is what they do in hydroponic farms, which is to water them several times each day, using a drip system. Rock proposes that creating healthy new circuits in the brain is similar: you need to pay regular attention.

Source: Adapted from Rock (2009).

Immune system

Our immune system is a system of biological structures and processes within an organism that protects us against disease by identifying and killing pathogens and tumor cells.

Much research has been carried out into the effects on the immune system of negative and positive emotions. It is an established fact that humor and laughter have a positive effect in addition to providing a number of positive physical processes, such as lowering blood pressure and certain stress hormones. Thus, women with breast cancer recovered better after their operation if they were exposed to forms of humor: humor was related to optimism and had a negative connection with stress. At the same time humor makes for an active approach to the illness, directly confronting it, resulting in stress reduction (Steptoe, Wardle, and Marmot, 2005; Lefcourt, 2005).

Self-efficacy also plays an important role in health. First of all, people with a higher self-efficacy will usually follow a healthier life pattern and show more commitment to stopping with harmful habits such as smoking and drinking alcohol. Secondly, a high self-efficacy will create favorable biological processes, like reduced reactions to stress and less vehement reactions of the immune system. A high self-efficacy also influences the production of certain neuro-transmitters, like endorphins, which are important in dealing with stress and illnesses.

Dopamine

Regulation of the neurotransmitter dopamine plays a crucial role in our mental and physical health. Neurons containing the neurotransmitter dopamine are clustered in the midbrain in an area called the substantia nigra. Research done by Hoebel, Avena, and Rada (2008) shows that approach behavior involves the release of dopamine, whereas acetylcholine is correlated with, or causes, avoid-ance. This is important in bulimia, for example, where clients have a difficult approach-avoidance conflict: they want to eat, but do not want to gain weight. Approach and avoidance goals are described in more detail in Chapter 6.

Isen (2005, p. 528) formulated a hypothesis about dopamine. She states that research revealed that people who feel happy are more likely to follow through their intentions and are more committed through their sense of social responsibility to charitable acts. They are more motivated to reach their goal, are more receptive to information, think more clearly, and record higher levels of satisfaction. Positive emotions promote more flexibility, creativity, and empathy, maintaining a connection with the release of dopamine:

"Dopamine may play a role in the effects of positive affect on cognition that have been observed. This dopamine hypothesis arose from the observation, at behavioural and cognitive levels, that positive affect fosters cognitive flexibility and the ability to switch perspectives (together with the understanding that dopamine in the anterior cingulate region of the brain enables flexible perspective-taking or set-switching)."

Bringing to mind problems brings them to mind (Rock, 2009). Unless you take care to label your emotions when they are at a high level (see Chapter 9), and not dwell on them, bringing problems to mind will increase limbic arousal, making it harder to solve them. Solving difficult problems involves getting around an impasse. This requires a quiet and generally positive and open mind. Getting lost in large amounts of history and detail does not make the brain quiet at all. The more negative connections you make, the less dopamine you have, the fewer resources you have for solving the next problem, and the more negative connections you make. In this low-energy state, everything looks hard. Increas-ingly risk adverse, you don't have the motivation to take action.

The decision to focus on a positive outcome instead of a problem impacts brain functioning in several ways:

1. When you focus on a positive outcome, you prime the brain to perceive information relevant to that outcome, rather than to notice information about the problem. You can't be looking for solutions and problems at the same time;

2. When you look for solutions, you scan your environment widely for cues, which activates more of the right hemisphere of the brain, rather than drilling down into information that activates the left hemisphere. Activating the right hemisphere is helpful for having insights, which is how complex problems are often solved;

3. When you focus on problems you are more likely to activate the emotions connected with those problems, which will create greater noise in the brain. This inhibits insight. Whereas focusing on solutions generates a toward state, because you desire something. You are seeking, not avoiding (see Chapter 6). This increases dopamine levels, which is useful for insight. And if you are expecting you might find a solution, these positive expectations help release even more dopamine. In all these ways, focusing on solutions can significantly increase the likelihood of having insights, and even make you feel happier.

Oxytocin

Oxytocin is a nine amino acid peptide that is synthesized in hypothalamic neurons and transported down axons of the posterior pituitary for secretion into blood. Oxytocin receptors are expressed by neurons in many parts of the brain and spinal cord, including the amygdala, ventromedial hypothalamus, septum, and brainstem. Oxytocin is released in response to stress, touch, and during breastfeeding. It has a role in social behaviors in many species and it seems likely that it has similar roles in humans. Oxytocin promotes the secretion of breast milk and stimulates the contraction of the uterus during labor. It increases trust and reduces fear and is often called the "tend and befriend" hormone. Animals prefer to spend time with animals in whose presence they have experienced high brain oxytocin in the past, suggesting that friendships may be mediated at least in part by the same system that mediates maternal urges.

In one study, volunteers were asked to play two types of games: a trust game and a risk game. In the trust game, subjects were asked to contribute money, with the understanding that a human trustee would invest the money and decide whether to return the profits, or betray the subjects' trust and keep all the money. In the risk game, the subjects were told that a computer would randomly decide whether their money would be repaid or not. The subjects also received doses of either oxytocin or a placebo via nasal spray. They chose oxytocin because studies had shown that oxytocin specifically increases people's willingness to trust others. During the games the subjects' brains were scanned using functional magnetic resonance imaging.

The researchers found that – in the trust game, not in the risk game – oxytocin reduced activity in two brain regions: the amygdala, which processes fear, danger, and possibly risk of social betrayal, and an area of the striatum, part of the circuitry that guides and adjusts future behavior based on reward feedback. Baumgartner *et al.* (2008) concluded that their findings showed that oxytocin affected the subjects' responses specifically related to trust. If subjects face the nonsocial risks in the risk game, oxytocin does not affect their behavioral responses to the feedback. Both subjects in the oxytocin group and the placebo group do not change their willingness to take risks after the feedback. In contrast, if subjects face social risks, such as in the trust game, those who received placebo respond to the feedback with a decrease in trusting behavior while subjects with oxytocin demonstrate no change in their trusting behavior although they were informed that their interaction partners did not honor their trust in roughly 50% of the cases.

Nasally administered oxytocin has also been reported to reduce fear, possibly by inhibiting the amygdala (which is thought to be responsible for fear response). Its effect lasts only for a few minutes though. Oxytocin also affects generosity by increasing empathy during perspective taking. In experiments, intranasal oxytocin increased generosity, but had no effect on altruism. Oxytocin, also named "liquid trust," can be bought as a nasal spray. Maybe therapists could use the spray to help clients to trust each other more than they usually do when starting therapy? Or maybe that is why a handshake or a light touch on the shoulder of the other person (touching releases oxytocin) can be so important.

Developing compassion for self and others, as a way to enhance well-being, has been central to Buddhist practice for the enhancement of well-being for thousands of years. For more details about Compassion Focused Therapy (CFT) see Chapter 3. Feeling cared for, accepted, and having a sense of belonging and affiliation with others is fundamental to our physiological maturation and well-being. These are linked to particular types of positive affect that are associated with well-being and a neuro-hormonal profile of increased endorphins and oxytocin (Panksepp, 1998).

Endorphins

Dunbar, Baron, Frangou, *et al.* (2011) did research on social laughter. Although laughter forms an important part of human nonverbal communication, so far it has received little attention. Relaxed (Duchenne) laughter is associated with feelings of well-being and heightened positive affect, possibly due to the release of endorphins. They tested this hypothesis in both the laboratory and naturalistic context, using pain threshold as an assay for endorphin release. The results show that pain thresholds are significantly higher after laughter than in the control condition. This pain-tolerance effect is due to laughter itself and not due to a change in positive affect. The researchers suggest that laughter, through an endorphin-mediated opiate effect, plays a crucial role in social bonding.

Cortisol

Cortisol is a hormone produced by cholesterol in the adrenal cortex. It plays a role in the digestion of food, our sleeping-waking rhythm, and our immune system. Cortisol is also called the "stress hormone" because all forms of stress, both physical and psychological, trigger its release. Its role is in breaking down certain proteins within the muscles and thereby releasing glucose (energy).

This energy is used to rebalance the body: at times of stress, adrenaline and noradrenaline are released, increasing alertness in the body and preparing the fight or flight response. Cortisol thereby compensated for this loss of energy. Much research in the field of stress has been directed at the role of cortisol. Moskowitz and Epel (2006) found that resilient people who were able to see beneficial aspects of stressful events and experienced positive emotions, showed a healthy fluctuation in their cortisol.

Another study done by Byrd-Craven, Geary, Rose, and Ponzi (2008) shows that extensive discussions of problems and encouragement of "problem talk," rehashing the details of problems, speculating about problems, and dwelling on negative affect in particular, lead to a significant increase in the stress hormone cortisol, which may predict increased depression and anxiety over time.

Gamma-aminobutyric acid

The GABA-receptors are a class of receptors that respond to the neurotransmitter gamma-aminobutyric acid (GABA), the chief inhibitory neurotransmitter in the vertebrate central nervous system.

Benzodiazepines, like Valium, are examples of GABA-receptors, they intensify the deceleratory action of GABA. Drugan (2000) experimented with resilient and nonresilient animals, which were susceptible to stress. With resilient animals the GABA-level increased, resulting in the animals experiencing less stress and fear. With nonresilient animals the GABA-level actually decreased. GABA-receptors ensure there is reduced recall of stressful events and less fretting. Contrarily, with the decrease in the GABA-level there is an increase in recall of stressful events and increased fretting. Drugan's conclusion is that active coping makes for an increase in the brain of the production of a valium-like substance with its calming, relieving, and relaxing effects.

The Body

Fredrickson (2009) sites an impressive amount of research in recent years, wherein there appears to be a positive relation between experiencing positive emotions and:

- a better immune system;
- less stress;
- lower blood pressure;
- less pain;
- fewer colds;
- better sleep pattern;
- fewer risks of affections like high blood pressure, diabetes, or a stroke;
- faster production of new cells in the body and in the brain;
- a longer life.

The standard fairy tale ending phrase is: "and they lived happily ever after." The research done in Positive Psychology and Solution-Focused Brief Therapy may give this ending phrase a whole new meaning. In the next section of the book you will find many applications of Positive CBT, which will hopefully contribute to a long and happy life for your clients and for yourself.

Part II
Applications

5

Enhancing the Therapeutic Alliance

If you want to build a ship
Don't drum up the men to gather wood
Divide the work and give orders
Instead, teach them to yearn for the vast and endless sea

Antoine de Saint-Exupery (1979)

Introduction

The concept of the therapeutic alliance has a long history. There is probably no psychotherapy book written in the past decades that has not referred to the alliance. Although it emerged as a contribution from the psychoanalytic tradition, it now stands as a necessary condition of change across all forms of psychotherapy. Therapeutic alliance has been defined in many ways and despite this diversity of definitions, the consensus is that the alliance represents a positive attachment between therapist and client, as well as an active and collaborative engagement of all involved in therapeutic tasks designed to help the client. Just a few facts from the research on alliance (Constantino, Castonguay, and Schut, 2002):

- The alliance is significantly related to client improvement and a robust predictor of outcome;
- Both the client and therapist contribute substantially to the quality of the alliance;
- Client and therapist relationship histories have an impact on the therapeutic relationship;
- The quality of the alliance is determined by complementary transactions between client and therapist, rather than by the separate action of either one of these participants.

Practicing Positive CBT: From Reducing Distress to Building Success, First Edition. Fredrike Bannink.
© 2012 John Wiley & Sons, Ltd. Published 2012 by John Wiley & Sons, Ltd.

Therefore, therapists should make explicit efforts to facilitate the creation of a positive and strong alliance in treatment. They should also systematically monitor the alliance with one of the now available instruments, rather than relying only on clinical impression. I will come back to this in Chapter 10.

It is important to keep in mind that the client's view of the alliance (and not the therapist's!) is the best-known predictor of outcome. Asking clients to fill out alliance measures should especially be measured early in therapy, because early session alliance is a good predictor of improvement, while poor early alliance predicts client dropout. Therefore close attention should be paid to the alliance as soon as therapy begins.

Building a Positive Alliance

Positive CBT starts with building "rapport" with the client. The therapist makes a positive start by asking questions about the daily life of the client: "What kind of work do you do?" Or: "What grade are you in?" when the client is a child, followed by questions such as: "What do you like about your work?" "What are you good at?" "What hobbies do you have?" or: "What is your best subject in school?" "Who is your favorite teacher?" These questions can be seen as icebreakers, but they may also be the start for uncovering useful information about strengths and solutions already present in the client's life. They set the tone for a more light-hearted conversation than the client may have been expecting.

After these questions the Positive CBT therapist may ask the client about his goal for coming to the therapy or about the concerns he wants to address in therapy. "What would be the best outcome of you coming to see me?" is a good way to start this part of the first session.

Many clients like to have the opportunity to talk about their problems, not least because they think that that is the intent of the therapy (I call this the "problem-focused therapy game"). The Positive CBT therapist will listen respectfully to their stories but will not ask for details of the problem, so there is no positive reinforcement of "problem talk" (see Chapter 2). With the question: "How is this a problem for you?" clients can often begin to talk about the problem in a different way. It may also be helpful to provide information about Positive CBT, because it makes it clear that nowadays there is another therapy game possible: the "strengths and solutions-therapy game." This game is about possibilities instead of impossibilities and strengths instead of weaknesses. The therapist may ask clients who adhere to the problem-focused game: "How many sessions do you think you need to talk about your problems and what is wrong with you before we can start looking at your future and what is right?"

It is also important to validate the client's point of view: "I am sure you must have a good reason for all this, please tell me more." In this way, the therapist shows that he respects the client's opinions and ideas. At the beginning of the first session the professional may also give the client(s) one opportunity to say "what definitively needs to be said" before switching to what clients want different in their lives. This has become a proven method in solution-focused conflict management (Bannink, 2008c, 2009b, 2009c, 2009d, 2010b).

The four – solution-focused – basic questions in Positive CBT, which I explained in detail in Chapter 4, are:

1. What are your best hopes?
2. What difference will that make?
3. What is already working?
4. What will be a next sign of progress/what will be your next step?

In Appendix A you find a protocol for the first session.

Offering Acknowledgment

Positive CBT would be impossible if the negative impact a problem has on the client goes unacknowledged. The client is often in great distress and generally wants to make that known during the session. The therapist respectfully listens to the client's story and shifts to a more positive conversation as soon as possible. It is a misconception, however, that there can only be sufficient acknowledgment if the problem is wholly dissected and analyzed or if the client is afforded every opportunity to expatiate on his or her view of the problem. Utterances by the therapist such as: "I understand that this must be an unpleasant situation for you" and "I can imagine how difficult it must be to get out of this impasse" offer that acknowledgment just as well and take up considerably less time than having a client describe the entire problem. Furthermore, the mood of the session can remain positive if the focus remains on what clients want to have instead of their problems.

Asking clients what they have tried so far to solve their problems also offers acknowledgment, since most clients have taken some steps to address their problems before therapy. However, a more positive question: "What have you tried so far, that has been helpful, even just a little bit?" invites clients to talk about their successes (however small) instead of their failures.

The therapist may present the client with the option by asking: "Would you like to conduct these sessions in a strengths- and solutions-focused or in a problem-focused way?", explaining both to the client. It has been my experience that clients who are motivated to change choose the strengths-focused approach. Clients who do not (yet) see themselves as part of the problem and/or the solution often choose problem-focused sessions. I guess they make that choice because it does not require them to take action yet. After all, in the problem-focused way, preceding any behavioral change, the problem must first be analyzed and explored or insight must be gained into the source of the problem or the reason for its perpetuation. In this way, this question also gives the therapist some insight as to which clients are motivated to change their behavior and which clients are not. Some questions to offer acknowledgment are:

- How do you cope?
- How do you ensure that the situation isn't worse than it is? How do you do that? Which personal strengths do you use?

- I can tell that this is a problem for you and I understand that this is an unpleasant situation for you. What would you like to be different?
- How is this a problem for you?
- I see what's important to you. What solutions would fulfill your wishes?
- Suppose you were given one opportunity to say what absolutely needs to be said before we proceed. What would you say?

Story 5.1: Acknowledging the Problem

Many years ago and far away there was a village. Its inhabitants were starving because they lived in fear of a dragon that they had seen in their fields, and they would not go to harvest their crops.

One day a traveler came to the village and asked for food. They explained that there was none because they were afraid of this dragon. The traveler was brave and offered to slay the dragon. When he arrived at the fields he couldn't see a dragon, only a large watermelon. So he returned to the village and said: "You have nothing to fear: there is no dragon, only a large watermelon." The villagers were angry at his refusal to understand their fear and hacked the traveler to pieces.

Some weeks later another traveler came to the village. Again, when he asked for food he was told about the dragon. He too was brave and offered to kill him. The villagers were relieved and delighted. When he arrived at the fields he also saw the giant watermelon and returned to the village to tell the villagers that they were mistaken about the dragon, they need have no fear of a giant watermelon. They hacked him to pieces.

More time passed and the villagers were becoming desperate. One day a third traveler appeared. He could see how desperate they were and asked what the problem was. The villagers told him and he promised he would slay the dragon so that they could go to the fields again to harvest their crops. When he got to the field he too saw the giant watermelon. He reflected for a moment, drew his sword, leaped into the field, and hacked the watermelon to pieces. He returned to the village and told them he had killed their dragon. The villagers were overjoyed. The traveler stayed in the village for many months, long enough to teach the villagers the difference between dragons and watermelons.

Source: Anonymous

Enhancing Hope

There are two situations that may lead to feelings of hopelessness: one may feel insecure because one fears that things will change in an undesired way, or one may feel that change is exactly what is needed, but be afraid that nothing will ever change. In both situations, there is an overarching sense that one has lost control over the future.

Since the 1950s, doctors and psychologists have pointed to the role of hope in people's health and well-being. In his address to the American Psychiatric Association, Menninger (1959) said that hope was an untapped source of power and healing. Menninger believed that hope is an indispensable factor in psychiatric treatments and psychiatric training. The interest in hope in psychotherapy was initially aimed at reducing despair rather than increasing hopeful thoughts. Given the link between despair and suicide, Beck, Weissman, Lester, and Trexles (1974, p. 864) focused on combating hopelessness. Their definition of hopelessness was: "a system of cognitive schemas whose common denomination is negative expectations about the future."

In the 1990s, Snyder and colleagues developed the "hope theory," in which they propose a two-factor cognitive model of hope that similarly focuses on goal attainment. Not only does Snyder focus on expectancies but also on the motivation and planning that are necessary to attain goals. He defines hope as "a positive emotional state that is based on an interactively derived sense of successful (a) agency and (b) pathways (planning to meet goals)." Based on this definition, hope's agency or "willpower" component provides the determination to achieve goals, whereas its pathways or "waypower" component promotes the creation of alternative paths to replace those that may have been blocked in the process of pursuing those goals. Hope has been shown to be applicable and to relate to performance in various domains, including the workplace (Youssef and Luthans, 2007).

The previous definitions tie hopeful thinking expressly to goals. By focusing on goal objects, we are able to respond effectively to our surrounding environment. Snyder and colleagues made the distinction between high-hope people and low-hope people. Compared with the vague and ambiguous nature of the goals for low-hope people, high-hope persons (Snyder, Michael, and Cheavens, 1999) are more likely to clearly conceptualize their goals.

In addition to setting goals, hope theory encourages therapists and clients to set goals that 'stretch' the clients (Snyder, 2002). In hope theory, goals that are difficult enough to be challenging but are easy enough to be accomplished, are called "stretch goals." Such goals encourage the clients not only to "patch up" problems but also to grow as an individual. For example, a stretch goal might be to increase well-being or connectedness, instead of "just" solving the problem. Continuously setting and meeting stretch goals is a way to move oneself toward a more positive, strengths-based stance.

Hope theory is considered to be a member of the Positive Psychology Family, as described in Chapter 4, along with optimism and self-efficacy: the power of believing you can. As an example of hope theory and self-efficacy theory we have seen the importance of "Audacity of Hope" and "Yes we can" used by Obama to become President of the USA. Hopeful thought reflects the belief that one can find pathways to desired goals and become motivated to use those pathways. Hope serves to drive emotions and well-being of people.

Exercise 5.1

If you want to (re)gain a glimmer of hope, even in crisis situations, ask yourself (or your client) the following questions:

- *What helped in the past, even if only marginally?*
- *How do I cope with everything that is going on and all I have gone through?*
- *How do I succeed in getting from one moment to the next?*
- *Could it be worse than it is? Why is it not worse?*
- *What does my social environment say I do well, also in very bad times?*
- *Imagine that in 10 or 15 years, when things are going better, I look back on today, what will have helped me to improve things?*
- *Suppose there is a solution, what difference would that make, what would be different – and, more specifically, better?*

The *first basic question* taps into hope and asks clients explicitly what they are hoping for: "What are your best hopes?" Hope theory states that hope can be seen as a journey. Three components are needed: a destination (goal), a road map (pathways), and a means of transport (agency). It is a thinking process that taps a sense of agency and pathways for one's goals. The pathway component involves a person's belief that he can set goals and devise multiple ways to reach them. Both short-term and long-term goals should be of value and be challenging but attainable. Once goals are set, a person's thoughts are focused on his ability to plan ways to reach these goals. When a route to a goal becomes blocked, those who are more hopeful devise alternate ways to pursue them. If a goal is permanently blocked, high hope people set a substitute goal that is satisfying. The agency component involves the person's conviction that he has the inner determination to implement his plans, even when faced with obstacles. Successful steps on the pathway towards a goal fuel a person's inner determination that, in turn, propels further progression towards the goal. To have a high hope level, a person must activate both components. *Goals* are the first component of hope. They are the mental targets of human action.

Hope theory research shows that setting goals of moderate certainty characterizes high hope, while it probably enhances hope because it increases motivation. When goals are perceived to be too difficult or too easy, people likely do not try as hard to reach them.

Pathway thinking is the second component of hope. It reflects the routes that people produce in relation to goals. Pathway thinking involves the perceived capacity to come up with mental road maps to reach goals. It is a way to link the present to the future through one's goals. Research on athletes shows that sports performances are increased when individuals envision the sequence of steps necessary to perform well. High-hope people are more skilled than low-

---

Story 5.2: The Archer

The Greek philosopher Aristotle cites the archer as his favorite example in describing moral wisdom. An archer comprehends his task if firstly he knows what his target is and secondly if he is aware of all circumstances (the means) that determine the situation in which he has to shoot. He has assessed the strength and direction of the wind, the characteristics of the arrow and the tension of the bow. Aristotle sees the wise person as such an archer, someone with knowledge of the target (the goal) and of the means to reach the goal (the pathways). The archer is more likely to hit the right mark if he has a target to aim at. Aristotle stated that striving for excellence is important but that knowledge of the goal is only useful if there is a striving to attain that goal (agency).

---

hope people at creating a detailed primary route to goal attainment. They are also better able to produce alternative routes to goals when those primary routes are impeded.

Agency thinking is the third component of hope. The ability to generate adaptive goals and perceived pathways will not result in actual goal attainment, unless the individual also has sufficient motivation to implement those routes. *Agency thinking* involves thoughts about one's ability to initiate and sustain movement along pathways toward desired goals, even when faced with impediments. Related to this point, there is evidence that high-hope individuals show a greater preference for agency-affirming statements than low-hope people: "I will find a way to get this done" or: "Yes we can!"

A key difference is between the words *can* and *will*, with the former pertaining to the capacity to act and the latter tapping intentionality to act.

Hope theory is built upon goal pursuit thinking. Positive emotions (see the "broaden-and-build theory of positive emotions" in Chapter 9) flow from perceptions of successful goal pursuit. Blockages to pathways or agency may impair coping. Negative emotions are the product of unsuccessful goal pursuits and undermine well-being. The perceptions of unsuccessful goal pursuit can stem from insufficient agentic and/or pathway thinking or the inability to overcome a thwarting circumstance. So goal-pursuit cognitions cause either positive or negative emotions.

High-hope individuals will find it easier to generate alternative pathways when the original pathway is blocked than low-hope individuals. Another finding is that high-hope people as compared with low-hope people have coping advantages when their goal pursuits are unimpeded, as well as when they are impeded (Snyder, 1994; Snyder *et al.*, 1998). High-hope people also learn to anticipate difficulties as a natural part of life and therefore are more resilient to stressful experiences. Another observation is that high-hope people naturally break big goals into small subgoals. Small steps can lead to big changes, so setting frequent short-term "stepping-stone" goals is important. The three components of hopeful thinking – goals, pathways, and agency – are so intertwined that the elicitation of any one should ignite the entire process of hopeful thought. Research also showed that optimism and hope are highly and positively correlated.

Story 5.3: The Power of Hope

A severely ill man was in hospital. The doctors had given up any hope of a recovery. They were unable to ascertain what the man was suffering from. Fortunately a doctor famous for his diagnostic skills would visit the hospital. The doctors said that maybe they could cure him if this famous doctor was able to diagnose him. When the doctor arrived the man was almost dead. The doctor looked at him briefly, mumbled moribundus (Latin for dying), and walked over to the next patient. A few years later the man – who did not know a word of Latin – succeeded in finding the famous doctor. "I would like to thank you for your diagnosis. The doctors had said that if you were able to diagnose me, I would get better."

Source: Anonymous

Reinforcing Strengths and "What Works"

Clients have personal qualities and past experiences that, if drawn upon, can be of great use in resolving their difficulties and creating more satisfying lives. These qualities, such as a sense of humor, resilience, caring for others, are the strengths of our clients. Useful past experiences are those in which the client thought about or actually did something that might be put to use in therapy. These experiences are the client's past successes.

Giving compliments – a way of positive reinforcement – to clients for their strengths, qualities, and past successes is a powerful tool and is widely used in Positive CBT. Cialdini (1984) states that giving compliments relates to two "weapons of influence": reciprocation and liking. By giving compliments the chances will be higher that the other person will be nicer too, because people who provide praise are liked better and because the rule of reciprocation will oblige the other person to do so. Cialdini cites a study done on men in North Carolina. The men in the study received comments about themselves from another person who needed a favor from them. Some of the men got only positive comments, some got only negative comments, and some got a mixture of both. There were three interesting findings. First, the men liked the evaluator who provided only praise best. Second, this was the case even though the men fully realized that the man who provided praise stood to gain from their liking him. Finally, unlike the other types of comments, pure praise did not have to be accurate to work. Positive comments produced just as much liking for the person who provided praise when they were untrue as when they were true.

Arts, Hoogduin, Keijsers, Severeijnen, and Schaap (1994) found that systematic use of compliments in psychotherapy not only ensures a positive alliance between therapist and clients but also enhances the outcome of psychotherapy no less than 30%, compared with psychotherapy in which compliments are not given.

There are different types of compliments. A "direct compliment" is a positive evaluation or reaction by the therapist in response to the client. It can be about something the client has said, done, or made, or about his appearance. A compliment can also be about the client's strengths or resources: You must be a real caring mother to . . . tell me more about that. Or: You must be a very determined person, please tell me more about this determination of yours.

An "indirect compliment" is a question that implies something positive about the client. One way to indirectly compliment is to ask for more information about a desired outcome stated by the client. These questions invite the client to tell a success story about himself: How did you do this? How were you able to . . . ? Where did you get this great idea?

When giving compliments to several people it is very important to share the compliments around evenly. Compliments can be given to each person individually or to the persons together: Apparently you all succeeded in the past to work together in a pleasant way. Could you tell me how you did that back then?

Indirect complimenting is preferable to direct complimenting because its questioning format leads clients to discover and state their own strengths and resources.

Many clients accept compliments easily. Others downplay or even reject them. But remember that the first goal in giving compliments is for clients to notice their positive changes, strengths, and resources. It is not necessary for them to openly accept the compliments.

Author and psychotherapist Yalom (2008) poses the question: what is it that patients remember when they look back on their therapy years later? Generally not the insights they had or the analyses the therapist made. Mostly they remember the positive and supportive remarks of the therapist.

From a solution-focused point of view our clients are invited to do more of what works and stop doing what does not work and do something else instead (see Chapter 4). Therapists should do the same: they should give positive reinforcement of everything that is working for the client and stop reinforcing what is not working for them. In learning theory terms this implies that they should give verbal and nonverbal positive reinforcement for what works and verbal and nonverbal negative punishment (or nonreward) for what is not working, as can be seen in reinforcing "solutions-talk" and nonrewarding "problem-talk."

Besides giving positive reinforcement to everything that works, normalizing and summarizing are also important. More information about these two interventions can be found in Bannink (2010a).

Exercise 5.2

In the next conversations that last longer than five minutes, give at least three compliments to those present and notice how the atmosphere of the conversations changes.

Enhancing Cooperation

Traditional CBT uses the concepts of "resistance" and "noncompliance." Positive CBT sees clients as always cooperating. They are showing the therapist how they think change takes place. As the therapist understands their thinking and acts accordingly, there will always be cooperation. If the therapist sees resistance in the other person, he cannot see his efforts to cooperate; if, on the other hand, he sees his unique way of cooperating, he cannot see his resistance.

Positive CBT uses the solution-focused terms for assessing the alliance between the client and himself: does it concern a "visitor-," a "complainant-," or a "customer-relationship"? For convenience, the terms are shortened to *visitor, complainant,* and *customer,* although they do not refer to a quality of the client as such, but always to the type of relationship between the therapist and each individual client. The challenge for all psychotherapists is to invite each client to become (or remain) a customer. It often happens that clients will start therapy from a visitor- or a complainant-relationship. This early assessment of each client's level of motivation is of essential importance for the strategy of the therapist and for any homework suggestions.

Prochaska, Norcross, and DiClemente (1994) developed a theory about the stages of behavior change, which can be broadly compared to the terms mentioned previously. When a person adopts an indifferent or unknowing attitude (the attitude of a client in a visitor-relationship), the emphasis is on providing information and on establishing a link between the behavior to be changed and the worries or problems that others experience. In the next stage, with someone who is contemplating change (the attitude of a client in a complainant-relationship), the emphasis is on deciding on and initiating the desired behavior. This is followed by the stages of change action (the attitude of a client in a customer-relationship), behavior maintenance, and (possibly) relapse.

In a *visitor-relationship* the client is mandated (by a doctor, parents, insurance company, employer). This involuntary client has no problem personally. Others have a problem with him or see him as the problem. Naturally he is not motivated to change his behavior. Often the mandated client's goal is to maintain the relationship with the person referring him or to free himself from this person as soon as possible.

The Positive CBT therapist creates a climate in which a call for help is made possible. What does the client want to achieve through his relationship with the therapist? What would the person referring him like to see changed in his behavior as a result of the therapy and to what extent is the client prepared to cooperate in this? Some tips:

- Assume that the client has good reasons for thinking and behaving in the way he does;
- Do not be judgmental; inquire into the perceptions of the client that make his – often defensive – attitude understandable;
- Ask what the client thinks the person referring him would like to see changed at the end of the therapy;
- Ask the client his opinion on this and what his minimum input might be.

Exercise 5.3

See who in your caseload may have been referred. Think about which of your clients have indicated that they want something out of their sessions with you.

Does the client himself want to achieve something by coming to you? Or are there others (e.g., family, parents, employer) who want something from the client and see him as having a problem or being the problem?

If the answer to the first question is no, your client has no goal (except maybe that of pleasing or shaking off the referrer). If your client says someone else is forcing him to come, you have an involuntary client, a "visitor."

In a *complainant-relationship* the client has a problem and is suffering from it, but he does not see himself as part of that problem and/or the solutions. He does not feel the need to change his own behavior; he thinks the other or something else is to blame for the problem and should change.

The therapist gives acknowledgment and asks about his competencies (for example: "How do you cope?"). He invites him to talk about exceptions: moments when the problem is or was there to a lesser extent or about the moments when there is already a sign or small part of what the client does want instead of what he does not want. Thus the client is invited to think and talk about his preferred future (without the problem) rather than focusing on the problem. Walter and Peller (1992) describe four strategies that may be applied in a complainant-relationship:

- I wish I could help you with this, but I am not a magician. I do not think that anyone is able to change anyone else. How else might I help you? Or: In what way is this problem a problem for you?
- Investigating the hypothetical solution: Imagine the other changing in the direction desired, what would you notice different about him? What would you notice different about yourself? What difference would that make to your relationship with him? At what moment is this already occurring?
- Investigating the future if the other is not changing: What can you still do yourself?
- Figuring out the hoped for outcome behind earlier attempts: What do you finally hope to achieve together?

Story 5.4: Misery I Love You!

Albert Ellis, one of the founders of CBT, was a well-known writer of song texts.

Here is an example of one of his "rational humorous songs" entitled "Oh, Misery I Love You," in which we can find the stance of clients in a complainant-relationship:

Oh, misery I love you!
I'm always dreaming of you!
If I should run and give you unemployment,
Then I might slyly have to try enjoyment!
Although my cares will flourish
Unless I wake and shake you free,
I always strive to keep alive and nourish
My beautiful misery!

Source: www.institutret.com

Exercise 5.4

Choose a partner for doing this exercise. Ask your partner to complain about a third person, which he would like to change. Ask him to talk about the same complaint every time, so you can practice with the four different strategies described previously. Notice the differences brought about by each strategy. Then change roles. In the role of the client you can learn a lot from the different types of questions that are asked of you.

In a *customer-relationship* the client sees himself as part of the problem and/or the solutions and is motivated to change. In the request for help the word "I" or "we" is present: What can I do to solve this problem? Or: How can we ensure that we re-establish a good relationship? Therapy with "customers" is often "the icing on the cake" (and gives some much needed positive reinforcement to the therapist that he is competent and is doing something which works).

In the first session it is common to find that clients are "complainants" and think that the other needs to change. Notice that the trichotomy between "visitor," "complainant," and "customer" is a value-free continuum: each position of the client is validated and accepted; the fact that he has shown up makes him already a "visitor" because he could also have chosen not to come. Cialdini (1984) states that the rule for reciprocation ("much obliged") and liking the other person (the therapist) are strong "weapons of influence." Giving compliments to clients for showing up helps in establishing a good relationship.

One of the principles of "motivational interviewing" (Miller and Rollnick, 2002) is unconditional acceptance of the client's position. The professional builds a relationship that is based on collaboration, individual responsibility, and autonomy. Miller and Rollnick state that the necessity of approaching the client in a nonmoralizing way is impeded if the professional is unprepared or unable to defer his own (mistaken) ideas about problem behavior and labels the client's behavior.

The professional reacts with empathy, avoids discussions, and strengthens the client's self-efficacy. Miller and Rollnick describe the term "change talk." This is a method of solution-focused communication used for enhancing the client's intrinsic motivation to change by stressing the advantages of the behavior change. This change talk assists the client in preparing for change. As methods for professionals to elicit change talk, they mention asking open-ended questions, such as: How would you like to see things change? How would you want your life to look in five years' time? By inviting clients to talk about their preferred future (their goal), their competences and successes, and to look for the exceptions, moments that were or are successful, the mediator will encourage visitors and complainants to transform into customers. Asking competence questions stimulates clients to talk about successes and to give self-compliments, which feeds their feeling of self-worth. Focusing on the preferred future facilitates change in the desired direction. Therefore: invite your clients to focus on what they do want instead of what they don't want.

Resistance

De Shazer (1984) proposes that what therapists see as signs of resistance are in fact the unique ways in which clients choose to cooperate. For example, clients who do not carry out the assigned homework, do not demonstrate resistance, but are actually cooperating because in that way they are indicating that this homework is not in accordance with their way of doing things. De Shazer assumes that clients are competent in figuring out what they want and in which way they can achieve this. It is the therapist's task to assist clients in discovering these competences and using them to create their preferred future. "With resistance as a central concept, therapist and client are like opposing tennis players. They are engaged in fighting against each other, and the therapist needs to win in order for the therapy to succeed. With cooperation as a central concept, therapist and client are like tennis players on the same side of the net. Cooperating is a necessity, although sometimes it becomes necessary to fight alongside your partner so that you can cooperatively defeat your mutual opponent." In this case the opponent is the problem. This view relates to the narrative approach (White and Epston, 1990) in which externalizing the problem, turning the problem into the enemy, is a much-used intervention. In Erickson's view (in: Rossi, 1980), resistance is cooperative: it is one of the possible responses people can make to interventions.

In sum: people are generally better persuaded by the reasons and solutions that they themselves discover than by those that have come into the minds of others.

If the therapist feels that he is becoming irritated, insecure, or demoralized, "counter-transference" is taking place: the negative reaction of the therapist to the behavior of the client. This may happen when the therapist – wrongly – considers the client a "customer" when it still concerns a visitor- or a complainant-relationship.

When clients are angry or seem to be unmotivated with regard to a particular topic, it is useful for the therapist to remind himself that clients are competent and that he has to look for a (better) way to cooperate with them. Then resistance becomes a signal that he needs to formulate a question about what the resistance suggests is important to the client, instead of concluding that the client is resistant or unmotivated. This applies equally to voluntary and involuntary clients.

Story 5.5: Everybody, Somebody, Anybody, and Nobody

This is a story about four people: Everybody, Somebody, Anybody, and Nobody. There was an important job to be done and Everybody was asked to do it. Everybody was sure that Somebody would do it. Anybody could have done it, but Nobody did. Somebody got angry (about that) because it was Everybody's job. Everybody knew that Anybody could do it, but Nobody realized that Somebody wouldn't do it. It ended up that Everybody blamed Somebody because Nobody did what Anybody could have done.

Source: Anonymous

6

Assessment

If a man is shot by a poisoned arrow and says "Don't take this arrow away before you find out exactly by whom and from where and how it was shot," this man's death is inevitable

Buddha

Introduction

Assessment in Positive CBT is different from assessment in traditional CBT or other problem-focused psychotherapies. Positive CBT is more interested in what clients want to change in their lives rather than exploring their problems in great detail, and it is more interested in what is right with clients than what is wrong with them. Therefore, the first challenge Positive CBT therapists encounter is inviting clients to shift from "problem talk" to "strengths and solutions talk" at the point at which they have had enough time to describe their problems to feel heard (often 10–15 minutes in the first session). Assessing what they want to be different (their goals), their strengths and resources (exceptions to the problem and their competences), their motivation to change, their progression, hope, and confidence are all part of the assessment and case conceptualization in Positive CBT.

In this chapter I will also explain how positive self-monitoring techniques and positive functional behavior analysis have their place in Positive CBT.

Case Conceptualization

Kuyken, Padesky, and Dudley (2009, p. 3) define CBT case conceptualization as follows: "Case conceptualization is a process whereby therapist and client work collaboratively to describe and then to explain the issues a client presents in therapy. Its primary function is to guide therapy in order to relieve client

Practicing Positive CBT: From Reducing Distress to Building Success, First Edition. Fredrike Bannink.
© 2012 John Wiley & Sons, Ltd. Published 2012 by John Wiley & Sons, Ltd.

distress and build client resilience." Case conceptualization is a process like that in a crucible: it synthesizes individual client experience with relevant theory and research. Collaborative empiricism is the "heat" in the crucible that drives the conceptualization process. It evolves over the course of CBT, progressing from descriptive to increasingly explanatory levels. Furthermore, it not only incorporates client problems but also client strengths and resilience.

They propose that therapy has two overarching goals:

1. To alleviate clients' distress;
2. To build resilience.

Conceptualization actively identifies and incorporates clients' strengths in order to apply existing client resources to presenting issues and to strengthen client awareness and use of strengths over time (e.g., building resilience).

"Most current CBT approaches are concerned either exclusively or largely with a client's problems, vulnerabilities, and history of adversity. We advocate for therapists to identify and work with client strengths at every stage of conceptualization. A strengths focus is often more engaging for clients and offers the advantages of harnessing client strengths in the change process to pave a way to lasting recovery" (p. 28).

Within the case conceptualization crucible, client experience includes client strengths.

CBT theories of "resilience" are highlighted and elaborated during the conceptualization process along with CBT theories relevant to problems. Clients are often not aware of the strategies they use to be resilient. Highlighting these in a case conceptualization increases the likelihood the person will consider their use during future challenges.

"Noticing the strategies a person employs to manage adversity is often an easy first step toward conceptualizing resilience. Strategies usually can be observed and may be behavioral (e.g., persisting in efforts), cognitive (e.g., problem solving, acceptance), emotional (e.g., humor, reassurance), social (e.g., seeking help), spiritual (e.g., finding meaning in suffering), or even physical (e.g., sleeping and eating well).

People who cope resiliently tend to construe events positively, including objectively challenging events. These interpretations involve positive expectancies (e.g., "I have faith this will work out"), self-efficacy (e.g., "This is tough, but I have coped with worse times"), and optimism (e.g., "We will manage this"). Sometimes clients are not aware of these thoughts. Conceptualizations of resilience bring these interpretative biases into awareness so clients can choose how to respond during challenging times" (p. 107).

Tedeschi and Calhoun (2004) and Bannink (2008b) state that results of several studies suggest that traumas need not be debilitating and that most people are resilient and even grow in the wake of a trauma. Understanding and highlighting the sources of this resilience and posttraumatic growth and focusing on hope and optimism help professionals foster these strengths in their clients, as opposed to focusing on what is wrong with them, which can has a discouraging effect. From a solution-focused perspective the focus in treatment shifts from posttraumatic stress to "posttraumatic success."

Exercise 6.1

A unique feature of resilience is that you can promote the factors of resilience independently of experiences of adversity. You can even engage in a game of "what if?" This means you can pretend an adversity or tragedy has occurred, and you can imagine what you would do to deal with it and which resilience factors you would use (Grotberg, 2003).

Assessing Goals

Setting goals emphasizes the possibility of change and begins to focus the client on future possibilities rather than on symptoms and problems. It also reinforces the notion that the client is an active member of the therapeutic relationship and that full involvement is required: the client will not be "done" to. Hawton *et al.* (1995) state that defined goals help to impose structure on treatment. They also prepare the client for discharge: making explicit that therapy will be terminated when goals are achieved, or that therapy will be discontinued if there is little progress towards them. This is not to say that goals cannot be renegotiated during treatment but that this should be done explicitly, together with the client, thus reducing the risk that client and therapist are pursuing different agendas. Finally, setting goals provides the opportunity for an evaluation of outcome related directly to the individual's presented problems.

Goals should be stated in *positive terms*, so that it is explicit what the client is moving towards rather than away from. As it is often difficult to turn the client away from symptoms, and towards positive goals, it may be useful to say something like:

"It's as though you've been wearing glasses which are very good at focussing on symptoms and problems. I want you to start wearing glasses, which pick up evidence that you're coping, evidence of success. So it's useful if we are clear what success would be like" (Hawton *et al.*, 1995, p. 42). Specific questioning may help to focus the client on positive targets. For example, a client said that she wanted to "stop being irritable all the time," and she was asked: "What would you do that was different if you were not irritable?" It may be useful asking the client to make "three wishes," or to describe a "typical ideal day."

Goals should be *specific and detailed*. Clients are often aware in general terms of how they would like to be. For example a client replied that she wanted "to be normal." The therapist asked: "Being normal means different things to different people. If you feel normal, how would you be different from how you are now?" "What would tell you that you were more like you used to be?" "What would you be doing that you are not doing now?" Or asking a client who is lacking in self-confidence: "How would you know if your self-confidence improved?" "What would you be doing that you are not doing now?" If possible, goals should be phrased so that more than one person could agree if the goal was achieved, as this is likely to increase the reliability of measures related to goal achievement.

Exercise 6.2

Take a moment to imagine a future in which you are bringing your "best possible self" forward. Visualize a "best possible self" that is very pleasing to you and that you are interested in. Imagine you have worked hard and succeeded at accomplishing your life goals. You might think of this as the realization of your life dreams and of your own best potentials. The point is not to think of unrealistic fantasies, rather, things that are positive, attainable, and within reason. After you get a fairly clear image, write about the details below. Writing your thoughts and hopes down helps to create a logical structure and help you move from the realm of foggy ideas and fragmented thoughts to concrete, real possibilities. Research shows this is a useful exercise in helping individuals with goal-setting and building optimism and hope.

Fantasy realization theory

Oettingen and Stephens (in: Moskowitz and Grant, 2009) state that the self-help industry would have us believe that to "think positive" is the single most effective means of getting what we want. And though empirical research does consistently find that optimistic beliefs foster motivation and successful performance, recent research reveals that alternate forms of positively thinking about the future (e.g., positive fantasies, wishful thinking, and other avoidant coping styles) are less beneficial for effortful action, performance, and well-being. Whether an individual indulges in a desired future (has positive fantasies about a desired future) or actually judges a desired future as within reach (has positive expectations about a desired future) has very different implications for effortful action and successful performance. In hope theory terms (see Chapter 5) this is called "agency thinking."

Oettingen proposes a model of fantasy realization that serves to turn free fantasies about a desired future into binding goals. The model assumes that mentally contrasting aspects of the future and reality activates expectations about attaining a desired future that in turn lead to persistent goal striving and effective goal attainment in the case of high expectations.

1. *Fantasy realization theory* (Oettingen, 1999; Oettingen, Hönig, and Gollwitzer, 2000) elucidates three routes to goal setting that result from how people elaborate their fantasies about desired futures. One route leads to expectancy-based goal commitment, whereas the other two routes lead to goal commitment independent of expectations.

   "Mental contrasting" is the expectancy-based route and rests on mentally contrasting fantasies about a desired future with aspects of the present reality. When people use the self-regulatory strategy of mental contrasting they first imagine a desired future and then reflect on the respective negative reality, emphasizing a necessity to change the present reality to achieve the desired future. This necessity to act should activate relevant expectations of success, which then informs goal commitment.

When engaging in mental contrasting individuals first elaborate a desired future, establishing the positive future as their reference point and only thereafter elaborate aspects of the present reality, thereby perceiving the negative aspects as obstacles standing in the way of attaining the future. Reversing this order (i.e., reverse mental contrasting) by first elaborating the negative reality followed by elaboration of the desired future, thwarts construal of the present standing in the way of the future and thus fails to elicit goal commitment congruent with expectations of success (Oettingen, Pak, and Schnetter, 2001).

2. *Indulging* consists of solely fantasizing about a positive future. There are no reflections on the present reality that would point to the fact that the positive future is not yet realized. A necessity to act is not induced and expectations of success are not activated and used.

3. *Dwelling* consists of merely reflecting on the negative reality, producing continual ruminations, as no fantasies about a positive future designate the direction to act. A necessity to act is not included and expectations are not activated and used.

Numerous studies have now shown that mental contrasting turns free fantasies into binding goals by activating expectations, thus influencing subsequent goal commitment and goal-directed behavior. Mental contrasting enables people to commit to their desired future and is effective in promoting commitment to goals that are initially hard to commit to. It can be used as a metacognitive strategy to help people manage and improve their everyday lives.

"Making fantasies come true is not merely the stuff of daydreams or fairy tales. To make our fantasies come true, a person needs the appropriate thought processes to activate expectations and commitment" (Oettingen and Stephens, 2009, p. 174).

In summary, inviting clients to design their desired future is important as a first step and is useful when it is followed by mental contrasting this preferred outcome with the present reality to help overcome the obstacles in the present. The solution-focused "reteaming model" is very much in line with this research. In "reteaming" designing the preferred future (goal) is the first step, which is later on followed by looking at the present moment and at obstacles and how to overcome them (see Chapter 13).

Exercise 6.3

This is a "mental contrasting" exercise. First you imagine that you will achieve your goal. Then you focus on obstacles, which are in your way. Grab a notebook or just a piece of paper and write down a wish or concern you currently have. Now think about what a happy ending would look like for this wish or concern. Write down one positive aspect of this happy ending. Next, think about an obstacle that stands in the way between where you are now and your happy ending. Now list another positive aspect of the happy ending. And another obstacle. And another positive aspect. And another obstacle. After doing this exercise, reflect on whether it was useful for you and, if so, how it was useful.

Case 6.1

In a Positive CBT therapy I explain to the client that my work is comparable to that of a taxi driver. The client states the destination of the taxi ride and it is my responsibility to drive her there safely. It is also my responsibility to see to it that the route is as short as possible and that the ride is as comfortable as possible. Therefore, my first question – being a taxi driver – is: "Where to?" instead of: "Where from?"

Approach and avoidance goals

We can only move toward or away from things, so "approach" and "avoidance" capture a lot of what we do in life. Approach motivation may be defined as the energization of behavior by, or the direction of behavior toward, positive stimuli (objects, events, possibilities), whereas avoidance motivation may be defined as the energization of behavior by, or the direction of behavior away from, negative stimuli (objects, events, possibilities) (Elliot, 2008). For example, weight control behavior is typically motivated by a desire to reach a positive goal, characterized by improvements in one's appearance and physical comfort, whereas smoking cessation is typically motivated by a desire to avoid the health threats associated with smoking.

Distinguishing approach motivation from avoidance motivation may be considered one of the oldest ideas in the history of thought about the behavior of organisms. The Greek philosopher Democritus articulated an ethical hedonism in which the immediate pursuit of pleasure and avoidance of pain were prescribed as the guide for human action. Freud construed the procurement of pleasure and the avoidance of pain (i.e., unpleasure) as the basic motivational impetus underlying psychodynamic activity.

Pavlov identified two types of reflexive responses to stimuli, an orienting response toward the stimulus and a defensive response away from the stimulus. Skinner distinguished between reinforcers that strengthen responses and punishing stimuli that weaken responses, and differentiated positive reinforcement (the provision of a positive) from negative reinforcement (the removal of a negative).

Both approach and avoidance motivation are integral to successful adaptation: avoidance motivation facilitates surviving, while approach motivation facilitates thriving.

Also, social relationships entail both pleasure and pain. Potential social incentives include affiliation, affection, intimacy, friendship, and love. The benefits of having positive social relationships are numerous and well documented. Diener and Seligman (2002) identified the happiest people (i.e., top 10%). The one aspect of their lives they all had in common was that they had strong positive social relationships. On the other hand, there are also potential threats inherent in relationships, including conflict, rejection, humiliation, competition, and jealousy.

Much recent work emphasizes the value of positive, approach-oriented emotions for "broadening" awareness and "building" social networks (Fredrickson, 1998). Research with couples indicates that stable relationships tend to have partners expressing five times as many positive approach emotions towards each other as negative emotions (a "positivity ratio" of 5 to 1, see Chapter 9), including both anger and avoidant emotions (Gottman, 1994).

From a functional point of view, both approach and avoidance goals are necessary for successful adaptation. Whereas approach motivation facilitates growth and flourishing, avoidance motivation facilitates protection and survival.

Tamir and Diener (2008) state that although it is beneficial to pursue at least some degree of both approach and avoidance goals, pursuing such goals may carry different implications for well-being. The pursuit of approach goals is more manageable than that of avoidance goals. According to cybernetic control models (Carver and Scheier, 1998) the pursuit of approach goals involves diminishing the discrepancy between a current state and a desired state. On the other hand, the pursuit of avoidance goals involves enlarging the discrepancy between a current state and an undesired state. From this conceptual viewpoint, the pursuit of approach goals should be more manageable than the pursuit of avoidance goals, because progress is more tangible and easier to monitor (Elliot, Sheldon, and Church, 1997).

In addition, the pursuits of approach and avoidance goals differ in the cognitions they give rise to. If goal pursuits involve constant comparisons of a current state to an end-state, the pursuit of approach goals involves constantly monitoring positive outcomes, making them more accessible during goal pursuit. On the other hand, the pursuit of avoidance goals involves constantly monitoring negative outcomes, making them more accessible during goal pursuit. Thus, the pursuit of approach goals maintains positive cognitions, whereas the pursuit of avoidance goals maintains negative cognitions (Elliot and Sheldon, 1998).

Tamir and Diener (2008) also state that research has shown that the feasibility of approach and avoidance goals varies as a function of basic motivational orientations. Pursuing approach goals may be more feasible for approach-oriented individuals, whereas pursuing avoidance goals may be more feasible for avoidance-oriented individuals. The pursuit of feasible goals is likely to promote well-being because it is more meaningful, the chances of success are higher, and success leads to more intense pleasant experiences. To maximize well-being, individuals may need to find the mix that fits them best.

When a young man marries a woman just because he cannot bear his loneliness any longer, we would not be surprised when this marriage does not bring him much happiness. Simply marrying somebody to avoid being alone does not guarantee marital happiness, common interests, personal well-being, or mutual understanding and growth, to name just a few approach goals neglected by the young man in the example. Avoidance goals, even when they are perfectly accomplished, terminate or prevent aversive states, but they do not necessarily promote the satisfaction of needs. Instead, avoidance motivation is associated with reduced subjective well-being, impaired subjective competence, and increased physical symptoms (Elliot and Sheldon, 1998).

Finally, experiments show differences between goals represented as "to do well on the task" or as "to avoid doing poorly on the task." How an individual intends to pursue a goal might be modulated by approach-avoidance motivation. Given the same goal, a relatively approach-oriented person might adopt a strategy designed to maximize rewards, whereas a relatively avoidance-oriented person might adopt one that minimizes punishments. These differential strategies also lead to effects on performance: approach goals are associated with better results than avoidance goals (Elliot and Church, 1997).

Since approach motives and goals are associated with better results and more well-being, it might be worthwhile to change from cognitions linked to avoidance to cognitions linked to approach. Behaviors linked to avoidance can also be changed to behaviors linked to approach. After explaining these two options to our clients, they are invited to explore some exceptions: When in a given situation was he already thinking in approach terms instead of avoidance terms? When was he already showing approach behavior instead of avoidance behavior? What were the consequences?

Although research shows that we generally benefit more from approach goals than from avoidance goals, there is considerable evidence that most people try harder to avoid losses than to obtain comparable gains. The effects of punishment and negative reinforcers on behavior are generally stronger than the effects of reward and comparable positive reinforcers, and people report more often trying to get out of bad moods than to get into or prolong good moods (Baumeister *et al.*, 2001). This means that in Positive CBT we invite our clients to change their focus from thinking and doing something that is probably contrary to what they would be thinking and doing automatically: obtaining gains instead of avoiding losses.

Case 6.2

Client A is depressed and her goal is to have more positive feelings (approach goal). Client B is depressed and her goal is to avoid becoming even more depressed (avoidance goal). Client A can monitor progress in her goal pursuit as she is feeling better. If she fails to feel better, she knows that she is not making progress toward her desired outcome. If however, she is feeling better, she knows that she is getting closer to obtaining her goal. Client A can monitor success and failure in her goal pursuit and experience pleasant or unpleasant affect as a result.

Client B may have a harder time monitoring her progress. If she is not feeling better, she knows that she is failing in obtaining her goal of keeping things as they are. What would indicate to her that she is succeeding in her goal pursuit? Finding indications of success in pursuing avoidance goals can often be challenging. Thus she may be more likely to detect failures than successes in her goal pursuit, making it more likely for her to experience unpleasant affect.

In addition the pursuits of approach and avoidance goals likely differ in the cognitions they give rise to. Clients A and B may have different thoughts accessible to them in their daily lives. Client A may think of what it would be like to be feeling better and such thoughts might engender pleasant affect. Client B on the other hand, may think of what it would be like if things don't get better and such thoughts may engender unpleasant affect.

Overall, the process of pursuing approach goals is different from the process of pursuing avoidance goals. Approach goals appear to be easier to monitor and more manageable than avoidance goals. In addition, whereas approach goals elicit positive cognitions by leading individuals to focus on desirable outcomes, avoidance goals elicit negative cognitions by leading individuals to focus on undesirable outcomes. Therefore, the pursuit of approach goals promotes more well-being than the pursuit of avoidance goals. Greater well-being results from experiencing more frequent pleasant and less frequent unpleasant affect and from having personally meaningful experiences in life.

Kuyken, Padesky, and Dudley (2009, p. 101) state: "Goals can be stated as increasing strengths or positive values (approach goal: e.g., be more considerate) as well as reducing distress (avoidance goal: e.g., feel less anxious). Therapists can routinely ask about positive goals and aspirations in early sessions and add these to the client's list of presenting issues. Discussions of positive areas of a client's life often reveal alternative coping strategies to those used in problem areas. These often more adaptive coping strategies can be identified as part of the same process that identifies triggers and maintenance factors for problems. When it is time for behavioural experiments to alter maintenance circles, the client can practice alternative coping responses drawn from more successful areas of life. Later in therapy, positive assumptions and core beliefs prove just as important as negative ones when forming longitudinal case conceptualizations."

De Shazer (1991, p. 158) states that too often the client is willing to accept the absence of the problem as "goal enough", but the absence can never be proved and, therefore, success or failure cannot be known by either therapist or client. Unless clearly established beforehand, even the presence of significant changes is not enough to prove the absence of the problem.

Walter and Peller (2000) state that clients sometimes speak only of what they do not want or what they want to eliminate from their lives (avoidance goal). In interactional situations, clients often speak of what they want the other person not to do. Their only course of action at that time has been to try to get the other person to stop doing what they consider to be problematic behavior. The other person is also in a strange position, in that the options are either to defend the present behavior or to stop what the other finds so problematic. She or he is still in the dark as to what the client does want to happen. Talking about what the client does want (approach goal) may open up the conversation in a more positive direction.

Story 6.1: Top Performers

How do top performers set goals? Jim Barrell, a performance improvement expert working with baseball players from the San Francisco 49ers and the Atlanta Braves states that there are toward goals and away goals. Which one you use has quite an impact on performance. Toward goals have you visualize and create connections around where you are going. You are creating new connections in your brain. What is interesting is that you start to feel good at lower levels with toward goals. There are benefits earlier. Away goals have you visualize what can go wrong, which re-activates the negative emotions involved.

Source: Anonymous

Some final remarks about goals are listed here:

1. It is not only the client himself who may define the changes he seeks to achieve in his life. The partner, children, colleagues, and referrer can be asked the same kind of questions about their goals and/or what they see as the goal for the client. In Appendix G you will find a questionnaire for the referrer;
2. Goals are not fixed or static but can rather be seen as a desired situation. They develop during the process and are refined and can even change as the process proceeds. Goals are not set to achieve an ideal state but, instead, to reach a situation that is "good enough" from the client's perspective;
3. Beijebach *et al.* (2000) found that setting clear goals predicts a twofold increase in success;
4. Walter and Peller (1992) state that well-defined goals should be: in a positive representation, in a process form, in the here and now (which means the client can start the solution immediately), as specific as possible, within the client's control, and in the client's language;
5. Setting the agenda is commonly used in traditional CBT. In Positive CBT setting the agenda can be used as well, but a question about goal formulation for each item is added before the agenda is addressed: "What would be the best result of discussing this item?" and "How will we know we can stop discussing this item?" (Bannink, 2010a);
6. A "stretch-goal," as described in hope theory, is defined as a goal that is beyond the client's current performance level. Stretch goals energize and often clients, who reach for what appears to be impossible at first, often actually do the impossible. Even when the client does not quite make it, he will probably wind up doing better than he would have done otherwise.

On this point, it should be noted that individuals reporting high levels of hope often prefer stretch goals that are slightly more difficult than previously attained goals.

Case 6.3

In a study conducted by King (2001), 81 participants were asked to write about one of four topics for 20 minutes each day for four consecutive days. They were randomly assigned to write about their most traumatic life event, their best possible future self, both of these topics, or a nonemotional control topic.

Mood was measured before and after writing and health center data for illness were obtained with participant consent. Three weeks later, measures of subjective well-being were obtained. Writing about life goals was significantly less upsetting than writing about trauma and was associated with a significant increase in subjective well-being.

Five months after writing, a significant interaction emerged such that writing about trauma, one's best possible self, or both were associated with decreased illness compared with controls. Results indicate that writing about self-regulatory topics can be associated with the same health benefits as writing about trauma.

Assessing Problems, Complaints, and Constraints

Positive CBT is by no means phobic to problems and complaints. Clients are given an opportunity to describe their problems or concerns, to which the therapist listens respectfully. But fewer details about the nature and severity of the problem are asked and possible causes of the problems are not analyzed. By asking about exceptions to the problem a form of differential diagnosis – removing diagnoses from the list – may reveal that some disorders can be eliminated (e.g., when asked about exceptions, a child who would otherwise be diagnosed with ADHD, appears to be able to sit still in the classroom).

Another way of conducting Positive CBT, granting due acknowledgment, is to first collect all symptoms, complaints, and constraints and then to "translate" all problem-descriptions into aspects of strengths and solutions: "What would you like to see instead?" "What is already working?" "How were you able to do that?" and then discard the collection of problems by tearing it up or just ignoring it in the next sessions when working with what clients want different in their lives. Another Positive CBT question would be: "If these problems/complaints/constraints would not be there, how would you or your life/relationship/work be different?"

Bakker, Bannink, and Macdonald (2010) state that one may choose to commence treatment immediately and if necessary pay attention to diagnostics of problems at a later stage. Severe psychiatric disorders, or a suspicion thereof, justify the decision to conduct a thorough diagnosis, since the tracing of the "underlying" organic pathology, for instance, has direct therapeutic consequences.

Ambulant intakes in primary or second-line health care are suitable for a Positive CBT approach. During the first or follow-up conversation it will automatically become clear whether an advanced diagnosis will be necessary, for example if there is a deterioration in the client's condition or if the treatment fails to give positive results. Analogous to "stepped care" one could think of "stepped diagnosis."

Duncan (2010), however, states that, unlike with medical treatments, diagnosis is an ill-advised starting point for psychotherapy. Diagnosis in mental health is not correlated with outcome or length of stay, and giving the dodo verdict (all psychotherapies are equal and have won prizes), cannot provide reliable guidance to clinicians or clients regarding the best approach to resolving a problem.

A final remark is about the importance of distinguishing between the person and the illness. When assessing problems it is important to always keep in mind that the client *is* not the problem or his diagnosis, but is someone who *has* a problem. Labels like "he is depressed" and "she is a borderliner" are not used in Positive CBT. After all, the client is much more than his problem or diagnosis. Instead of saying, "Henry is depressed," one might say: "He suffers from depressive episodes." Or: "Ann has a borderline personality disorder." In this way, openings are created for strengths and resources. O'Hanlon and Rowan (2003, p. 49) have also emphasized the importance of distinguishing between person and illness and of examining the effects of the illness on the person: "Ask not what disease the person has, but rather what person the disease has."

Assessing Strengths and Resources

Peterson (2006) developed the Values in Action Signature Strengths (VIA) test, available on the Authentic Happiness web site at www.authentichappiness.org. This survey has been developed to reliably classify people on the basis of 24 character strengths (see Chapter 4). The taxonomy of strengths and virtues is meant as a positive alternative to the DSM-IV-TR taxonomy of psychiatric disorders (and can also be used in combination with the DSM-IV-TR).

Assessment in Positive CBT may take the form of inviting clients to take the VIA test online and bring the printed outcome with them to the next session. The therapist and client then pay attention to the rank order of the strengths of each client. Then clients are asked to list their five highest strengths and are invited to provide some examples of how they used these strengths lately (or in the past).

The key to extracting more than a temporary high out of listing these strengths, however, is to invite clients to reshape their lives in such a way that they are able to apply their strengths more often. Seligman, Steen, Park, and Peterson (2005) discovered that the boost in positivity that comes from learning about one's strengths is significant, but temporary. By contrast, the boost in positivity that comes from finding new ways to apply these strengths is significant and lasting.

On the recently mentioned website more tests can be found, including emotion questionnaires, engagement questionnaires (among which is the Brief Strengths Test, measuring the 24 Character Strengths), meaning questionnaires, and life satisfaction questionnaires. More Positive Psychology questionnaires are : the PANAS (Positive and Negative Affect Schedule); the Gratitude Questionnaire (GQ-6); the Hope Scale (HS); the Inspiration Scale (IS); the Meaning in Life Questionnaire (MLQ); the Mindful Attention Awareness Scale (MAAS); the Quality of Life Inventory (QOLI); and the Personal Growth Initiative Scale (PGIS). A number of Positive Psychology questionnaires can be found at: www.ppc.sas.upenn.edu/ppquestionnaires.htm.

Exception-finding questions are frequently used in Positive CBT. They are another useful way of looking at already existing strengths and resources. Those questions are new to many clients, who are more accustomed to problem-focused questions. When asked about exceptions, which are the keys to solutions, they may start noticing them for the first time. Solutions are often built from formerly unrecognized differences. One can distinguish between exceptions pertaining to the desired outcome (the goal) and exceptions pertaining to the problem (see Appendix B).

- Exceptions pertaining to the goal are: "When do you already see glimpses of what you want to be different in your life?" "When was the last time you noticed this?" "What was it like?" "What was different then?"
- Exceptions pertaining to the problem are: "When was the problem less severe?" "When was the problem not there for a short period of time?" "When was there a moment you were able to cope a little bit better?"

The therapist, having heard and explored these exceptions, then compliments the clients for all the things they have already done.

A scaling question can be used: On a scale where 10 equals you have reached your preferred future and 0 equals the worst situation you can image, where would you say you are right now? By means of a scaling question, the therapist can help clients to express complex, intuitive observations about their past experiences and estimates of future possibilities. Scaling questions invite clients to put their observations, impressions, and predictions on a scale from 10 to 0. For example, you may ask your client: "On a scale from 10 to 0, where 10 means you are confident that you can reach your goal and 0 means you are not confident at all, where would you say you are now?"

Lamarre and Gregoire (1999) describe a technique called "competence trans-ference" in which they invite their clients to talk about other areas of competence in their lives, such as sports or a hobby or a special talent. They then ask clients to bring those abilities to bear in order to reach their goals. For instance, they describe how a client suffering from a panic disorder learned to relax by applying his knowledge of deep-sea diving whenever he experienced anxiety.

Case 6.4

Cindy had for years suffered from the mood swings of her husband. She tried everything but without success. Cindy, as a horse trainer, had a special talent for training supposedly untameable horses. When asked the secret of her success, she replied that she always rewarded the horse for its achievements, even if the results were minimal.

She also explained that she resisted disciplining the horse or becoming angry and abandoning it. At that point she would stop for the day and try again the next day. Then Cindy realized that she could use her talent in precisely the same way when dealing with her husband.

Walter and Peller (2000) give three competence questions, which invite their clients to relate their success stories:

- How did you do that?
- How did you decide to do that?
- How did you manage to do that?

The first question is based on the assumption that the client has done something and therefore supposes action, competence, and responsibility. The second question is based on the assumption that the client has taken an active decision, affording him the opportunity to write a new life story, with influence on his own future. The third question invites the client to relate his successes.

Assessing Progress, Motivation, Hope, and Confidence

The Greek philosopher Heracleitus (540–480 BC) is often credited with saying that nothing is permanent but change: "Panta rhei." Exploring what is different about better versus worse days, times without the problem versus times when the problem seems to get the best of clients, can help therapists to use the description of such fluctuations as a guide to activity.

Studies done by Weiner-Davis *et al.* (1987) show that 15–66% of clients experience positive treatment-related gains prior to the formal initiation of treatment ("pretreatment change"). Simply scheduling an appointment may help set the wheel of change in motion and present the possibility for an emergent story of competence and mastery.

Therapists may view their clients through a change-focused lens. Shining a spotlight on change illuminates existing client resources and allows their enlistment. A change-focus requires that the therapist believes, like Heracleitus, in the certainty of change and creates a context in which to welcome, explore, and develop new or different perspectives and behaviors. Of special interest is what the clients have done to bring about this change and how the clients make sense of it all. Questions about "pretreatment" change are:

- Since you made the appointment for this therapy and our session today, what is better (even just a little bit)?
- Many clients notice that, between the time they call for the appointment and the actual first session, things already seem different. What have you noticed about your situation?
- What is already different/better between you?
- How were you able to do that?
- What would you need to do (or what needs to happen) for you to experience more of that?
- As you continue to do these things, what difference will that make to you tomorrow? How will your day go better?
- What are these positive changes saying about you as a person?

Walter and Peller (2000, p. 7) describe their own development as therapists: "As we weighed the frequency of problem patterns versus exception patterns, we asked, even more radically, how useful it was to interpret clients' experiences as stable patterns. Perhaps the notion of stable patterns was just a construct that was limiting our ability to observe change. Perhaps it would be more productive to think of change as constant and randomness of behaviour as the norm, rather than enduring interactional patterns as the norm. We began to think that the assumption 'change is occurring all the time' might be a more useful starting point than 'behaviour is constant and repetitious'."

So-called "scaling questions" can be used to assess progress, motivation, hope, and confidence. The client is invited to indicate to what degree his goal has already been achieved (when progress is assessed) on a scale of 10 to 0, with 10 being the most desirable outcome and 0 the worst things have ever been. "Where would you say you are right now on this scale?" "What did you do to (already) reach this score?" "How come it is not lower than it is?" "How did you do that?" "What would one point higher on the scale look like?" "What would you then be doing differently?" "What point on the scale do you want to reach for you to consider the goal (sufficiently) achieved?" "At what number would you deem yourself ready to conclude the therapy?"

Scaling questions can also make clear which part of the road is already traveled. Most clients are not at a complete 0 when they come in for therapy (although sometimes they are, in which case the therapist may extend the scale a bit and ask: "How do you manage?" or "How come it is not minus 10?"). As mentioned before, scaling questions can be the starting point for an operant conditioning technique called "successive approximation" (or "shaping") of desired behavior.

Usually, when clients have a clear sense of what they want to achieve and when they have already been able to achieve to some extent what they want, it will be relatively easy for them to choose the next steps forward. Rothman (2000) found that the decision criteria that lead people to initiate a change in their behavior are different from those that lead them to maintain that behavior.

Decisions regarding behavioral initiation depend on favorable expectations regarding future outcomes, whereas decisions regarding behavioral maintenance depend on perceived satisfaction with received outcomes. Also a comparison with the preferred situation is particularly beneficial and motivating at the start of the therapy, but during the therapy the client will become more motivated to continue, when making regular comparisons with the past before changes were initiated. As you will see in the following story, people find it more motivating to be partly finished with a longer journey rather than at the starting gate of a shorter one.

Story 6.2: At the Car Wash

A local car wash ran a promotion featuring loyalty cards. Every time customers bought a car wash, they got a stamp, and a free wash when they filled up their cards with eight stamps. Other customers got a different loyalty card. They needed to collect ten stamps (rather than eight) to get a free car wash – but they were given a "head start": two stamps had already been added.

The "goal" was the same: buy eight additional car washes, get a reward. But the psychology was different: in one case, you're 20 percent of the way toward the goal; in the other case you're starting from scratch. A few months later 19 percent of the eight-stamp customers had earned a free wash, versus 34 percent of the head-start group (and the head-start group earned the free wash faster).

People find it more motivating to be partly finished with a longer journey than to be at the starting gate of a shorter one. To motivate action is to make people feel as though they're closer to the finish line than they might have thought.

Adapted from: Goldstein, Martin and Cialdini (2007).

In traditional CBT, scaling questions are frequently used. The difference, however, is that in problem-focused therapy the scales are always about the problem: a depression scale, an anxiety scale, or SUD (Subjective Units of Distress) in Eye Movement Desensitization and Reprocessing (EMDR). On these scales the highest point is where the depression or stress is at its peak and the 0 is where the negative feeling is absent. The absence of negative feelings does not say anything about the presence of positive feelings, as we have seen in the previous chapters.

In Positive CBT scales are used in a different way. A "depression-scale" is not used, but a neutral "mood-scale," where the highest point (10) stands for the best possible mood and the 0 stands for the worst possible mood. An "anxiety-scale" is not used, but again a neutral scale, where the 10 stands for complete relaxation and the 0 stands for stress at its worst.

Case 6.5

In a clinical setting for adolescents with a drug- and/or alcohol addiction the (problem-focused) therapists frequently ask their clients a scaling question about their craving, for which they developed a "craving-scale." "How high are you right now on this scale, where 10 stands for the craving being at its worst and 0 stands for no craving at all?" Often the clients answer: "My craving was rather low till you brought it up, but now you mention it, I feel it right away!" A Positive CBT scaling question might have been: "Where are you now in having control over your addiction, where 10 stands for: I have every control and 0 stands for: I have no control at all?"

Assessing Motivation to Change

It would be nice if both clients and therapist could begin with the assumption that therapy is being used as intended: to find solutions to solve a problem or to put something behind them. For this, sometimes changes in personal behavior are required. However, commitment to therapy and the motivation to make changes are not synonymous. If a client is willing to come to therapy (commitment) this does not necessarily signify that he is also willing to change his own behavior. Often clients will (silently) hope that the therapist will solve the problem or will see the other person as the one who is to blame for the problem. In Positive CBT it is the task of the therapist to assist clients to make changes and help them to leave the ditches they dug themselves into. Chapter 5 discusses the method of assessing the clients' motivation to change and how this change can be encouraged, so a positive outcome in therapy is enhanced. In this process the therapist assesses the type of relationship he has with each client to optimize cooperation: does it concern a "visitor-relationship," a "complainant-relationship," or a "customer-relationship"?

Positive Self-monitoring

In traditional CBT self-monitoring of symptoms is used to gain a more accurate description of behaviors (rather than relying on recall) to help adapt the intervention in relation to client progress and to provide clients with feedback about their progress.

It is a means of helping clients to become active, collaborative participants in their therapy by identifying and appraising how they react to events (in terms of their own physiological reactions, behaviors, cognitions, and feelings).

93

Self-monitoring is often integrated into the therapy, both in the sessions and as part of homework assignments.

The difference between traditional CBT and Positive CBT is that self-monitoring in Positive CBT is not about clients' symptoms and problems but about clients' strengths and about exceptions to the problem. When clients use this form of positive self-monitoring they feel more competent and can choose to do more of what works to change their situation for the better. I will discuss three forms of positive self-monitoring.

1. The first method of positive self-monitoring is through the use of the "thought record" as seen in Table 6.1. In traditional CBT the thought record is used to help clients understand which thoughts trigger their problem behavior, whereas in Positive CBT it is used to help clients understand which thoughts trigger their desired behavior. Positive CBT therapists may also invite their clients to fill in both problem-focused and strengths and solutions focused records.

2. The second method of changing the focus in self-monitoring from negative to positive is the observation of positive changes. Clients are invited to answer the following questions:
    *   Please indicate an area in your life in which you desire change the most;
    *   Evaluate the current situation on a scale of 10–0 (10 meaning very good, 0 meaning very bad);
    *   Describe briefly what is happening in this area that prompted you to choose this number and not a lower one (what is already working?);
    *   Suppose some day things will change and everything in this area of your life will be the way you want it to be. Describe briefly how you will know that everything is going very well (the 10 on the scale);
    *   Think what you could do in the near future in order for your evaluation on the scale to increase by at least one point (indicating that your situation became a little bit better). Make the actions as specific as you can;

Table 6.1 Thought record.

Situation	Mood (rate 100–0%)	Automatic thoughts (images)	Behavior

© Fredrike Bannink

Table 6.2 Observation form of exceptions to the problem.

Date	Event	What changed in desired direction?	What did you do to make this change?	What thoughts or emotions did this raise?	Further possible actions

© Fredrike Bannink

- When you would take these actions, what will change in this area of your life? How would this be helpful for you and/or others in your life?
3. The third method of positive self-monitoring is the monitoring of exceptions to the problem as seen in Table 6.2. In doing so, special attention should be paid to the ways in which this exception was different from problem times. Whereas in traditional CBT the therapist would explore the who, what, when, and where of client problems, the Positive CBT therapist is interested in exploring the who, what, when, and where of exceptions. Exceptions-finding questions are:
   - When didn't you experience the problem after expecting that you would?
   - What happens as the problem ends or starts to end?
   - Could the problem be worse? Why isn't the problem worse?
   - When was the problem less of a problem (even just a little bit)?
   - What is better already?

More exceptions-finding questions can be found in Bannink (2010a).

Notice that exceptions can either be deliberate or random. To find out about the "how" of an exception, the therapist inquires about who did what and when to make that happen. If the client is able to describe how an exception happened, the exception is deliberate. If, however, the client responds by shrugging his shoulders and saying "I don't know," this is a random exception. The importance of this distinction will be explained in Chapter 5 because it plays a key role in determining which homework suggestions are given to the client.

Positive Functional Behavior Analysis

Functional analysis methodology identifies variables that influence the occurrence of problem behavior and has become a hallmark of behavioral assessment.

Functional Behavior Analysis (FBA) is considered to be a problem-solving process for addressing client problem behavior. FBA looks beyond the behavior itself: the focus is on identifying significant factors associated with the occurrence (or nonoccurrence) of specific behaviors. This broader perspective offers a better understanding of the function or purpose behind the behavior. In FBA each problem is analyzed in terms of the A-B-Cs: the Antecedents, Behaviors and Beliefs, and Consequences. Each of these factors may increase or decrease the probability that the behavior will occur.

In traditional CBT a functional behavior analysis is made of the ABC's of problem behavior, whereas in Positive CBT an FBA is made of the exceptions of the problem behavior to identify their Antecedents, Behaviors and Beliefs, and Consequences. The Positive CBT therapist may choose to use both problem-focused and positive FBAs.

The contexts in which the problems (or the exceptions to the problems) arise, the "Antecedents," are those conditioned stimuli that cue the behavior. The "Behavior" of "Belief" may become reinforced via operant conditioning by removing aversive states or by the memory of achieving a desired goal, thus maintaining the behavior or belief (the "Consequences").

In other words: problem-focused FBA is used to describe the contexts in which the problem arises, to look at the factors which modulate the intensity of the problem, and to assess the consequences, including the avoidance, of them; Positive FBA on the other hand is used to describe the same for the desired behavior in the future and exceptions to the problem that already take place.

Behavioral research demonstrates that behaviors can be learned and extinguished on the basis of patterns of association, reward, and punishment.

During the descriptive stages of case conceptualization, functional analysis can be used to map how, when, and where behaviors occur, noting the consequences across different contexts (Kuyken, Padesky, and Dudley, 2009). Traditional FBA usually starts with a detailed description of the problem behavior, whereas Positive CBT starts with a detailed description of the exceptions to the problem behavior. Questions that may be asked are:

- When is/was the problem not there or there to a lesser extent (even just a little bit)?
- When is/was there already something of what you want different?
- When is/was there a moment when the problem is/was there, but you are/ were able to handle it a bit better?
- What do you do when you overcome the urge to . . . (drink too much, smoke, use drugs, eat too much)

Having built up a reasonable picture of the conditions under which the problem or the exceptions to the problem, or both, are most likely to occur, the next step is to look at what is maintaining the problem or what is maintaining the exceptions to the problem, with a focus on the immediate consequences of the behavior.

In traditional CBT the problematic behavior has positive consequences that need to be undermined, whereas the negative consequences need to be emphasized. The positive short-term consequence of feeling calm while smoking a cigarette should be undermined and the negative long-term consequence of getting lung cancer should be emphasized. Exceptions to the problem have positive consequences as well, which of course do not have to be undermined, but be emphasized instead. When a client tells his therapist that he is able to sometimes overcome the urge to drink too much alcohol, this exception should be emphasized, instead of undermined. When clients become more aware of their ability to stop themselves instead of following their usual patterns, the instances in which they stop themselves become perceived exceptions and something on which to build.

Sometimes, however, these exceptions can also hold negative consequences for the client, for example there can also be less attention from the family when the problem is solved or is less apparent.

Questions that may be asked are:

- What kind of positive effects will it have, if what you want different would happen?
- What are the apparent benefits of this behavior? What difference does this make to other important persons in your life?

In traditional CBT this understanding will then allow the client to choose an intervention that is more likely to be effective. In Positive CBT the client does more of what already works: there is no need to try something different, because the solution is already present. The client then reports on the helpfulness of the intervention and collects further observations by self-monitoring, and the cycle of FBA repeats itself.

By identifying the client's strengths and exceptions, intervention plans can focus on increasing the use of appropriate skills the client already possesses rather than relying solely on manipulating antecedents and consequences to reduce negative behaviors.

Questions that may be asked are:

- What is better (since the last time we met)?
- What is different (since the last time we met)?
- What has been helpful (even just a little bit)?

Positive FBA Interview in 7 questions

1. Suppose tonight while you are sleeping, a miracle happens and your problems that we talk about today are all solved. But because you are asleep, you don't know that this miracle happens. What will be the first thing you notice tomorrow morning when you are waking up that would tell you that this miracle has happened? What will be the first thing you notice yourself doing differently that will let you know that this miracle occurred? What else? And what else?
2. Please tell me about some recent times when you were doing somewhat better or (part of) the miracle was happening, even just a little bit.
3. When things are going somewhat better for you, what have you noticed that you or others do differently then? What other consequences have you noticed?

4. On a scale of 10–0 (10 being the miracle has happened and 0 being the worst), where would you say you are at today?
5. What will you be doing differently that will tell you/others that you are one point higher on the scale?
6. What will be better for you/others when you are one point higher on the scale? What other consequences will you notice?
7. What/who will help you to achieve one point higher on the scale? (Also see Appendix D.)

7

Changing the Viewing

Every problem is an opportunity in disguise

Benjamin Franklin

Introduction

O'Hanlon (2000) states that when someone is not happy or is not getting the results he wants, he has to do something different. Therefore, the client has to change either the doing of the problem or the viewing of the problem, or both. This will almost certainly result in a change in the feeling of the problem.

In changing the viewing of the problem the focus is on changing how a person thinks and what he pays attention to as a way to change his situation for the better. This can involve five things:

1. Acknowledge feelings and the past without letting them determine what he can do;
2. Change what the person is paying attention to in a problem situation;
3. Focus on what the person wants in the future rather than on what he does not like in the present or the past;
4. Challenge unhelpful beliefs about himself and his situation;
5. Use a spiritual perspective to help him transcend his troubles and to draw on resources beyond his usual abilities.

Acknowledging Feelings and the Past

In dealing with emotions it is useful to, on the one hand, acknowledge the negative emotions like anger, frustration, or sadness and, on the other hand, to look for possibilities by saying something like: "I see that your feelings are very strong about this topic. What would you like to feel instead in the future when

Practicing Positive CBT: From Reducing Distress to Building Success, First Edition. Fredrike Bannink.
© 2012 John Wiley & Sons, Ltd. Published 2012 by John Wiley & Sons, Ltd.

the problem is solved?" Positive CBT represents those efforts of therapists to help people optimize human functioning by acknowledging their strengths and deficiencies as well as environmental resources and stressors. This book shows how Positive CBT is about balancing acknowledgment and possibilities for change. The role of the therapist is to, on the one hand, acknowledge the impact of the problem and to, on the other hand, help clients to focus on possibilities for change instead of impossibilities.

O'Hanlon (1999) states that there are four types of negative stories that can be changed to positive stories. These negative stories are:

1. Blame stories, in which someone is bad or wrong, has bad intentions, or gets the blame for the problem;
2. Impossibility stories, in which change is seen as impossible in a given situation;
3. Invalidation stories, in which someone's feelings, desires, thoughts, or actions are seen as wrong or unacceptable;
4. Unaccountability stories, in which people are excused from responsibility for their actions by claiming that they are under the control of other people or some other factor that is beyond their control.

Negative stories can be changed to positive stories by first acknowledging the impact of the problem and the facts of the situation instead of evaluating, judging, or explaining it. Then counterevidence can be found that contradicts the unhelpful problem stories and clients can be reminded that whatever story they have, that story is not all there is to them. Creating compassionate and helpful stories and finding a kinder, gentler view of themselves, the other, and/ or the situation is also helpful (O'Hanlon, 1999; Gilbert, 2010).

The present and future determine how we look at our past: it is said that it is never too late to have a happy childhood. Furman (1998), a solution-focused psychiatrist, asked the readers of two Finnish magazines who had endured difficult childhoods to reply to three questions relating to their experiences:

1. What helped you survive your difficult childhood?
2. What have you learned from your difficult childhood?
3. In what way have you managed in later life to have the kind of experiences that you were deprived of as a child?

The nature of the replies convinced him of the ability of human beings to survive almost any trauma. This gave him the belief that people can view their past – including even the most extreme suffering – as a source of strength rather than of weakness. "Our past is a story we can tell ourselves in many different ways. By paying attention to methods that have helped us survive, we can start respecting ourselves and reminisce about our difficult past with feelings of pride rather than regret" (p. 56). Asking questions about how clients survived and what strengths and competences they used, sometimes renders unnecessary exposure to the negative past: here certainly the "least burden principle" applies.

Furman states that it is natural to think that our past has an effect on how our future will turn out, but we rarely look at it the other way around. The future

– that is what we think it will bring – determines what our past looks like. If you are depressed, the past appears darker; if you are in love it may appear somewhat brighter.

Case 7.1

A client said in a weary voice that, because of his depressive moods, I was the fourth therapist he was consulting in a time frame of about 15 years. He had seen a psychoanalytic psychotherapist for three years; he had been in client-centered group psychotherapy for two years; had done bodywork with a Pesso psychotherapist; and so on. But despite taking antidepressant medication, which proved of little help, he was still suffering from depressive episodes.

I decided to ask him the three questions about his childhood as proposed by Furman. In answering the first question: "What do you think helped you survive your difficult childhood?", he answered that he had never thought of it this way. He had always seen himself as a victim of his aggressive and abusive father, with no control over the situation. He discovered that he actually had done something active: he tried to stay away as long and as much as possible and found a refuge with the parents of his school friend. Now, the realization that he had actually achieved something to be safe and escape his father, transformed for the first time in his life his vision of himself from victim to a (partly) successful survivor. This change in vision enhanced his self-efficacy and generated further positive emotions.

Changing What the Client is Paying Attention to

The point of departure is that a problem does not always manifest itself to the same degree. What is the client doing differently, or what is different at those moments when the problem is absent or is less of a problem, or when is the client better able to cope with the problem? When were there periods or moments in the client's life during which he was doing well or the problem was absent or less of a problem?

Directing attention to the client's past or present successes instead of his failures and failings generates a positive expectation: clients begin to see themselves or the situation in a more positive light. Finding exceptions to the problem is one of the basic solution-focused tools. Heath and Heath (2010) give the following impressive example of finding these exceptions, which they call "the bright spots."

Story 7.1: Finding the "Bright Spots"

To pursue "bright spots" is to ask the solution-focused question: "What is working and how can we do more of it?" instead of asking: "What is broken and how do we fix it?" This is the story about Jerry Sternin, who in the 1990s was working for Save the Children. The Vietnamese Government had invited the organization to help fight malnutrition. When Sternin arrived with his family, the welcome was less than warm: he was given only 6 months to produce results. The conventional wisdom about malnutrition was that it was the result of a number of huge problems: poverty, ignorance, poor sanitation, and lack of access to clean water.

According to Sternin, all these problems were "TBU": True But Useless. The millions of kids could not wait for all those problems to be solved: he would not be able to fight the "root causes" of the malnutrition. So Sternin decided to do something else: he traveled to rural villages and met with the local mothers. The mothers were divided into teams and went out to weigh and measure every child in their village. The results were surprising: they found kids who were bigger and healthier than the typical child.

Sternin's idea was to search for so-called "bright spots," exceptions to the problem: people whose behaviors create better results than their neighbors having the same resources. They discovered that the bright-spot mothers fed their kids more meals in a day (using the same amount of food). Healthy kids were also actively fed while unhealthy kids ate on their own. In addition, the bright-spot mothers collected shrimps and crabs from the rice fields (which were considered adult food) and sweet potato greens (which were considered a low-class food) and mixed them in with the rice, making the meal more nutritious.

Sternin ensured that the solution would be a native one. He invited the mothers to practice the new behaviors and it spread to other villages. It was hugely successful: over the next six months 65% of the kids were better nourished and stayed that way and the program reached 2.2 million Vietnamese people in 265 villages. What is remarkable about this story is that Sternin and his team weren't experts and did not have the answers when they started. But they did have a deep faith in the power of finding exceptions: the "bright spots."

Adapted from: Heath and Heath (2010).

Psycho-education

Psycho-education is the education offered to clients (and their family members) who live with a psychological disturbance. A goal is for the client to understand and be better able to deal with the disorder or illness. In Positive CBT the client's own strengths, resources, and coping skills are also reinforced, in order to avoid relapse and contribute to their own health and wellness on a long-term basis.

Psycho-education also has the function of contributing to the destigmatization of psychological disorders and to diminish barriers to treatment. Through an improved view of the causes and the effects of the illness, psycho-education frequently broadens the client's view of their illness and this increased understanding can positively affect the client. The relapse risk is lowered and clients and their family members, who are better informed about the disease, feel less helpless. Important elements in psycho-education are:

- Information transfer (symptomatology of the disorder, causes, treatment concepts);
- Emotional discharge (understanding to promote exchange of experiences with others, etc.);
- Support of a medication or psychotherapeutic treatment, as cooperation is promoted between the mental health professional and client (compliance, adherence);
- Assistance to self-help (e.g., training, as crisis situations are promptly recognized and what steps should be taken to be able to help the client).

In Positive CBT psycho-education is somewhat different from traditional CBT in the sense that clients are considered to be co-experts. They are invited to share their – already existing – knowledge:

- What do you already know about the disorder/diagnosis?
- What have you read about it so far (or googled)?
- How and where could you find more information if you want to?
- What do you want to know about the disorder in the first place (because some clients do and some clients don't want to know)?
- What/who has been helpful to you so far in coping with the disorder?
- What do you know about how other people (including family members who may have a similar disorder) deal with their problems and what has been helpful to them?
- How are you using your personal strengths and resources to deal with the disorder?

The Positive CBT therapist may then add information – if still necessary or useful – to the clients' knowledge or invite the client to find out (more) about the disorder.

Cognitive bias modification

Cognitive accounts of depression and anxiety disorders emphasize the importance of cognitive biases. For example, depression and other mood disturbances are characterized by negative interpretation biases (Beck, 1967), that is a tendency to interpret information in a negative way. Depressed mood is also associated with a deficit in generating positive imagery about the future. A Cognitive Bias Modification (CBM) paradigm targeting both interpretation bias and positive imagery may therefore have particular potential in developing innovative treatments for depression (Holmes, Lang, and Deeprose, 2009).

They propose that negative intrusive imagery, a lack of positive imagery, and negative interpretation bias serve both independently and interactively to maintain depressed mood. Recent research (Blackwell and Holmes, 2010) shows some preliminary evidence for its effectiveness, paving the way for the development of a novel computerized treatment for depression. Positive imagery was done through 64 different positive training paragraphs each day, of which the structure was designed so that the positive outcome only became clear towards the end of the statement. For example: "You ask a friend to look over some work you have done. They come back with some comments, which are all very positive." After each training paragraph the participants rated the vividness of their imagery on a 5-point scale.

Imagery

Imagery interventions can be used to remove and transform negative images or create and build positive ones (also see Chapter 3). The recent years have seen a growing interest in the use of imagery rescripting (ImRs) interventions in CBT, especially with clients who struggle with distressing, intrusive imagery. It is an imagery technique in which a distressing image is modified in some way to change associated negative thoughts, feelings, and/or behaviors. ImRs is most often used as a component of trauma-related nightmare treatments, such as imagery rehearsal therapy (IRT), and is also used in Compassion Focused Therapy (CFT). The effectiveness of IRT has been typically examined in a group setting over one to three sessions (Krakow, 2004). The session(s) generally include psycho-education and cognitive skills training regarding insomnia and nightmares, an imagery rescripting component, and follow-up to discuss progress and review concerns/experiences. One set of instructions for the imagery rescripting component is as follows: Choose a nightmare and modify it any way you wish; rehearse the modified nightmare for at least several minutes daily; and modify additional nightmares as necessary every 3 to 7 days, rehearsing no more than one or two new dreams per week. ImRs is a good way to modify negative thoughts and images into positive ones.

Case 7.2

As a client told me: "I imagine the scene again, just as it occurs in my flashbacks. Only this time, my adult self goes right over to the little girl (me), picks her up, and takes her away, saying soothing, kind words and holding her gently but firmly close. I am protecting her (me) from my aggressive mother. This may sound crazy, but it feels great."

Positive imagery in CBT is used in goal setting, skills training, and in checking, appraising and adjusting to solve problems and fine-tune skills. All three elements are central to creating "new ways of being," a new orientation that clients, who have previously held strong persistent negative beliefs, are encouraged to develop towards themselves. The focus is on envisioning new ways of being or desired states. For example, treating oneself with kindness and compassion rather than disgust may create fundamental changes. Since imagery has a more powerful effect on positive emotion than verbal thoughts about the same information, imaginal strategies appear to be particularly useful tools for generating positive new ways of being (Hackmann, Bennett-Levy, and Holmes, 2011). In this vein, positive imagery in CBT is very much in line with Solution-Focused Brief Therapy and Positive Psychology interventions.

Changing perspectives

Positive CBT uses so-called "relationship questions" to invite clients to construct descriptions of interactional events as well as their meanings. The therapist finds out who are the client's significant others and weaves them into the questions so as to encourage clients to describe their situations and what they want different in interactional terms. They are a good way to invite clients to amplify their solutions. A relationship question might be: "Suppose the two of you could get along a little bit better in the future, what would he notice you do instead of losing your temper?" Or: "What would your boss say will be different between you and your colleague when things were somewhat better?"

Walter and Peller (1992) introduced the *interactional matrix* (see Table 7.1). This matrix is a tool for facilitating the building of solutions from an interactional view and to invite clients into areas of difference. Across the top of the matrix are the frames used in Positive CBT. These are the frames of: goal, hypothetical solutions, and exceptions. Along the left side of the matrix are the different reporting positions of the question and response. The first is the "for self" position. Questions of this position invite clients to answer from their own position. The next position is "for the other." Questions from this position invite clients to answer questions as if they were listening and reporting for someone else. For example, in a relationship therapy the partners are asked what they think their children will say about certain topics. In order to answer this question, the person has to suspend his own way of thinking for the moment and imagine the other(s) answering the question. He has to put himself in the other's shoes briefly or at least think of what the other person might say if he was responding to the question. This usually induces a search for new and perhaps different information.

The third row of the matrix is reporting "for the detached position." This position is of someone who is detached from the problem and is merely observing: "If I were a fly on the wall observing you and your partner, what would I see you doing differently when things are better?" This question invites clients

Table 7.1 Interactional matrix.

Reporting position	Goal	Hypothetical solution/Miracle question	Exception
Self	What is your goal in coming here?	What will you be doing differently? What will the other person be doing differently?	What are you doing differently? What is the other person doing differently?
Other	What would the other person say is your goal in coming here?	What would the other person say you will be doing differently?	What would the other person say you are doing differently?
	What would the other person say is his goal in coming here?	What would the other person say he will be doing differently?	What would the other person say he is doing differently?
Detached	What would I say or what would the fly on the wall say is your goal in coming here?	What will I or the fly on the wall see you doing differently?	What would I or the fly on the wall see you doing differently?

Source: Adapted from Walter and Peller, 1992, p. 174.

to answer from a neutral position. Each question or row of the matrix invites clients into an area of experience different from their usual way of thinking. Also see Appendix F.

Exercise 7.1

Think of a situation where you have a problem with another person. Ask yourself every question from the interactional matrix or let someone else ask you these questions. Keep the same order as in the schedule: from goal to hypothetical solutions/miracle to exceptions. Notice the differences in your reactions and how this changes your personal film. Then choose the next row with another viewpoint and notice again how this changes your reaction. What differences do you notice in your personal film? Which questions are most useful to you?

Case 7.3

During a therapy session about a conflict at work Peter, head of administration for a nonprofit organization, expresses his belief that the working atmosphere is failing and beyond repair. He has no plans to return to work. Because of the situation he had decided to stay at home and not attend the office, claiming sickness benefit.

The therapist asks: "Suppose there might still be some way forward for you, what might be the first step that you could take or that others should take?" The therapist also asks some questions from the interactional matrix:

- What would you like to see different at your workplace (for self-position)?
- What would your wife say about what you will be doing differently that will allow her to say you are making progress (for the other position)?
- If I were a fly on the wall and I could see that there still remains a faint hope of the possibility of your returning to work, what differences in your behavior would I see (for the detached position)?

Exercise 7.2

You can practice your Positive CBT skills by asking your clients some other questions using different perspectives. It is important to use the following sequence, starting with Question 1 and then moving on to 2 and 3, especially in the case where clients want someone else to change.

1. *When this problem will be solved, what will you notice is different about the other person? What will you see him/her doing differently? What else?*
2. *When this problem will be solved, what will this other person notice what is different about you? What will this other person see you doing differently? What else?*
3. *When this problem will be solved and you are being watched by an outside observer, what will he/she notice that is different about your relationship with the other person? What will this observer see both of you doing differently? What else?*

Third-person perspective

A common goal of psychotherapy is to change the self, so clients who visit a psychotherapist should be particularly interested in assessing how they have changed since beginning treatment. Assessing change matters because it constitutes critical determinants of satisfaction and well-being (Carver and Scheier, 1998) and also guides future courses of action: "Am I getting any thinner?", "Are we getting over the problems in our relationship?"

Self-change influences people's memory perspective. Third-person recall produces judgments of greater self-change when people are inclined to look for evidence of change, but lesser self-change when they are inclined to look for evidence of continuity. Research by Ross and Wilson (2002) shows that recalling an old, pre-change self from the third-person perspective helps to deal with the challenge of maintaining personal change. Greater perceived change leads to greater satisfaction with one's efforts thus far and, therefore, to make it easier to summon the resources necessary to maintain one's efforts. In sum: psychologically distancing oneself from negative past selves and remaining close to positive past selves promotes well-being.

Libby, Eibach, and Gilovich (2005) found that there are two ways of seeing oneself as successful: as an observer from the first and third-person perspectives. Libby and colleagues found that there is a much greater change or continuing with desired behavior when one considers oneself from a third-person perspective. This theory builds on the research that we have a tendency to interpret the behavior of others as being indicative of their personality; whereas we tend to interpret our own behavior as being indicative of the situation we are in. Therefore, seeing ourselves from the third-person perspective, such as an observer would, allows us to see the sort of person who engages in that sort of behavior. Seeing oneself as the type of person who would engage in a desired behavior increases the likelihood of engaging in that behavior.

Vasquez and Buehler (2007) found that people feel more motivated to succeed on a future task when they visualize its successful completion from a third-person perspective rather than a first-person perspective. Actions viewed from the third-person perspective are generally construed at a relatively high level of abstraction – in a manner that highlights their larger meaning and significance – which heightens their motivational impact. They found that students experience a greater increase in achievement motivation when they imagine their successful task completion from a third-person perspective rather than from a first-person perspective. Moreover, research shows that third-person imagery boosts motivation by prompting students to construe their success abstractly and to perceive it as important.

Victim or survivor

Clients who have gone through terrible events may see themselves as a victim or as a survivor. If they see themselves as a victim, it becomes more difficult to play an active role in shaping their life. The client was unable to do anything about what has happened to him and he expects that he cannot change much about the way the rest of his life pans out. He probably feels powerless and feels that he has lost control. However, when the client sees himself as a survivor, the possibility of a more active role becomes apparent. It offers the opportunity to organize and take control of his life, despite what he has experienced. This initiates a spiral of positivity and more control. The following four-step exercise can help clients to find out which role they want to play in the rest of their lives, that of victim or survivor.

Exercise 7.3

1. *How would you like to see your life in a month's time? The same people and circumstances are still present, but you feel a little less influenced by what you have experienced.*
2. *If you think about your answer to the previous question, that is, your goal in a month's time, how would you then think and feel, and how would you behave in order to reach your goal if you see yourself as a victim?*
3. *Answer the same question, but now from the perspective of a survivor.*
4. *What differences do you notice? What will you be doing differently? Which attitude is the most helpful to you?*

Dolan (1998) states that overcoming the immediate effects of abuse, loss, or other trauma and viewing yourself as a survivor rather than as a victim are helpful steps but are ultimately not sufficient to help people fully regain the ability to live a life that is as compelling, joyous, and fulfilling as it used to be. People who remain at the survivor stage see life through the window of their survivor-hood rather than enjoying the more immediate and unobstructed vision of the world around them that they previously held. All experiences are evaluated in terms of how they resemble, differ from, mitigate, or compound the effects of past events. This diminishes their ability to fully experience and enjoy life and is responsible for the flatness and depression reported by so many people who categorize themselves as survivors. In this vein a third position may be added to the exercise, which I would like to call the position of a "thriver."

Fredrickson (2009, p. 230) states: "A few years ago I came across a greeting card that read: 'Life gives us negativity on its own. It's our job to create positivity.' I like this phrasing because it reminds us that positivity is a choice – a choice we all need to make again and again, day after day. I'd like to remind you that your emotions are as far from random as they are from being fixed by your genes. They stem to a large degree from your daily activities and your entrenched mental habits. Perhaps more than you ever thought possible, you get to choose them. Sure enough, negativity that's necessary will always know where to find you. But you can choose to minimize the gratuitous kind. And the more you value positivity, the more often its upward spiral will lift you to new heights."

Story 7.2: The Dog I Feed Most

A Native American elder once described his own inner struggle in this manner: "Inside of me there are two dogs. One of the dogs is mean and evil, the other dog is good. The mean dog fights the good dog all the time".

When asked which dog wins, he reflected for a moment and replied: "The one I feed most."

Source: Anonymous

Exercise 7.4

When clients suffering from posttraumatic stress syndrome (PTSS) are invited to draw a circle and then to draw a point, which represents the most traumatic event in their life, they often draw this point right in the middle of the circle, symbolic for the central place the event plays in their lives. The Positive CBT therapist may ask the client whether putting the event in this central place is helpful for the client or would he rather have the point a bit less central in the circle or even outside the circle in a better future.

For each point the client chooses, the therapist may ask what difference that makes for the client and important others in his life. The therapist may also ask about helpful exceptions and how the client is or was able to bring them about.

ACT and mindfulness

A well-known serenity prayer is: "God grant me the serenity to accept the things I cannot change, the courage to change the things I can, and the wisdom to know the difference." Acceptance and Commitment Therapy (ACT), rather than trying to teach people to better control their thoughts, feelings, sensations, memories, and other private events, teaches them to "just notice," accept, and embrace their private events, especially previously unwanted ones.

Mindfulness-Based Cognitive Therapy (MBCT) has been developed as an approach that combines the mindfulness mediation rooted in Buddhist thought and the western tradition of CBT approaches. It is an intervention that helps increase a wide, open awareness as well as focused attention and reduces automatic responding. The power of mindfulness is that it can literally sever the link between negative thoughts and negative emotions. Both ACT and mindfulness promote positive emotions (see Chapter 9) and this positivity is what enables people to see the big picture, appreciate the now, and find the good within the bad.

> **Story 7.3: Shake it Off and Step Up**
>
> *Once upon a time there was a farmer who had an old mule. The mule fell into a deep dry well and began to cry loudly. Hearing his mule cry, the farmer came over and assessed the situation. The well was deep and the mule was old and heavy. He knew it would be almost impossible to lift the animal out.*
>
> *Because the mule was old and the well was dry, the farmer decided to bury the animal in the well. In this way he could solve two problems: put the mule out of his misery and have his well filled. He asked his neighbors to help him and so shovel full of dirt after shovel full of dirt began to fall on the mule's back. The mule became hysterical.*
>
> *Then all of a sudden an idea came to the mule. Each time they would throw a shovel of dirt on his back he could shake it off and step up! Now exhausted and dirty, but quite alive, the mule stepped over the top of the well and walked through the crowd. What a great attitude! What a great way to approach life! Shake it off and step up! Too often we hold on to what has happened to us! Let it go and you will feel free because you are no longer buried in the well. Once you are on your feet again you can take some action and you can decide where you want to grow in life and which direction you want your life to take.*
>
> Source: Anonymous

Externalization of the problem

Externalization of the problem can help clients see the problem as something separate from themselves that affects them but does not always control every aspect of their lives. This intervention is retrieved from narrative therapy by White and Epston (1990). They grant their clients, with the externalization of the problem, the freedom to separate themselves from their problematic self-image. In asking how the problem affected their lives and relationships, they offer their clients the opportunity to gain more control. The problem can be seen as something that lies outside the clients and usually has a negative influence on them. The problem is then seen as an "enemy" by both clients and the therapist and can be fought jointly. De Shazer (1984) stated that therapist and client(s) should be as tennis players on the same side of the net, with the problem as the opponent.

Externalizing the problem can also be brought about by drawing it or designing a symbol for it. Clients first give a name to the problem like "Depression," "Tension," or "ADHD Monster." A noun (X) is best for this. The question to the client is: "How would you name the problem that bothers you?" Then questions are asked about the times when the problem (X) is not there or is less (exceptions) and what clients do to bring that about. Clients can also be asked to talk about the times when X is present and how they deal with it. Depending on the needs of the clients more or less time can be spent on finding out how X controls their lives. The competence of the clients can be highlighted and thereby increase their confidence that more control is possible. Also the tendency to apportion blame to the other(s) for the problem can be minimized as they reap the benefits of collaboration in gaining control over X.

During each meeting, clients can indicate on a scale of 10–0 the extent to which the problem (X) has control over them: 10 means the problem has complete control over them and 0 means they have complete control over X. It is apparent that in most cases the problem will more or less disappear as the control of the clients increases. Scaling questions in externalizing the problem are:

- On what mark on the scale 10–0 are you today?
- What was the mark in the previous week/the previous meeting?
- If the mark is higher than last week/the last meeting: How did you succeed in doing that?
- If the mark is the same as the mark for last week/the last meeting: How did you manage to maintain the same mark?
- If the mark is lower than last week/the last meeting: What did you do earlier on to go ahead again? What have you done in the past in a similar situation that has been successful?
- What have significant others in your life noticed about you in the last week? How did that influence their behavior towards you?
- What are you doing together when X has control over you?
- How does X manage to do that?
- What do you do (differently) when you have control over X?
- What do you do when you are planning to attack X?
- How are you able to fool X?

(See also Appendix E for the externalization of the problem.)

Exercise 7.5

Think of a current personal problem. Ask yourself the questions listed previously. What name would you give the problem? Discover where you are already on the scale of control: what is already working and how you may reach a higher mark.

Using a whiteboard or flip chart

Many traditional CBT therapists use a whiteboard or flip chart to group problems into a case conceptualization or to challenge dysfunctional cognitions and beliefs (for example with a so-called "pie chart"). Here the therapist is the active one who writes on the whiteboard or chart; the clients listen and may add to what the therapist is saying.

In Positive CBT, however, the therapist and the client use a whiteboard or a flip chart to outline in drawing and/or writing the solution-focused steps of goal formulation, exceptions, and scaling. It is recommended that the therapist lets his clients do as much of the drawing and writing as possible in order to stimulate an active attitude on their part. As soon as the goal has been formulated, one can also draw a circle on the board or paper and write the goal down in it. Next to the circle, one may draw a vertical scale and indicate where on the scale the client currently is if 10 is the goal and 0 is the worst moment he has ever experienced. The therapist can then ask scaling questions: "How do you manage to be at that number?" "What would one point higher look like and what is helpful for you to get there?" "And what else?"

Around the circled goal formulation, a second circle is drawn in which the therapist (or, better yet, the clients) writes down all the things that can bring the client closer to the goal, that is, the exceptions that have helped in the past and all the other possibilities that might help as well. When all this has been noted in the second circle, the therapist asks with which of these possibilities the client wants to get started and how others can help make that possibility a success. One or more of these means can be assigned as homework suggestions.

Using metaphors

The Greek term metaphor means to "carry something across" or to "transfer." A metaphor is a figure of speech in which a comparison is made between two things, based on resemblance or similarity, without using "like" or "as." Metaphors enliven ordinary language, encourage interpretation, and are more efficient than ordinary language, because they give maximum meaning with a minimum of words. They imply rather than state relationships and can get clients to think about what they are hearing. Just about any word of phrase can be used as a metaphor.

Sometimes clients talk about their problems using a metaphor. They say: "I feel stuck" or "There is an icy atmosphere in our relationship." The Positive CBT therapist may then invite the clients to think of another, more positive metaphor: what would they like to have instead? When clients do not come up themselves with a metaphor, the therapist may introduce this concept and invite clients to think about their problem in this way. How would they depict the problem and/ or the solution?

Metaphors are an accurate description of the clients' way of being in the world. The technique of "Clean Language" (Tompkins and Lawley, 2003) can be applied to discover how clients use metaphors and what needs to happen for them to change so that they have a different perception of the world. Clean language is optimized to have clients discover and develop personal symbols and metaphors, without contamination or distortion of the developing metaphor landscape through the way the questions are put.

Clean Language was developed in the 1980s as a method of resolving clients' traumatic memories. Many clients naturally describe their symptoms in metaphor, and when the therapist inquires about these using their exact words, often their perception of the trauma begins to change.

Padesky uses the metaphor of "prejudice" (International Cognitive Therapy Newsletter, 1991) to teach clients with personality disorders about schemas and information processing theory. She asks clients if they know what prejudice is and then find an example of someone they know who has a particular prejudice against some sort of person where they can see that this prejudice is wrong. Once clients have picked someone, the Socratic questioning proceeds to recall specific instances of this persons' responses to information discrepant with their belief. This should continue until clients have presented several processes used to distort information contrary to an active schema. The most important processes to uncover are distortion, discounting, calling the observation an exception and not noticing. The therapist then asks how clients would go about trying to change this person's prejudice.

Finally the therapist may ask clients why they think the therapist has been talking with them about prejudice after they discussed their core beliefs. At this point most clients have the realization that the therapist may think their core beliefs are a sort of prejudice. The final task in using this metaphor is to explore with clients if their belief does act like a prejudice and review examples from the prior months of therapy when the clients distorted, discounted, talked about data as an exception, or did not notice relevant information in and outside of the session. The advantage of using a metaphor instead of simple didactic teaching in therapy is that clients may learn and remember what they have learned through this process of active engagement. These types of collaborative metaphors are an extension of the process of Socratic questioning and can help clients construct their own learning and change.

Case 7.4

In a solution-focused mediation the team members describe their team as a stony and cold desert. Moving is difficult because of the conflicts and problems in their team, and nobody seems to be caring for the others anymore. When the mediator asks the team members which metaphor they would rather have instead in the future, they come up with the metaphor of a boat, floating on a beautiful lake in summer. The mediation continues using this positive metaphor. When were there times in the past when the team had been functioning as a boat on a lake in summer? How were they able to achieve this? On a scale from 10 to 0, where would they say the team is right now? How come they are not lower? Which steps are they willing to take to get closer to this image? At this point the team members decide to make a painting together of their wished for boat on the lake and hang the painting in the meeting room for all to see and to remind them every day of their journey towards their preferred future.

Focusing on What the Client Wants in the Future

Setting goals about what clients want different in the future emphasizes the possibility of change and begins to focus clients on future possibilities rather than on their symptoms and problems. Chapter 6 addresses the importance of the formulation of goals for therapy. Well-defined goals should be stated in positive terms so that it is explicit what the client is moving towards rather than away from. They should also be in a process form, in the here and now (which means the client can start the solutions immediately), as specific as possible, within the client's control, and in the client's language.

Whereas approach motivation facilitates growth and flourishing, avoidance motivation facilitates protection and survival. Both approach and avoidance motivation are integral to successful adaptation: avoidance motivation facilitates surviving, while approach motivation facilitates thriving. Here are some goal-related questions:

- If tomorrow were different, how/what would that look like?
- Suppose a miracle would happen tonight while you were asleep and tomorrow all your problems would have disappeared, but you did not know because you were sleeping. What would be the first thing you would notice tomorrow morning that would tell you that this miracle has happened? What else? (the so-called "miracle question").
- What are your best hopes? What will be different when your best hopes are met?
- What do you want to have instead of the problem?

More questions about goal formulation can be found in Bannink (2010a).

Challenging Unhelpful Beliefs

From the perspective of quantum mechanics an objective world independent from personal perceptions is not real. Human problems are per essence subjective because they originate in the dynamics of personal thoughts, emotions, and beliefs of the people involved. The sources of personal problems are the result of the perceptions of persons. Einstein (1954) stated: "Problems cannot be solved by the level of awareness that created them." Einstein also postulated that information and knowledge are not sufficient for problem-solving. Imagination is more important than knowledge, for knowledge is limited, whereas imagination embraces the entire world, stimulating progress, giving birth to evolution: most people see what is and never see what can be. The world of knowledge has its limits, whereas the world of imagination is boundless.

As this book shows imagination is widely used in Positive CBT by asking the miracle question (see Chapter 6) and other projections into the future, as well as using positive imagery and imagery rescripting.

As I already pointed out in Chapter 2, the first – problem-focused – strategy in cognitive therapy of assisting clients to identify and reality-test unhelpful cognitions, which underlie repeated negative patterns of emotion and behavior, is not used in Positive CBT. The second – strengths and solutions focused – strategy of developing and testing more adaptive cognitions that can give rise to a more positive experience of the self, others, and the world, is frequently used. It is important to note that often these (more) adaptive cognitions and beliefs do not have to be developed, because they are already present (the exceptions to the problems) and may be used again ("If it works, do more of it," see Chapter 4).

Exercise 7.6

The following exercise is about using actions to create empowering beliefs. It is derived from NLP (Neuro Linguistic Programming).

1. *Think of something you want to believe about yourself but which you aren't quite sure is true;*
2. *State your desired belief in a positive form. Make sure it's truly yours, something you can do something about;*
3. *Ask yourself: What would a person with this desired belief naturally do? Imagine many different actions and list them;*
4. *Select a specific time and place in your future where you would like to have your desired belief;*
5. *Select an action from your list that is evidence of your desired belief and is appropriate for that specific future time and place;*
6. *See yourself in your selected future time and place doing the action. Watch the scene (as though it were a movie) of that "future you" completing the actions of your desired belief. Revise the scene if it is necessary so that it is positive and appropriate;*
7. *Rewind that scene to the beginning. Step into it and go through this future time as if you are living it now. See the scene around you. Feel the feelings. Hear yourself state your belief with conviction. Go through the scene to the end.*

Repeat steps 4 through 7 three more times. Select a different appropriate action from your list of actions for your desired belief each time, each with another future time and place.

Learned optimism

Seligman (2002), one of the founders of Positive Psychology, shifted his attention from "learned helplessness" to "learned optimism." He undertook research into the factors that lead people to perceive an event as positive or negative and their reasoning behind this. Pessimistic people attribute negative events particularly to stable, global, and internal factors. They say: "Things never go right with me" (stable), "I will never be happy again" (global), and "I am good for nothing" (internal). They attribute positive events to temporary, specific, and external factors. They say: "That was only luck, which had nothing to do with me," if something positive happens.

Optimistic people think in the opposite way. They attribute positive events to stable, global, and internal factors. If something positive happens, that does say something about them, for example: "I really am valuable." Optimists attribute negative events particularly to temporary, specific, and external factors. They might say: "I could not do anything about it, because he threatened me." Thinking in a pessimistic way, especially about negative events, leads to expectations of hopelessness.

Einstein said: "I would rather be an optimist and a fool than a pessimist who is right." Churchill said: "The pessimist sees difficulty in every opportunity; the optimist sees the opportunity in every difficulty."

Beck (1967) similarly underscores the importance of optimistic cognitive styles in protecting people from depression. According to the cognitive perspective, people with optimistic cognitive styles are at lower risk for depression than people with pessimistic cognitive styles. However, a little pessimism at times cannot hurt. It forces people to confront reality, and depressed people tend to have a more realistic view of the world. Every day could be your last; you could be involved in a traffic accident or catch a fatal disease. Depressed people harbor few illusions about how safe and predictable the world and life actually is. Yet it turns out that we feel better and happier if we do hold these illusions and are able to preserve them.

Optimism and pessimism are relatively stable personality traits, but they can be influenced by the way someone acts and by what he is focusing on. Optimism contributes to more adaptive survival strategies, namely more positive reappraisal, better coping abilities, and more use of positive distractions (hobbies and exercise).

Research has shown that even people with a pessimistic nature felt happier if over the course of a week they made notes of when in the past they had been at their best; every day during a week they would note down something about their strengths, express gratitude to someone whom they had not yet properly thanked, or made a note of "three good things" that were happening in their lives. Six months later these people were still feeling happier, although the exercise took place over a period of only one week. Research has also shown that happy people are optimistic about their future and that optimistic people are in better health than pessimistic people. Four positive elements significantly contribute to a happy life (Bannink, 2007a). 1. Happy people like themselves, 2. are mostly extrovert, 3. have the idea that they are in control, and 4. are optimistic. The question relevant to all four is: does optimism make people happier (A) or are happy people more optimistic (B)? It turns out that A leads to B and B leads to A. Questions, which enhance optimism, are:

- What makes you optimistic that you will reach the desired result?
- Which indications do you have that you will reach your goal?
- What fuels your hope?
- Which good arguments do you have to be optimistic?
- What will be the first sign that things are going to work out well?

Exercise 7.7

This is an exercise aimed at increasing optimism. Every night before going to bed write down a sentence about the most pleasant event of that day, as if the event was brought about by something general, global, and within your control (because I am . . . or because I can . . .). As an example: Today my colleague offered to help me out, because I am also someone who would help another person if needed and he knows that.

Also every night write down a sentence about the most unpleasant event of that day, as if that event was brought about something specific, temporary, and outside your control (because X, then Y). As an example: Because the bus was delayed, I was not able to get to the appointment with my dentist on time.

Exercise 7.8

Ask your very pessimistic client to imagine the "worst case scenario" before the dreaded event takes place and then compare what actually happens to this scenario to see if he can even come close (most of the time they can't).

Rational Emotive Behavior Therapy

Rational Emotive Behavior Therapy (REBT) is both a psychotherapeutic system of theory and practices and a school of thought established by Ellis. Originally called "rational therapy," its appellation was revised to "rational emotive therapy" in 1959, then to its current appellation in 1992. REBT was one of the first of the cognitive behavior therapies. Precursors of fundamental aspects of REBT have been identified in ancient philosophical traditions, particularly Stoicism.

One of the premises of REBT is that humans do not merely get upset by unfortunate adversities but also by how they construct their views of reality through their language, evaluative beliefs, meanings, and philosophies about the world, themselves, and others. In REBT, clients usually learn and begin to apply this premise by learning the A-B-C-model of psychological disturbance and change. This model states that it normally is not merely an A, adversity (or activating event), that contributes to disturbed and dysfunctional emotional and behavioral Cs, consequences, but also what people, B, believe about the A, adversity. A, adversity can be either an external situation or a thought or other kind of internal event, and it can refer to an event in the past, present, or future. The Bs, beliefs that are most important in the model are explicit and implicit philosophical meanings and assumptions about events, personal desires, and preferences. The Bs, beliefs that are most significant are highly evaluative and consist of interrelated and integrated cognitive, emotional, and behavioral aspects and dimensions. Through REBT people then begin to D, dispute, refute, challenge, and question these beliefs, distinguish them from healthy constructs, and subscribe to more constructive and self-helping constructs.

By using different cognitive, emotive and behavioral methods and activities, the client, together with help from the therapist and in homework exercises, can gain a more rational, self-helping, and constructive rational way of thinking, feeling, and behaving. By attaining and ingraining a more rational and self-constructive philosophy of themselves, others, and the world, people often are more likely to think, behave, and feel in more life-serving and adaptive ways.

Exercise 7.9

This is an exercise to contradict your negative thoughts as quickly as possible. Write down a negative thought that pops up in your mind, such as "I can't do this" or "Everybody hates me." This negative sentence represents your inner critic that you sometimes hear and tries to undermine you. Write these thoughts on index cards. After you have written the cards with some of your regular negative thoughts, pick one up at random and read it out loud. Then rapidly dispute the negative beliefs with every argument you can come up with. This is called: "Rapid Fire Facts": you rapidly fire contradicting positive facts at your negative sentence. When you run out of facts, pick another card and repeat the positive rapid fire facts. Coming up with contradictory facts will get easier and easier with each card.

With this tool you learn to become quick at contradicting your negative thoughts. You "nip them in the bud" before they get a chance to depress you. This exercise can also be done with a team.

Upward arrow technique

So-called core beliefs are central, absolute beliefs about self, others, and the world. People develop both positive and negative beliefs. The automatic thoughts and underlying assumptions lead therapist and client toward relevant core beliefs. The "downward arrow technique," used in traditional CBT, is one of the ways to identify beliefs that underpin negative reactions to a given situation. Questions used in the downward arrow technique are: "What does that matter?" "What is so bad about . . . ?" "What would be the 'worst case scenario' here?"

The questions are repeated in response to each answer the client provides.

The "upward arrow technique," which I designed to use in Positive CBT, is different in that the focus is on positive reactions to a given situation, or to exceptions to the problem. Questions used in the upward arrow technique are:

- How would you like the situation/yourself/others to be different?
- What will be the best outcome?
- What will be the "best case scenario" here?
- Suppose that would happen, what difference will that make (for yourself, for others)?
- And what difference will that make?

Then repeat these questions in response to each answer the client provides. The final outcome in using the upward arrow technique for most people is: calmness and happiness.

In Chapter 3 two other ways of challenging unhelpful beliefs are addressed in more detail: Compassion Focused Therapy (CFT) and Competitive Memory Training (COMET).

Exercise 7.10

With a partner do the following exercise in downward and upward arrow techniques. Think about problems or worries in your life, which are causing you concern. Invite your partner to spend some minutes posing a range of questions relating firstly to the downward arrow technique and then to the upward arrow technique. Discuss the changes you have noticed, both as interviewer and interviewee. Now change roles.

Schema therapy

Schema Therapy (ST) is described in more detail in Chapter 3. ST seeks to replace maladaptive schemas by more healthy schemas and thus repair early negative experiences. The basic philosophy of ST is that if basic safety, care, guidance, and affection are not met in childhood then maladaptive schemas begin to develop and often lead to unhealthy/unstable relationships, poor social skills, unhealthy lifestyle choices, self-destructiveness, and overall poor functionality. By building caring bonds and enforcing self-examination, Schema Therapy aims to help a person to gain the self-confidence needed in order to achieve their ultimate goals.

Kuyken, Padesky, and Dudley (2009) not only focus on negative core beliefs of schemas but also on existing positive client values. These values can be understood as beliefs about what is most important in life. Incorporating values into conceptualizations as part of a client's belief system enables the therapist to better understand clients' reactions across different situations. An example of such a positive value is: It is important to show love to my children. Besides personal values also positive cultural values may play an important role and can be a source of power in the clients' life (e.g., dignity, faith).

Discussions of positive areas of a client's life often reveal alternative coping strategies to those used in problem areas. These often more adaptive coping strategies can be identified as part of the same process that identifies triggers and maintenance factors for problems. "When it is time for behavioural experiments to alter maintenance cycles, the client can practice alternative coping responses drawn from more successful areas of life. Later in therapy, positive assumptions and core beliefs prove just as important as negative ones when forming longitudinal case conceptualisations (p. 101)." In this form of Schema Therapy there is a close collaboration with the client, the therapeutic alliance is used to encourage and motivate clients, Socratic methods are used to help construct new belief systems rather than to test out the old, behavioral experiments are used for the construction of new behavior patterns and the focus is on building the client's resilience and a new set of positive emotions that are far more adaptive than the old ones. In creating new belief systems positive imagery plays an important role: clients are encouraged to imagine the best possible outcomes they can think of ("How would you like to be?"), thus increasing motivation and producing greater potential for change.

Research examining "possible selves" (Oyserman, Bybee, and Terry, 2006) has explored people's self-generated images of what they could become (see Chapter 6, Exercise 21 re Best Possible Self). A positive image of oneself in the future motivates action by helping people to articulate their goals clearly and develop behaviors that will allow them to fulfill those goals. Research in social cognition illustrates that the very act of imagining future events not only can make those events seem more likely but also can help to bring them about. Similar imagery techniques have been shown to enhance athletic performance and have been used to alter behavior of children with impulsive disorders, to reduce relapse rates among people with alcohol abuse, and to reduce the premature termination of therapy. More research on mental simulation – the cognitive construction and rehearsal of hypothetical scenarios – sheds further light on how and why imagining a desired future aids in goal attainment. Mental simulation appears to facilitate goal-directed behavior by increasing people's expectations of success, increasing their motivation and emotional involvement, and prompting concrete plans and activities. For example, students who simulated their successful performance on a midterm exam began studying earlier, studied longer, and received higher grades than those who did not.

De Boer and Bannink (article forthcoming) conducted a pilot study showing positive results, using a solution-focused form of ST in a prison population. This new approach in ST will be further developed as part of a scientific research program. In solution-focused ST the focus is on what clients want to have instead of their maladaptive schemas, their preferred future. The focus is also on clients' competences and resources. Clients are invited to use these strengths and competences in building more adaptive schemas. This is similar to Kuyken *et al.* in the sense that therapists no longer focus on reducing maladaptive schemas, but help clients to build healthy schemas and behavior patterns instead (see Chapter 3).

Young *et al.* (1994) state that their aim is to isolate and modify self-defeating life patterns, which they call "lifetraps." They found that many of these schemas originate from events in early childhood. Just to name a few examples of these schemas: abandonment/instability, mistrust/abuse, or emotional deprivation. They offer, however, a final assumption about change, which involves the need to create a personal vision and state that change is not just the absence of lifetraps. Each person must discover who he wants to be and what he wants from life. It is vital to have this direction before going too far along the change process. It is therefore important to look beyond the elimination of individual lifetraps to an image of what will lead finally to feel fulfilled, happy, and self-actualized.

Positive CBT agrees with Young *et al.* in stressing the importance of looking beyond reducing maladaptive schemas to what clients want different in their lives (their preferred future). When using Young's "language" of lifetraps, Positive CBT therapists will always ask about exceptions and competences:

- When was there a time when you could prevent yourself from falling into this lifetrap?
- How did you manage to do that?
- What would be helpful in doing this more often?
- If you have fallen into one of these lifetraps, what/who is helpful to get out again?
- What do you know about how other people do this?

Metacognitions

Central to the metacognitive model in the treatment of Generalized Anxiety Disorder (GAD) (Wells, 1995; 1997) is the difference between the content of worrying and client's beliefs about worrying, the so-called metacognitions (e.g., "I have to worry to stay in control"). As the content of GAD worrying cannot be differentiated from "normal" worrying, Wells assumed that is was not the content (referred to as "type-I worrying") that is causing the disorder but the clients' own perceptions of their worrying (referred to as metacognitions or beliefs about worrying). Worrying may been seen as a coping or safety strategy for real or imagined problems, based on positive beliefs the client holds about worrying (e.g., "worrying helps me to be prepared to deal with problems," referred to as "type-II worrying" or "meta-worrying").

However, worrying will be strengthened and be used more often and in the long run can result in a greater sensitivity to "danger related" information. This means that clients start to interpret more and more neutral situations as dangerous, and focus on the negative aspects of a situation. Constant worrying also results in thinking of more and more possible negative outcomes, each of which may lead to more worrying (van der Heiden, 2011).

Metacognitions can either be negative or positive. Negative metacognitions are based on negative appraisal, such as "worrying is harmful" or "worrying is uncontrollable." These may lead to feelings of anxiety and fear. These emotional responses can be interpreted as a confirmation of the negative metacognitions, which ultimately increase the negative feelings.

Positive metacognitions are learned by modeling and reinforcement. For example, if a feared event does not occur, clients may attribute this to the act of worrying about it, which may lead to the development of beliefs such as "worrying helps me prevent negative events" or "worrying helps me to be prepared to deal with problems." Note that here the connotation "positive" is different from "positive" in Positive CBT, because in itself positive metacognitions are negative.

Metacognitive therapy (MCT) is different from other GAD treatment programs, because it is not aimed at the content of worrying (type-I worrying) and does not teach ways to control worrying. MCT consists of four phases:

1. Case conceptualization and socialization to the model;
2. Examining negative metacognitions;
3. Examining positive metacognitions;
4. Modifying cognitive bias and strategy shifts.

Regarding the fourth phase – modifying strategy shifts – client are invited to examine new endings for old worries by generating positive outcomes in brainstorm sessions. Instead of controlling their worries, they may also practice "letting go of thoughts," to increase awareness of worrying without doing anything with it. A third strategy is the use of exposure and response prevention exercises to abandon avoidance and safety behavior, such as no longer asking for reassurance.

From a Positive CBT point of view the same metacognitive model and the same "language" are used, again with a focus on exceptions to the problems. Clients are invited to think and talk about successful exceptions to their negative and positive metacognitions. Questions are:

- When were you (recently or in the past) able to let go of these thoughts (even just a little bit)?
- What difference did that make?
- How were you able to do that?
- What else was helpful in these situations?
- When was there a time when you could prevent yourself from thinking these thoughts in the first place?
- What resources or personal strengths have you used in the past to let go of these thoughts?
- How could you use these strengths again now or in the future?

Another metacognitive model is the *intolerance-of-uncertainty model* of GAD, in which intolerance of uncertainty (IU) is the cornerstone. The IU model (Dugas, Freeson, and Ladouceur, 1997) refers to the tendency to react negatively to uncertain and ambiguous events, independent of their probability of occurrence and their associated consequences.

From a Positive CBT point of view clients may again be asked about exceptions to this intolerance or uncertainty. Questions are:

- When were you able to tolerate uncertainty (even just a little bit) in specific situations in the past?

- What difference did that make?
- How were you able to do that?
- How might you use this ability again in the present or in future situations?
- What else was helpful back then?

Using a Spiritual Perspective

O'Hanlon (1999) describes the three C's of spirituality as sources of resilience. "Connection" means moving beyond your little, isolated ego or personality into connection with something bigger, within or outside yourself. "Compassion" means softening your attitude towards yourself or others by "feeling with" rather than being against yourself, others, or the world. And "contribution" means being of unselfish service to others or the world.

You may remember that one of the 24 character strengths mentioned earlier in this book is spirituality/sense of purpose/faith/religiousness. You have strong and coherent beliefs about the higher purpose and meaning of the universe. You know where you fit in the larger scheme. Your beliefs shape your actions and are a source of comfort to you. Seligman (2011, p. 261): "After a half-century of neglect, psychologists are again studying spirituality and religiosity in earnest, no longer able to ignore their importance to people of faith. Do you have an articulate philosophy of life, religious or secular, which locates your being in the larger universe? Does life have meaning for you by virtue of attachment to something larger than you are?" There is now considerable evidence that a higher level of spirituality goes hand in hand with greater well-being, less mental illness, less substance abuse, and more stable marriages (Myers, 2000).

Clients may be asked to imagine that many years later they are an older and wiser version of themselves. They are still healthy and have all intellectual capabilities. They may ask this older and wiser version of themselves questions like:

- If you look back on your life, what advice would you give to your younger version?
- If you look back on your life, what do you like most about the life you have lived?
- Is there anything you would rather have done differently?
- What do you hope your children would like to remember about their lives with you?
- On a scale from 10 to 0, to what extent have you achieved these wishes in your present life?
- What would be the smallest step you can take to reach a higher mark?

Clients can also go for a walk with the older and wiser version of themselves and ask for advice regarding their problem, as in the exercise that follows.

Exercise 7.11

Imagine you have become an old and wise person and you look back on this difficult period of your life. What do you think this old and wise person would advise you to do in order to get through the present phase of your life? What would this person say that you should be thinking of? What would this person say that would help you the best to recover from the past? What would this person say how you could console yourself? (And how, from this person's view, could psychotherapy (if needed) be most useful to you?)

Grief and resilience

People often say that one of the positive outcomes of the loss they suffered was that it signaled a "wake-up call." Priorities in their lives underwent a change. No longer was it all about pursuing success in work but about cherishing and improving their relationships with people who were dear to them. People also mentioned that they live more in the present and are not so pre-occupied with the past or future. Enjoying a sunny day or admiring the beauty of nature, and enjoying good company with nice people becomes more important than before. Theories about coping state that taking stock of your resilience after a setback, or reconsidering the meaning of life or indeed the importance of relationships with significant others, can prevent feelings of loss or helplessness. This, in return, can lead to experiencing existence as significant, connected to feelings of well-being and self-respect. A traumatic incident or the loss of a loved one can also ensure further development in life, perhaps because you had to adopt a new role such as that of widow or head of family.

Nolen-Hoeksema (2000) interviewed people in bereavement at intervals of 6, 13, and 18 months after their initial loss. She found those people who after 6 months could report something positive, experienced less fear and depression than people who did not experience a positive dimension 6 months after the loss. Research shows that it is not a question of how many positive things someone can find but whether someone can find anything positive at all. Research into coping mechanisms of the bereaved found that those who found something positive used different coping styles from those who did not. The former group really tried hard to find something positive, sought out more support, expressed their emotions more, and were actively seeking diversion. "Although the loss of a significant loved one can be a highly distressing experience, the majority of bereaved people report finding something positive in their loss experiences. Common positive themes included having a sense of personal growth and personality change, a realization of personal strengths, a reprioritizing of life goals, a greater appreciation of relationships, and a diminished sense of fear about death. Being an optimist not only seemed to contribute to engaging in more positive coping strategies, but also to finding something positive in the loss. In turn, people who found something positive in their losses showed better psychological adjustment to the loss, both shortly after the loss and long afterwards" (p. 123).

Research also shows that people who, amidst feelings of grief for the loved one, can experience something positive, recover much faster (Ong *et al.*, 2006). Some, reflecting on the qualities of the loved one and the years they spent together, find contentment in the wonderful time they had together. Others find consolation in the comfort and support they receive from family and friends at such difficult times. Another group find significance in their lives through altruistic acts, like starting a self-help group or doing voluntary work. Whatever it is, there will be space to develop plans and set goals for the future, whereby a further widening can take place and creativity can increase (compare the broaden-and-build theory of Fredrickson). People often report that they have become stronger and that their resilience has increased. Fredrickson (2009) states that it could well be this positivity that is the deepest resource in times of crisis, because that is what is required to stop the downward spiral of negative emotions and to be able to bounce back.

Nolen-Hoeksema and Davis (2005) discovered a strong link between optimism and finding significance in life after a loss. People who, in general, have positive expectations, optimists, are actively committed to seeking ways of transforming bad times into good times. They actively search for positive ways to look at the situation. And the more they pre-occupy themselves with that the greater the chance they will find something positive. Compare this with what the Greek philosopher Epictetus said: it is not about what happens to you but about how you deal with it.

Nolen-Hoeksema and Davis found that the majority of people who face a major trauma such as the loss of a loved one are able to find some benefit in their experience, usually some way they have grown, have gained perspective, or have enhanced relationships with others. A focus on recovery from a loss to a previous level of functioning misses the true process of change that many people experience following a loss. It is important that psychotherapists could more clearly see, at times of loss and trauma, whilst still acknowledging the pain of that loss, positive emotions in discovering a new significance in life. The psychotherapist's focus should not be merely on "return to normal," but they should, together with their clients, look at how positive emotions can contribute to personal growth and new levels of functioning.

Exercise 7.12

This is an exercise aimed at finding a new significance in life and positive aspects after the loss of a loved one. In the saying "it is better to have loved and lost than never to have loved at all," nestles a kernel of positivity. This morning one of my clients telephoned me to cancel his appointment: his 85-year-old mother had just died. He told me that he was very sad but relieved that she was spared a long period of suffering, dependency, and loss of dignity. He also found consolation in the fact that she hardly suffered.

However sad you are, and however difficult you may find it in the beginning, attempt to discover something positive in your situation. Perhaps there is some-

thing for which you can be grateful? Could something have been even worse? What is it about your situation that prevents it from being even worse? It can also help to talk things over with someone, possibly with a professional. Research shows that it really does not matter how small the positive aspect is, so long as you can find something positive. This very small aspect can be the seed which you sow in order to harvest more positivity in the future.

8

Changing the Doing

Insanity is doing the same thing over and over again and expecting different results
                                                                Albert Einstein (attributed)

Introduction

One way to solve a problem is not to analyze why the problem arose but to change what you are doing to solve it. The way to do that is to determine how you keep acting in the same way over and over again (the problem pattern), stop behaving that way, and begin to experiment with doing something different (breaking the pattern). In changing the *doing of the problem* the focus is on concrete actions someone can take to make these changes by doing two things:

- Pay attention to repetitive patterns that the client is caught up in or that others are caught up in with him and change anything possible about these patterns;
- Notice what the client is doing when things are going better, and let him do more of that.

Story 8.1: For a Change Do Something Different

If you always do what you have always done
You will always get what you've always got
So for a change do something different
And do something different for a change

Source: Anonymous

Practicing Positive CBT: From Reducing Distress to Building Success, First Edition. Fredrike Bannink.
© 2012 John Wiley & Sons, Ltd. Published 2012 by John Wiley & Sons, Ltd.

Changing Repetitive Patterns

O'Hanlon (1999) states that most psychotherapists have the idea that it takes years to make a significant change, especially with serious, long-standing problems, but the solution-focused approach has shown that people can make changes rapidly. The solution-focused approach focuses on the present and the future and encourages people to take action and change their viewpoint. The past is important in the sense that it has influenced us and has brought us to where we are today, but letting it determine your future is a mistake. Instead, this approach suggests acknowledging the past and then getting on with changing things. O'Hanlon offers three keys for breaking repetitive problem patterns.

Key 1: Change the doing of the problem. To solve a problem or change things that are not going as well as you would like, change any part you can of your regularly repeated actions in the situation. Do something different when you have the problem. Pay attention to what you usually do when you have the problem and do it differently. For example: when you are feeling depressed, instead of staying in bed, go outside and take a short walk.

Key 2: Use paradox. Go with the problem or try to make it worse (more intense or more frequent) or try to deliberately make the problem happen. Or just try to avoid having the problem and instead embrace it and allow it to happen. Stop trying to fix the problem or make the situation better. This works best for emotional or bodily problems like insomnia, anxiety, phobias, panic, and sexual problems. For example: when you are feeling anxious, instead of avoiding the situation, stay and use a mindfulness exercise instead and watch your anxiety come and go.

Key 3: Link new actions to the problem pattern. Find something that you can do every time that you have the problem – something that will be good for you. Find something that you think you should do but usually avoid or put off. Every time you feel the urge to "do" the problem, do this avoided action first. If you are not able to do that, do the avoided action for the same amount of time as the problem action, after the problem is over. Make the problem an ordeal by linking it to something that you find unpleasant. Add something new, usually something burdensome, to the situation, every time the problem occurs. For example: when you have had a few drinks too many, do some extra fitness exercises the next day.

Insight or understanding

Instead of focusing on the inner life of clients and why the problems arose, invite clients to move into action. Research by Grant and O'Connor (2010) shows that problem-focused questions (e.g., questions like: Why am I having this problem? What's wrong with me? Why is this always happening to me?) reduce negative affect and increase self-efficacy, but do not increase the understanding of the nature of the problem or enhance positive affect. The solution-focused approach (e.g., questions like: What else can I do to change the situation? How have I managed before? What might be helpful now?) increases positive affect, decreases negative affect, increases self-efficacy, and also increases participants' insight and understanding of the nature of the problem.

One of the differences between traditional CBT and Positive CBT (see Table 2.1) is that in traditional forms of psychotherapy insight or understanding is a precondition for change, whereas in Positive CBT insight or understanding comes during or after the change and is not necessary for psychotherapy to be successful (Klaver and Bannink, 2010). Therefore, "why" questions often lead people in the wrong direction, seeking explanations and going over the same problem again and again. Positive CBT uses "what," "how," and "when" questions instead, since these questions are often more productive.

Story 8.2: Sail Away From the Safe Harbor

Mark Twain once said: "Twenty years from now, you will be more disappointed by the things that you did not do than by the ones you did do. So throw off the bowlines. Sail away from the safe harbor. Catch the trade winds in your sails. Explore. Dream. Discover."

Building "positive addictions"

Habits are those behaviors that have become automatic, triggered by a cue in the environment rather than by conscious will. When we think of habits, most of the time we think of bad ones: biting our fingernails, procrastinating, eating sweets when we are anxious, and so on. But of course we also have good habits: jogging or brushing our teeth. Positive CBT therapists want to assist their clients not only in breaking unhealthy habits and negative addictions, but also in helping them building healthy habits and "positive addictions" instead.

How long does it take to build a healthy habit, you may wonder. Research on healthy habit formation (Lally, van Jaarsveld, Potts and Wardle, 2010) shows that the most common pattern of habit formation was for early repetitions of the chosen behavior to produce the largest increases in its automaticity. Examples of healthy behavior or positive addictions are: going for a 15 minute run before dinner, eating a piece of fruit with lunch, or doing 50 sit-ups after morning coffee. The average time to reach maximum automaticity was 66 days, much longer than most previous estimates of the time taken to acquire a new habit. Participants who had chosen exercise behavior took about one and a half times as long to reach their automaticity plateau compared with the participants who adopted new eating or drinking behaviors. Contrary to what was thought earlier, a single missed day had little impact on later automaticity gains.

Action triggers

Gollwitzer (1999) found that making a "mental plan" is quite effective in motivating action. Setting so-called "action triggers" implies that you have made the decision to execute a certain action (go jogging) when you encounter a certain situational trigger (tomorrow morning; coming home after work). Noticing in advance exactly *when and where* you intend to execute the action make a huge difference. Gollwitzer argues that the value of action triggers resides in the fact that we are pre-loading a decision. They protect goals from tempting distractions, bad habits, or competing goals. In essence, action triggers create an "instant habit." One study showed that the single biggest predictor of whether women gave themselves a monthly breast examination was if they had a habit of doing so. When another group of women who didn't have such a habit were asked to set action triggers, they ended up doing just as well as the women with long-time habits. By pre-loading a decision, they created an instant habit.

People can delegate the initiation of goal-directed behavior to environmental stimuli by forming so-called implementation intentions (if-then plans of the format: If situation X is encountered, then I will perform behavior Y). Forming implementation intentions facilitates detecting, attending to, and recalling the critical situation. Moreover, in the presence of the critical situation the initiation of the specified goal-directed behavior is immediate, efficient, and does not need a conscious intent.

Noticing What the Client is Doing When Things are Going Better

Thomas Edison once said: "If we did all the things we are capable of doing, we would literally astound ourselves." In Positive CBT it is the task of the therapist to move attention away from the problems and symptoms of their clients to improve their well-being and quality of life and to invite their clients to astound themselves. In Chapter 5 I explained the concept of setting so-called "stretch goals": goals that encourage the clients not only to "patch up" problems, but also to grow as an individual. For example, a stretch goal might be to increase well-being or connectedness, instead of "just" solving the problem. Continuously setting and meeting stretch goals is a way to move oneself toward a more positive, strengths-based stance.

O'Hanlon (1999) offers four keys to find and use solution patterns.

Key 1: As yourself: When didn't I experience the problem after I expected I would?

Find a time that is an exception to the usual problem pattern and mine it for changes you can make in the situation by deliberately repeating whatever action worked. For example: when was there a moment when you expected to have another fight with your partner, but somehow you avoided it. What did you do differently and what difference did that make in your relationship?

Key 2: Notice what happens as the problem ends or starts to end. Then deliberately do some of the helpful actions you do then, but much earlier in the problem situation. For example: how do your fights usually end?

Key 3: Import some solution patterns from other situations in which you felt competent. Examine your patterns at work, in your hobbies, with friends, and in other contexts to find something that you can use effectively in the problem situation (see the description of "competence transference" in Chapter 6). For example: is there anything in your areas of competence that would be helpful now in changing the problem?

Key 4: Ask yourself: Why isn't the problem worse? Then use your own natural abilities to limit the severity of the problem you have been using without noticing. For example: Ask yourself how come my overweight is not worse than it is right now? What have I done and what I am doing to prevent the problem from getting worse? Or when your weight is more or less stable, ask yourself how you managed to do that. Most of the time our clients know very well – often better than we as therapists do – what works and what doesn't work , but for a change they have to actually do something different from what they are currently doing.

Enhancing self-control

Self-control is defined as a set of responses that can be taught; learning and using those responses reduces the need to depend on external control by others.

Self-control is also known as "impulse control" or "self-regulation." Some psychologists prefer the term "impulse control" because it may be more precise. The term self-regulation is used to refer to the many processes individuals use to manage drives and emotions. Therefore, self-regulation also embodies the concept of willpower. Self-regulation is an extremely important executive function of the brain. A lack of self-control/regulation is often found in a large number of psychological disorders including ADHD, Antisocial Personality Disorder, Borderline Personality Disorder, addictions, eating disorders, and impulse control disorders.

A CBT way to look at self-control is the S > R > C scheme, whereby S = stimulus; R = response; C = consequences. In traditional CBT the focus is on the problematic behavior: S (stimulus that triggers the undesired behavior) > R (the response: the undesired behavior) > C (the positive and negative consequences of undesired behavior).

Positive CBT uses the same S > R > C scheme, whereby the S (stimulus) remains the same, but now the R (response) is the desired behavior in the future or the already existing exceptions to the problem. The C (consequences) are the positive – and sometimes also negative – products of desired behavior. Questions that may be asked are:

- What would you like to do instead of the undesired behavior?
- When didn't you experience the problem after you expected you would?
- What do you do when you overcome the urge to . . .
- What do you know about how others overcome to urge to . . .
- How much confidence do you have that you could do this (again)?

Beginning in the late 1960s and early 1970s, Mischel pioneered work illuminating the ability to delay gratification and to exert self-control in the face of strong situational pressures and emotionally "hot" temptations. His studies with preschoolers (four-year-old children) in the late 1960s, often referred to as "The marshmallow experiment," examined the processes and mental mechanisms that enable a young child to forego immediate gratification (one marshmallow) or to wait instead for 15 minutes for a larger desired but delayed reward (two marshmallows). Continuing research with these original participants has examined how preschool delay of gratification ability links to development over the life course, and may predict a variety of important outcomes (e.g., social and cognitive competence, educational attainment, and drug use), and can have significant protective effects against a variety of potential vulnerabilities. This work also opened a route to research on temporal discounting in decision making and most importantly into the mental mechanisms that enable cognitive and emotional self-control, thereby helping to demystify the concept of "willpower" (Mischel, Shoda, and Rodriguez, 1989; Mischel and Ayduk, 2004).

They concluded that self-control is correlated with various positive life outcomes, such as happiness, adjustment, and various positive psychological factors. On YouTube you can see a great film about the marshmallow experiment: www.youtube.com/watch?v=6EjJsPylEOY

Story 8.3: Chocolate-chip Cookies

Baumeister et al. (1998) showed that self-control is not synonymous with willpower, but rather an exhaustible resource. College students participated in a study about "food perception" (or so they were told). They had been asked not to eat for three hours beforehand and were led to a room that smelled great: the researchers had baked chocolate-chip cookies. On a table there were two bowls: one held the chocolate-chip cookies, the other bowl held radishes.

The researchers told the students they had selected the cookies and radishes because they have highly distinctive tastes and that the next day they would contact them and ask them about their memory of their taste sensations. Half the participants were asked to eat two or three cookies, but no radishes. The other half was asked to eat two or three radishes, but no cookies. Despite the temptation, all participants ate what they were asked to eat, and none of the radish-eaters sneaked a cookie.

At that point the experiment was "officially" over, and a new group of researchers entered with a supposedly unrelated study: they wanted to find who is better at solving problems, college students or high school students. The college students of course wanted to show they did better. They were presented with some puzzles that required them to trace a geometric shape without retracing any lines and without lifting their pencils from the paper. In reality, the puzzles were unsolvable. The researchers wanted to see how long the students would persist in a frustrating task before giving up. The students who were given the chocolate-chip cookies and therefore had not had to resist them spent 19 minutes on the task and made 34 attempts to solve the problem. The radish-eaters, who had had to resist the cookies, gave up after 8 minutes – less than half the time – and they managed only 19 solution attempts.

Small steps

De Shazer (1985, p. 33) assumed: "Minimal changes are needed to initiate solving complaints and, once the change is initiated (the therapists' task), further changes will be generated by the client (the 'ripple effect')." In Positive CBT the focus is on one small step forward instead of a big leap, even in situations with big problems. When problems are large, taking small steps may be even more powerful. Small steps are often the only way to start tackling overwhelming problems. Small steps (also called "babysteps") have the following advantages: there is a low threshold, there is low risk, chances of successes are bigger, and there can be a positive snowball-effect of bigger changes.

Research on hope theory (see Chapter 5) shows that high-hope people naturally break big goals into small subgoals. Small steps can lead to big changes, so setting frequent short-term "stepping-stone" goals is important. Clients, who often lack hope at the beginning of therapy, are invited to design and choose their own small steps forward. Suggestions by the therapist are often not necessary, because of the clients' need for autonomy and their expertise of what might be working in the right direction.

If clients do not (yet) have any ideas about which step forward they might take, an observation suggestion as a homework assignment might be useful:

- Between now and the next time we meet, could you observe when things are just a little bit better and what you did to make that happen?
- Do you think it might be useful to observe situations when the problem is there to a lesser extent, even just a little bit?

In traditional CBT the "modification procedures" for changing the doing (like self-control procedures or behavioral experiments like exposure) are advised by the therapist, whose role is that of the expert on what works for this client, in this context and at this moment. In Positive CBT this is different: the modification procedures are already available: the client, whose role is that of the co-expert on what works for him, in this context and at this moment, is competent to make changes and has made changes before. Also there are always exceptions to the problem. Therefore, the modification procedures may be the same as advised by the therapist in traditional CBT, with the difference that in Positive CBT the client himself comes up with the modification procedures, which have helped before, and are therefore "evidence-based" and may be repeated. In this vein, the term "learning new behavior" is replaced by the term "becoming better at." This term is often more positive to the client, who sometimes has a very negative connotation regarding the word "to learn."

Exercise 8.1

Write a short description of how you would like to have your life relayed to your grandchildren (or a young child whom you care about). A few days later, review the summary and take stock in what is missing in your life and the changes that would be helpful to make the summary a reality. Take a first small step to get closer to your goal and see what difference that makes.

Exercise 8.2

Ask your client to consider a particular skill in which he is now proficient but which in the past he had failed to develop. Ask him to explain how he managed to bring about this change.

Building resilience

The American Psychological Association (APA; www.apa.org) describes 10 ways to build resilience. These ways are very much in line with the assumptions of Positive CBT:

1. Make connections. Good relationships with close family members, friends, or others are important. Accepting help and support from those who care about you and will listen to you strengthens resilience. Some people find that being active in civic groups, faith-based organizations, or other local groups provides social support and can help with reclaiming hope. Assisting others in their time of need also can benefit the helper.
2. Avoid seeing crises as insurmountable problems. You can't change the fact that highly stressful events happen, but you can change how you interpret and respond to these events. Try looking beyond the present to how future circumstances may be a little better. Note any subtle ways in which you might already feel somewhat better as you deal with difficult situations.
3. Accept that change is a part of living. Certain goals may no longer be attainable as a result of adverse situations. Accepting circumstances that cannot be changed can help you focus on circumstances that you can alter.
4. Move toward your goals. Develop some realistic goals. Do something regularly – even if it seems like a small accomplishment – that enables you to move toward your goals. Instead of focusing on tasks that seem unachievable, ask yourself, "What's one thing I know I can accomplish today that helps me move in the direction I want to go?"
5. Take decisive actions. Act on adverse situations as much as you can. Take decisive actions, rather than detaching completely from problems and stresses and wishing they would just go away.
6. Look for opportunities for self-discovery. People often learn something about themselves and may find that they have grown in some respect as a result of their struggle with loss. Many people who have experienced tragedies and hardship have reported better relationships, greater sense of strength even while feeling vulnerable, increased sense of self-worth, a more developed spirituality, and heightened appreciation for life.
7. Nurture a positive view of yourself. Developing confidence in your ability to solve problems and trusting your instincts helps build resilience.
8. Keep things in perspective. Even when facing very painful events, try to consider the stressful situation in a broader context and keep a long-term perspective. Avoid blowing the event out of proportion.

9. Maintain a hopeful outlook. An optimistic outlook enables you to expect that good things will happen in your life. Try visualizing what you want, rather than worrying about what you fear.
10. Take care of yourself. Pay attention to your own needs and feelings. Engage in activities that you enjoy and find relaxing. Exercise regularly. Taking care of yourself helps to keep your mind and body primed to deal with situations that require resilience.

Additional ways of strengthening resilience may be helpful. For example, some people write about their deepest thoughts and feelings related to trauma or other stressful events in their life. Meditation and spiritual practices help some people build connections and restore hope. The key is to identify ways that are likely to work well for you as part of your own personal strategy for fostering resilience.

Behavioral experiments

The operational definition of behavioral experiments according to Bennett-Levy *et al.* (2004, p. 8) is: "Behavioural experiments are planned experiential activities, based on experimentation or observation, which are undertaken by patients in or between cognitive therapy sessions. Their design is derived directly from a cognitive formulation of the problem, and their primary purpose is to obtain new information, which may help to:

• Test the validity of the patients' existing beliefs about themselves, others, and the world;
• Construct and/or test new, more adaptive beliefs;
• Contribute to the development and verification of the cognitive formulation."

There are three types of experiments possible:

1. Experimental manipulation of the environment. This necessitates doing something, which is different to what the client would usually do in a particular situation. For example, the client may try to answer the question: If I go to the supermarket alone and do not take my usual precautions, will I actually faint (as my existing belief would predict) or will I just feel anxious (the prediction of an alternative theory).
2. Observational experiments, in that it is either not possible or not necessary to manipulate key variables. Instead clients set out to observe and gather evidence, which is relevant to their specific negative thoughts or beliefs. For example, a client may try to answer the question: Will people think I am stupid or abnormal if I sweat in social situations?
3. Discovery-oriented experiments, when clients have little or no idea what will happen when they undertake a behavioral experiment and need to collect data systematically in order to "build a theory." For example, a client may try to answer the question: What would happen if I acted "as if" I was valued by others? Or the client may be encouraged to try out different ways of

behaving in order to collect those data (How might a valued person act in these circumstances?).

Positive CBT employs the same types of behavioral experiments, but the difference is that now a positive focus is used:

1. Regarding experimental manipulation of the environment: clients are invited to explore exceptions to the problem: What has the client done – even slightly – differently before? How has that been helpful? Does the client think it might be a good idea to use this solution again?
2. Regarding observational experiments, clients are invited to observe and gather evidence, which is relevant to their specific *positive* thoughts and beliefs. For example, the client may try to answer the question: Will people think I am likable if I go to this party? When they pay attention to their positive thoughts or beliefs, chances are that clients will find evidence for these positive ones, whereas when they pay attention to their negative thoughts or beliefs, chances are that clients will find evidence for the negative ones too. What you focus on expands!
3. Regarding discovery-oriented experiments, clients are invited to act "as if" the miracle has happened (when the miracle question is posed) or "as if" their preferred future has already arrived. During the session individuals/couples/families are invited to pretend things are going better and show the therapist (for some minutes) how their life/relationships will be different and how this will appear.

More information about behavioral experiments as homework assignments can be found in Chapter 10.

De Shazer, one of the founders of Solution-Focused Brief Therapy (1985, p. 136) states: "In some sense, the therapy really adds nothing. The therapist does not tell the clients what to do differently and does not teach the clients any new techniques. These interventions are minimally intrusive and yet their impact seems inordinately large."

9

Changing the Feeling

Downward spiral or upward spiral, as I see it, that's your choice
Fredrickson (2009, p. 16)

Introduction

In traditional forms of psychotherapy many questions are about feelings. "How do you feel about having these nightmares?" "How did you feel when your children were taken away from you?" "How do you feel when you start drinking?" It is widely believed that getting clients to explore and express their negative emotions is important in helping them.

But reducing negative emotions does not automatically increase positive emotions. So far little attention has been paid to theories of (building) positive emotions in psychology and psychotherapy. This may well reflect the spirit of the age in which most disciplines have focused on problems and it may also reflect the nature of emotions themselves. The literature in psychology between 1970 and 2000 has 46 000 papers about depression and only 400 papers about joy (Myers, 2000).

Positive emotions are fewer in number than negative emotions, generally a ratio of 3 to 4 negative emotions to 1 positive emotion are identified. Positive emotions are less differentiated than negative emotions and this imbalance is also reflected in the number of words in most languages that describe emotions.

In this chapter I shall explain how negative emotions can be reduced, positive emotions built, and how balancing positive and negative emotions plays a major role in Positive CBT.

Reducing Negative Emotions

Beck (2011, p. 158) states that emotions are of primary importance in CBT. She adds – using a problem-focused perspective – "After all, the major goals of treatment are symptom relief and a remission of the patient's disorder."

Practicing Positive CBT: From Reducing Distress to Building Success, First Edition. Fredrike Bannink.
© 2012 John Wiley & Sons, Ltd. Published 2012 by John Wiley & Sons, Ltd.

In this vein traditional CBT aims to obtain a clear picture of situations which are distressing to clients by helping them to clearly differentiate thoughts from emotions, it empathises with their emotions throughout the process, and it helps them to evaluate the dysfunctional thinking which has influenced their mood. The therapist's job is to minimize the negative effect: by dispensing drugs or in instigating psychological interventions, thereby rendering people less anxious, angry, or depressed. Seligman, however, describes some disappointing results with this approach (2011, p. 54): "As a therapist, once in a while I would help a patient get rid of all of his anger and anxiety and sadness. I thought I would then get a happy patient. But I never did. I got an empty patient. And that is because the skills of flourishing – of having positive emotion, meaning, good work, and positive relationships – are something over and above the skills of minimizing suffering."

Research by Lieberman *et al.* (2007) shows different results. They found that putting feelings into words – by simply putting the name to the emotion – the response in the amygdala portion of the brain that handles fear, panic, and other strong emotions decreases and become less intense. What lights up instead is the right ventrolateral prefrontex cortex, the part of the brain that controls impulses. That is why talking to a therapist, or even a sympathetic bartender, often makes people feel better. The same strategy of putting feelings into words is seen in mindfulness meditation practice. This involves a regular practice in stepping back and observing the flow of experience, with labeling as one tool that can help this process.

Lieberman and colleagues conducted four studies examining the effect of affect labeling on self-reported emotional experience. In study 1, self-reported distress was lower during affect labeling, compared with passive watching, of negative emotional pictures. Studies 2 and 3 added reappraisal and distraction conditions, respectively. Affect labeling showed similar effects on self-reported distress as both of these intentional emotion regulation strategies. In each of these three studies, however, participant predictions about the effects of affect labeling suggest that unlike reappraisal and distraction, people do not believe affect labeling to be an effective emotion regulation strategy. Even after having the experience of affect labels leading to lower distress, participants still predicted that affect labeling would increase distress in the future. Finally, study 4 employed positive emotional pictures and here affect labeling was associated with diminished self-reported pleasure, relative to passive watching. This suggests that affect labeling tends to dampen affective responses in general, rather than specifically alleviating negative affect.

These findings may be in line with the disappointing results of research showing that unexplained positivity lasts longer than positivity which we analyze until we fully understand it (Wilson *et al.*, 2005). They found that the cognitive processes used in making sense of positive events reduce the pleasure people derive from them.

As an example of how reducing negative affect does not automatically increase positive affect, research in a coaching context done by Grant and O'Connor (2010) shows that problem-focused questions reduce negative affect and increase self-efficacy, but do not increase understanding of the nature of the problem or enhance positive affect. Solution-focused questions increase positive affect, decrease negative affect, increase self-efficacy as well as increase participants' insight and understanding of the nature of the problem.

Building Positive Emotions

Although emotions do not have to be singled out for special conversation in order to build a positive cooperative relationship with clients, a demonstration of natural, empathic understanding is required and helpful when clients are describing what they find difficult and painful in a given problem. Empathic affirmation of the client's perspective is useful: "I understand that things have been getting worse lately." Then the therapist can move on to explore what the clients want different in their lives or what the clients are doing to keep their heads above water. In dealing with emotions it is useful to, on one hand, acknowledge the negative emotions like anger, frustration, or sadness and, on the other hand, to look for possibilities by saying something like: "I see that your feelings are very strong about this topic. What would you like to feel instead in the future?" Remember that moving from minus 10 (for example, feeling very depressed) to 0 (for example, not feeling depressed anymore) requires different strategies than moving from 0 (not feeling depressed anymore) to plus 10 (for example, feeling great and flourishing).

The transparency of the Positive CBT method can also ensure that the potential emotional charge of the focus is reduced. The therapist announces, that together with the clients, he will focus on all positive elements, which can replace the problem: what is desirable rather than what is undesirable. This proposal meets with the approval of most clients.

Selective Attention Theory describes that what you focus on expands. This theory has obvious applications in relation to emotions. If there is a focus on negative emotions, such as anger, then the anger will increase. If you focus on sadness, you will feel sadder. An example of this would be the psychoanalytical "catharsis" method, whereby there is the assumption that emotions must be aired in order to activate a purifying process.

In Positive CBT the focus is instead on positive emotions and on balancing positive and negative affect: "How will you feel when your hoped for outcome is reached?" "What will you be thinking, doing, and feeling differently when you notice that the steps you take are in the right direction?" Also bringing back the best from the past by asking questions about previous successes and competences triggers positive emotions.

The "broaden-and-build theory of positive emotions" (see later) suggests that negative emotions narrow our thought-action repertoires, whereas positive emotions broaden our awareness and encourage novel, varied, and exploratory thoughts and actions. The power of asking open questions in Positive CBT ("How will you know this session has been useful?" "How will you know the problem has been solved?" "What has been working well?" "What is better?") all serve to widen the array of thoughts and actions. Using imagination as in the "miracle question" (see Chapter 6) also creates positive emotions and has a powerful impact on our capacity to expand our ideas and activities. While this is highly speculative, it is possible that the miracle question by engaging our imagery, which is consistent with right hemisphere processing, also engages the global processing capacities of the hemisphere enabling us to expand our thinking. The right hemisphere sees the forest; the left hemisphere sees the trees. The use of compliments and competence questions ("How did you manage to do that?" "How did you decide to do that?") also elicit positive emotions. The focus of the Positive CBT therapist is on noticing skills and resources of his clients and to compliment or play those resources back to them.

In sum, focusing on positive goals, focusing on hope and what difference it would make if the things hoped for become reality, focusing on exceptions to the problem and the competences of the clients to make that happen, all help to create an atmosphere in which positive feelings can flourish and the problem can be transformed into something positive: the preferred future of our clients.

Exercise 9.1

Ask your clients to draw some happy events from their lives and invite them to explain them to you. Or ask your clients to draw themselves while they are doing something they are proud of.

Isen (2005) states that a growing body of research indicates that positive emotions facilitates a broad range of important social behaviors and thought processes. For example, work from approximately the past decade shows that positive affect leads to greater creativity, improved negotiation processes and outcomes, and more thorough, open-minded, flexible thinking and problem solving. And this is in addition to earlier work showing that positive affect promotes generosity and social responsibility in interpersonal interactions.

In a negotiation study, positive affect induced by a small gift (a pad of paper) and a few cartoons significantly increased the tendency of bargainers who were face-to-face to reach agreement and to obtain the optimal outcome possible for both of them in the negotiation. Isen: "Relative to control groups, people in positive-affect conditions have better negotiation outcomes and enjoy the task more, and they can take the other person's perspective."

The literature indicates that under most circumstances, people who are feeling happy are more likely to do what they want to do, want to do what is socially responsible and helpful and what needs to be done, enjoy what they are doing more, are more motivated to accomplish their goals, and are more open to information and think more clearly. In the case of positive emotions, one of the most clear and most distinctive cognitive effects observed is increased flexibility and creativity. This may be mediated by release of the neurotransmitter dopamine. Dopamine may play a role in the effects of positive affect on cognition that have been observed. This "dopamine hypothesis" arose from the observation, at behavioral and cognitive levels, that positive affect fosters cognitive flexibility and the ability to switch perspectives (together with the understanding that dopamine in the anterior cingulate region of the brain enables flexible perspective-taking or set-switching).

Another type of research was done by Isen and Reeve (2005), showing that positive emotions foster intrinsic motivation, as reflected by choice of activity in a free-choice situation and by rated amount of enjoyment of a novel and challenging task, but also promotes responsible behavior in a situation where uninteresting tasks need to be done. This has implications for the relationship between positive affect and aspects of self-regulation, such as self-control.

Exercise 9.2

This exercise is called: "You at your best." Remind yourself of a time when you were at your best. Remember where you were, who was there with you, and what you were thinking, doing, and feeling. This could be an experience that brings forth pleasant memories, such as a birthday, wedding, a job interview, or a time when you accomplished something important in your life. You might find benefit in doing this exercise with physical memorabilia – photo albums, trinkets collected from a vacation, trophies or awards, meaningful letters or printed e-mails, or college degrees. After recalling the event, take a few minutes to simply bask in the past success and pleasant feelings this experience brings forth in you. Bring your attention to the details and your positive emotions. Don't analyze the experience where you are picking the experience apart and trying to figure out why certain things happened; this is often counterproductive with positive experiences and is not truly savoring. Instead, focus on the "replaying" of the experience. This exercise has been shown to build positive emotions and build confidence.

Broaden-and-build theory of positive emotions

The "broaden-and-build theory of positive emotions" (Fredrickson, 2003) suggests that positive emotions (interest, contentment, enjoyment, serenity, happiness, joy, pride, relief, affection, love) broaden one's awareness and encourage novel, varied, and exploratory thoughts and actions. Over time, this broadened behavioral repertoire builds skills and resources. For example, curiosity about a landscape becomes valuable navigational knowledge; pleasant interactions with a stranger become a supportive friendship; aimless physical play becomes exercise and physical excellence.

This is in contrast with negative emotions, which promote narrow, immediate survival-oriented behavior. Positive and negative emotions are different in their links to action. For example, the negative emotion of anxiety leads to the specific fight-or-flight response for immediate survival. To survive, we immediately focus our attention on a specific behavioral response such as running or fighting, and therefore we do not expand our thinking to other behavioral alternatives. Positive emotions, on the other hand, do not have any immediate survival value, because they take one's mind off of immediate needs and stressors. However, over time, the skills and resources built by broadened behavior enhance survival.

Fredrickson states that it is this narrowing effect on our thought-action repertories that distinguishes negative and positive emotions. When we are experiencing negative emotions that accompany problems, our attention narrows and we limit our behavior repertoire that does not offer solutions: we feel "stuck." The usual approach of trying to find solutions by delving further into the problem – sometimes with the help of the therapist – perpetuates the situation by creating more negative emotions that continue to narrow our attention and further the sense of being stuck.

Fredrickson proposes that in contrast to negative emotions that narrow our thought-action repertoires, positive emotions broaden our thought-action repertoires and build enduring personal resources physically, intellectually, psychologically, and socially.

People who are feeling positive show patterns of thought that are more flexible, unusual, creative, and inclusive. Their thinking tends to be more efficient and more open to information and options. It is suggested that positive emotions enlarge the cognitive context, an effect recently linked to increases in brain dopamine levels.

The broaden-and-build theory is an exploration of the evolved function of positive emotions and has substantial support. Fredrickson has conducted randomized controlled lab studies in which the participants were randomly assigned to watch films that induce positive emotions such as amusement and contentment, negative emotions such as fear and sadness, or no emotions. Compared with people in the other conditions, participants who experience positive emotions show heightened levels of creativity, inventiveness, and "big picture" perceptual focus. Longitudinal intervention studies show that positive emotions play a role in the development of long-term resources such as psychological resilience and flourishing. Individuals who express or report higher levels of positive emotions show more constructive and flexible coping, more abstract and long-term thinking, and greater emotional distance following stressful negative events.

Exercise 9.3

A book is made up of many chapters. You can see your own life in this way. If you were to write the story of your life as an exercise, then you should begin with the second chapter instead of beginning at chapter one. Any problems, which you are currently experiencing, can be omitted. What positive differences would there be in your life description? Which persons would you omit and which persons would you include to make them part of chapter two? Which strengths and resources do you have in chapter two? Which good ideas from chapter two could you be already using? As an exercise write your own life story but begin it at chapter two.

Undoing effect

Fredrickson (2000) found that positive emotions also serve as particularly effective antidotes for the lingering effects of negative emotions, which narrow individuals' thought-action repertoires. In other words, positive emotions have an undoing effect on negative emotions, since positive emotions are incompatible with negative emotions. In addition, to the extent that a negative emotion's narrowed thought-action repertoire (i.e., specific action tendency) evokes physiological changes to support the indicated action, a counteracting positive emotion, with its broadened thought-action repertoire, should quell or undo this physiological preparation for specific action. By returning the body to baseline levels of physiological activation, positive emotions create physiological support for pursuing the wider array and actions called forth. Positive emotions have a unique ability to down-regulate the lingering cardiovascular after-effects of negative emotions. Beyond speeding physiological recovery, the undoing effect implies that positive emotions should counteract any aspect of negative emotions that stems from a narrowed thought-action repertoire. For instance, negative emotions can entrain people toward narrowed lines of thinking consistent with the specific action tendencies they trigger. When angry, individuals may dwell on getting revenge or getting even; when anxious or afraid, they may dwell on escaping or avoiding harm; when sad or depressed, they may dwell on the repercussions of what has been lost.

Exercise 9.4

We all have the power to turn positivity on and off for ourselves. Experiment with this and turn positivity on right now. Take a moment to notice your physical surroundings. Whether you are in your living room, bathroom, on the bus or train, ask yourself: What is right about my current circumstances? What makes me lucky to be here? What aspect of my current situation might I view as a gift to be treasured? How does it benefit me or others? Taking time to think in this manner can ignite the inner glow of gratitude. Take a few moments to savor and enjoy the good feeling you have created for yourself.

Now turn positivity off. Positivity spoiling questions are: What is wrong here? What is bothering me? What should be different and better? Who is to blame? Try asking yourself these kinds of questions and follow the chain of thoughts they produce and how quickly your positivity plummets (Fredrickson, 2009).

Research on the positive affect "gratitude" (cited in Seligman, 2002) shows that:

• Expressing gratitude has a short-term positive effect (several weeks) on happiness levels (up to a 25% increase). Those who are typically or habitually grateful are happier than those who are not;
• People who noted weekly the things they were grateful for increased their happiness levels 25% over people who noted their complaints or were just asked to note any events that had occurred during the week;
• People who scored as severely depressed in a depression inventory were instructed to recall and write down "three good things" that happened each day for 15 days. 94% of them went from severely depressed to mildly to moderately depressed during that time.

Balancing Positive and Negative Emotions

"When I started out as a therapist almost forty years ago, it was common for my patient to tell me: 'I just want to be happy, Doctor'. I transformed this into: 'You mean you want to get rid of your depression'. Back then I did not have the tools of building well-being at hand and was blinded by Sigmund Freud and Arthur Schopenhauer (who taught that the best humans can ever achieve is to minimize their own misery); the difference had not even occurred to me. I had only the tools for relieving depression. But every person, every patient, just wants 'to be happy', and this legitimate goal combines relieving suffering and building well-being. Cure, to my way of thinking, uses the entire arsenal for minimising misery – drugs and psychotherapy – and adds positive psychology" (Seligman, 2011, p. 54).

Beck (2011, p. 158) shares the same goal: "The aim of cognitive behaviour therapy is not to get rid of all distress; negative emotions are as much a part of the richness of life as positive emotions and serve as important a function as does physical pain, often alerting us to potential problems that may need to be addressed. In addition, you will seek to increase patients' positive emotions, through discussion (usually relatively brief) of their interests, positive events that occurred during the week, and positive memories. You will often suggest homework assignments aimed at increasing the number of activities in which the patient is likely to experience mastery and pleasure."

As an example of how to decrease the negative effect and increase the positive, Kranz, Bollinger, and Nilges (2010) studied the relationship between chronic pain acceptance and affective well-being from a coping perspective. 150 patients from a multidisciplinary pain center provided self-report data including measures of pain acceptance, positive and negative affect, and accommodative flexibility. The bivariate and multiple correlation patterns were consistent with the assumption that pain willingness (the attitudinal component of pain acceptance including the recognition of the uncontrollability of pain) primarily reduces negative affect, whereas activity engagement (the behavioral component of pain acceptance including the pursuit of life activities despite pain) additionally produces positive affect. The data furthermore suggest activity engagement as a mediating link between pain willingness and positive affect. Moderation analysis shows that accommodative flexibility (the general readiness to adjust personal goals to situational constraints) facilitates both pain willingness and activity engagement – especially when average pain intensity is high. In sum, the results support the view that chronic pain patients' well-being is closely tied to the maintenance of life activities which presupposes an accepting attitude towards pain.

We all want to feel pleasure and avoid pain, as I explained in more detail in Chapter 6, and although people generally prefer happiness, they may sometimes prefer being angry or anxious as they see this emotion as providing long-term benefits. Tamir, Mitchell, and Gross (2008) state that people typically prefer to feel emotions that are pleasant (e.g., excitement) and avoid those that are unpleasant (e.g., anger). They tested whether people prefer to experience emotions that are potentially useful, even when they are unpleasant to experience.

They tested whether individuals are motivated to increase their level of anger when they expect to complete a task where anger might enhance performance. Participants were told that they would either play a violent or a nonviolent computer game. They were then asked to rate the extent to which they would like to engage in different activities before playing the game. They found that participants preferred activities that were likely to make them angry (e.g., listening to anger-inducing music, recalling past events in which they were angry) when they expected to play a violent game. In contrast, participants preferred more pleasant activities when they expected to play a nonviolent game.

To examine whether preferences to increase anger resulted in improved performance, participants were assigned at random to either an angry, neutral, or excited emotion induction and then played a violent and a nonviolent computer game. As expected, angry participants performed better than others in the violent game, by successfully killing more enemies. However, angry participants did not perform better than others in the nonviolent game, which involved serving customers. Such findings demonstrate that what people prefer to feel at any given moment may depend, in part, on what they might get out of it. A factor that ought to be considered, where anger is concerned, is that it can be very arousing, and thus can feel actually good in a certain way. Interestingly, people sometimes opt for less arousing and less pleasant feelings such as fear. This is particularly true when people are pursuing avoidant, rather than approach goals (see Chapter 6). Approach goals seek out a positive outcome, such as: I want to go to bed early tonight, because I want to feel fit tomorrow morning. Avoidance goals seek to avoid a negative outcome such as: I don't want to go to bed late tonight, because I don't want to be sleepy at work tomorrow morning. Tamir and colleagues found that people prefer fear when they are pursuing avoidance goals. Despite the unpleasantness of fear, people appear to recognize that it will help them better achieve certain types of goals.

Positivity ratio

Fredrickson's (2009) "positivity ratio" – comparing positive and negative thoughts, emotions, and activities during our day to day lives – shows a tipping point in the ratio around the 3 to 1 mark, where people experience transformed lives through positivity. For those with positivity ratios below 3 to 1, positivity is inert and useless, for those with ratios exceeding 3 to 1, positivity forecast both openness and growth. "Only those people truly enjoyed the sweet fruits of positivity" (p. 135).

Gottman (1994) developed several ways to compute the positivity ratio of a marriage. He divided the marriages into two groups: one group was made up of marriages that lasted and that both partners found to be satisfying, the so-called "flourishing marriages." The other group was made up of marriages that had fallen apart, the partners had become dissatisfied, estranged, separated, or divorced. He found that among flourishing marriages positivity ratios were about 5 to 1. By sharp contrast, languishing and failed marriages had positivity ratios lower than 1 to 1.

He states that in order for a relationship to flourish, for every disapproving remark or negative signal, there must be five positive ones. In relationships where the partners separated, the ratio often fell to 1 to 1. It was more often a case of negative emotions than positive ones. He was able to predict with 94% accuracy which of 700 couples, who participated in the research, would ten years later still be together, or would have separated, based on his observations of a 15 minute film of each couple from which he scored the ratio of their positive and negative interactions.

Fredrickson (2009, p. 133): "For individuals, marriages – and business teams as well – flourishing, or doing remarkably well, comes with positivity ratios above 3 to 1. By contrast, those who don't overcome their depression, couples who fail in their marriages, and business teams that are unpopular and unprofitable each have ratios in the gutter, below 1 to 1." Below 3 to 1, positivity may be inert, swamped as it is by the greater potency of negativity. Positivity needs to accumulate and compound to a certain degree before it reaches the crucial tipping point. Only then will the broaden-and-build effects of positivity emerge. Only then will people see the astonishing benefits of positivity blossom in their own lives, relationships, and work. On the other hand, the upper bound for flourishing is around 11 to 1 in the USA. This may be different in other cultures.

Story 9.1: Consider a Sail-boat

Consider a sail-boat. Rising from a sail-boat is an enormous mast that allows the sail to catch the wind. Below the waterline is the keel, which can weigh tons. You can take the mast going up as positivity, and the keel down below as negativity. If you've ever sailed, you know that you can't get anywhere without the keel. If you tried, at best you'd slide aimlessly across the water, or at worst you'd capsize. Although it is the sail hanging on the mast of positivity that catches the wind and gives you fuel, it is the keel of negativity that keeps the boat on course and manageable. And just as the keel matters most when you're going upwind, appropriate negativity matters most in hard times.

Fredrickson (2009, p. 137)

Exercise 9.5

Make your own positive "mood board." Mood boards are often used by (graphic) designers to enable a person to illustrate visually the direction of style that they are pursuing. However, mood boards can also be used to visually explain a certain style of writing or an imaginary setting for a storyline. In short, mood boards are not limited to visual subjects but serve as a visual tool to quickly inform others of the overall "feel" (or "flow") that a designer is trying to achieve. Creating mood boards in a digital form may be easier and quicker, but physical objects often tend to have a higher impact on people because of the more complete palette of sensations physical mood boards offer.

Exercise 9.6

This exercise is called: "savoring your day." Reflect on your day for 2–3 minutes on two pleasurable experiences or moments and allow/make the pleasure last as long as possible. This taps into the intensification or elongation of positive emotions through focused attention on the present moment.

Story 9.2: The Nun Study

"And they lived happily ever after." Handwritten autobiographies from 180 Catholic nuns, composed when participants were a mean age of 22 years, were scored for emotional content and related to survival during ages 75 to 95. A strong inverse association was found between positive emotional content in these writings and risk of mortality in late life. As the quartile ranking of positive emotion in early life increased, there was a stepwise decrease in risk of mortality resulting in a 2.5-fold difference between the lowest and highest quartiles. Positive emotional content in early-life autobiographies was strongly associated with longevity 6 decades later.

Source: Danner, Snowdon, and Friesen (2001).

Positive Emotions in the Medical Setting

In this section are some studies showing that positive affect matters, also in medical settings.

Are all psychiatrists equally effective when prescribing medication? This question led to research done by McKay, Imel, and Wampold (2006) showing that both psychiatrists and treatments contributed to outcomes in the treatment of depression. Given that psychiatrists were responsible for more of the variance in outcomes it can be concluded that effective treatment psychiatrists can, in fact, augment the effects of the active ingredients of antidepressant medication as well as placebo.

In another study, Ankarberg and Falkenstrom (2008) argue that available empirical evidence indicates that depression treatment with antidepressants is primarily a psychological treatment. This conclusion has far-reaching consequences for the scientific status of contemporary treatments for depression. It also affects what the doctor should focus on in a treatment with antidepressants and how to act when the patient is treatment resistant. In order to achieve the results obtained in clinical trials, the quantity and quality of support from the doctor is more important than pharmacological concerns, such as adequate doses of medicine. When faced with a treatment resistant patient, relationship factors rather than pharmacological factors should be in focus.

The risk of being sued for malpractice seems to have very little to do with how many mistakes a professional makes. Analysis of malpractice lawsuits show that there are highly skilled doctors who get sued a lot, and doctors who make lots of mistakes and never get sued. In other words, patients do not file lawsuits because they have been harmed by shoddy medical care. Patients file lawsuits because they have been harmed by shoddy medical care and something else happening to them.

The medical researcher Levinson (in: Gladwell, 2005) recorded hundreds of conversations between a group of physicians and their patients. Roughly half of the doctors had never been sued. The other half had been sued at least twice, and Levinson found that just on the basis of those conversations, she could find clear differences between the two groups. The surgeons who had never been sued spent more than three minutes longer with each patient than those who had been sued (18.3 minutes versus 15 minutes). They were more likely to make "orienting" comments, such as: "First I will examine you, and then we will talk the problem over," which helps patients get a sense of what the visit is supposed to accomplish and when they ought to ask questions. They were more likely to engage in active listening, saying things such as: "Go on, tell me more about that." And they were far more likely to laugh and be funny during the visit. Interestingly, there was no difference in the amount or quality of information they gave their patients; they did not provide more details about medication or the patient's condition. The difference was entirely in *how* they talked to their patients.

Psychologist Ambady listened to Levinson's tapes, zeroing in on the conversations that had been recorded between surgeons and their patients. For each surgeon, she picked two patient conversations. Then, from each conversation, she selected two 10 second clips of the doctor talking, so she had a total of forty seconds. Then she removed the high-frequency sounds from speech that enable us to recognize individual words. What is left is a kind of garble that preserves intonation, pitch, and rhythm but erases context. She found to her surprise that by using only those ratings, she could predict which surgeons got sued and which ones didn't. The judges of the tapes knew nothing about the skill level of the surgeons or how experienced they were, what kind of training they had, or what kind of procedures they tended to do.

They did not even know what the doctors were saying to their patients. All they were using for their prediction was their analysis of the surgeon's tone of voice. In fact, it was even more basic than that: if the surgeon's voice was judged to sound dominant, the surgeon tended to be in the sued group. If the voice sounded less dominant and more concerned, the surgeon tended to be in the nonsued group. Malpractice sounds like one of those complicated and multidimensional problems. But in the end it comes down to a matter of *respect*, and the simplest way that respect is communicated is through tone of voice, and the most corrosive tone of voice that a doctor can assume is a dominant tone.

A study done by Estrada, Isen, and Young (1994) investigated whether creative problem solving and reported sources of satisfaction from the practice of medicine are influenced by the induction of positive affect among physicians.

Physicians (internists) randomly assigned to the positive affect group received a small package of candy; the control group received nothing. The physicians were told that the reason for the study was to analyze how an internist solves a clinical case. The positive affect group was told that the bag of candy was a small token of appreciation for their willingness to volunteer for the study.

The affect group scored better on the creativity measure than did the control group. Regarding practice satisfaction, all physicians perceived humanism as more important than extrinsic motivation as a source of satisfaction from the practice of medicine. However, a significant interaction between affect and source of satisfaction revealed that the affect group attributed more importance to humanism and less relative importance to extrinsic motivation compared with the control group. In contrast, physicians in a third condition, in which they read phrases reflective of the humanistic satisfactions from medicine, did not differ from the control group in the creativity test or in the practice-satisfaction questionnaire. They conclude:

- Induction of positive affect among physicians improves their creative problem solving and influences the source of practice satisfaction they report;
- Induction of positive affect in clinical settings seems possible, despite the serious nature of the work that takes place in these settings. Feelings of success and competence, pleasant interactions with co-workers and patients, a sense of helping people and being appreciated, as well as the everyday events that sustain enjoyment in many work settings are only a few of the ways in which positive affect may be introduced in clinical settings;
- In facilitating creativity, positive affect promotes the clinician's ability to see relatedness among concepts, ideas, and symptoms, enabling him to formulate an appropriate diagnostic list and thus enhancing medical diagnosis and decision making;

- Induction of positive affect sensitises physicians to humanistic concerns.

Hershberger, a family physician, promotes mental and emotional well-being (2005). As part of health promotion or primary prevention, a family physician may frequently encourage patients to be physically active. Although not currently part of the culture of family medicine, it is reasonable to think about mental health promotion and the development of life satisfaction in a similar vein. While some of the most common physician-patient communication strategies appropriately emphasize eliciting negative emotions, similar strategies can be used for helping patients share good experiences and the associated positive emotions. Happy people have better quality of life, and research in the behavioral, social, and medical sciences is continuing to identify other benefits of happiness, including better health. The promotion of mental and emotional well-being can legitimately be viewed as synergistic with the promotion of physical health. One of the identified, and perhaps most influential, pathways between positive outlooks/moods and better physical health is health behavior. This has been found in the relationship between optimism and health and also in longitudinal research demonstrating that individuals with positive views of aging tend to live longer. Perhaps family physicians who begin to give more attention to their own happiness, satisfaction, and meaning in life will be most likely to promote the same in patient care. Family medicine educators, in particular, are in an excellent position to emphasize the promotion of emotional well-being as an important part of comprehensive care. The starting point is the adoption of the perspective that such an endeavor can (and arguably should) be a part of family medicine.

10

Homework Assignments

Only a small change is needed

Steve de Shazer (1985, p. 33)

Introduction

In traditional CBT, homework assignments are considered important. For example, self-monitoring is the most widely used adjunct to CBT and is almost invariably used both at the initial assessment stage and to monitor subsequent change.

In Positive CBT, self-monitoring and other homework assignments are only important if the client thinks it is useful, because change in the viewing, doing, and feeling already occurs during and not only after the sessions. Some clients even struggle with the terms "homework" and "task." They remind them of their school days and not everyone has positive memories of doing homework. Instead of saying "homework," the Positive CBT therapist may speak of "suggestions for something to do between now and the next appointment," thus avoiding any possible negative associations. Presenting homework or tasks as an "experiment" or even a "small experiment" may also make it easier for clients to try it, because it alleviates the pressure to be successful at accomplishing the task. Before coming up with these suggestions, it is useful to ask clients whether they want to do homework anyway. If clients say that they don't have any need for it, they will probably have a good reason: perhaps they don't consider it necessary or useful, or maybe they don't have time before the next session. In those instances, the therapist needn't come up with suggestions.

Practicing Positive CBT: From Reducing Distress to Building Success, First Edition. Fredrike Bannink.
© 2012 John Wiley & Sons, Ltd. Published 2012 by John Wiley & Sons, Ltd.

The importance of homework as seen in traditional CBT is no longer deemed useful in Solution-focused Brief Therapy. De Shazer (1985, p. 21): "We found that we could get as much information when the client did not perform the task as when the client did perform the task. Not only that, we also found that accepting non-performance as a message about the client's way of doing things (rather than as a sign of 'resistance') allowed us to develop a cooperating relationship with clients which might not include task assignments. This was a shock to us because we had assumed that tasks were almost always necessary to achieve behavioural change. Thus, we became more successful with more clients in a fewer number of sessions."

General Suggestions

At the end of each Positive CBT session, the therapist has the option to offer the client some suggestions. These are intended to direct clients' attention to those aspects of their experiences and situations that are most useful in reaching their goals. In offering these suggestions, it is important for the therapist to keep the following three questions in mind:

1. Do I have a visitor-, a complainant-, or a customer-relationship with this client? (See Chapter 5 for a detailed description of these terms.)
2. Does the client have a well-defined goal?
3. Are there spontaneous or deliberate exceptions related to the client's goal?

In a visitor-relationship, in which the client is mandated, no assignments are given. After all, the problem has not yet been defined, nor is there any talk of a goal or related exceptions. It may be that persons in the client's environment have a problem with him or feel concern. In that case, with these persons in the environment there is often a complainant-relationship. The professional goes along with the client's worldview; extends acknowledgment and compliments the client on his personal strengths and resources and for coming to the therapist's office, and he proposes another appointment to continue to find out with the client what would be the best thing for him to do.

In a complainant-relationship, in which the client does not see himself as part of the problem and/or solution but thinks someone else or something else has to change, only observational tasks are assigned. To a client in a complainant-relationship, who cannot name exceptions or a goal or who has vague complaints, the therapist may assign one of the following observational tasks:

- Pay attention to what happens in your life that gives you the sense that this problem can be solved;
- Reflect on what you would like to accomplish with these sessions;
- Pay attention to what is going well and should stay the same or pay attention to what happens in your life that you would like to continue to happen;
- Observe the positive moments in your life so that you can talk about them next time we meet;

- Pay attention to the times when things are going better so that you can talk about them next time;
- If a scaling question (see Chapter 6) has been asked: Observe when you are one point higher on the scale and what you and/or (significant) others are doing differently then;
- Pay attention to what gives you hope that your problem can be solved.

The use of an observation task implies that the exceptions can occur again and can contribute to the client feeling more hopeful. Observation tasks also indicate that useful information is to be found within the client's own realm of experience (De Jong and Berg, 2002).

De Shazer (1988) found it useful to add an element of prediction. He believes that the value of such a task derives from its suggestive power. If there are exceptions already, a "prediction task" suggests that they will occur again, maybe even sooner than the client imagines. If the client predicts a better day, he or she will be more inclined to look for signs of confirmation (a "positive self-fulfilling prophecy"). A client in a complainant-relationship, who is able to describe spontaneous exceptions, receives a prediction task:

- Predict what tomorrow will be like, find an explanation for why the day turned out the way it did tomorrow evening, and then make a new prediction for the following day;
- Pay attention to exactly what happens when an exception manifests itself so that you can tell me more about it: What is different then, and what are (significant) others doing differently?
- With a client in a complainant-relationship, who thinks the other person is the problem: Pay attention to the times when the other person does more of what you want, to what is different then, and to what he/she sees you do then that is helpful to him or her;
- Pay attention to what the other person does that is useful or pleasant and to the difference it makes so that you can talk about it next time.

In a *customer-relationship*, in which the client sees himself as part of the problem and/or solution and is motivated to change, behavioral *and* observational tasks may be assigned. If the client in a customer-relationship is able to clearly formulate his or her goal and find exceptions, the therapist can make the following suggestions:

- Continue with what works and pay attention to what else you're doing that is helpful that you hadn't noticed before (a combination of a behavioral and an observational task);
- Continue to find out what works best for you (a combination of a behavioral and observational task);
- Do more of what works;
- Do the easiest thing that works;

- Think about what else might help;
- Do a piece of the miracle or the goal (as an experiment);
- Discover more about seemingly coincidental exceptions;
- Predict the seemingly coincidental exceptions and explain the result.

If the client in a customer-relationship seems motivated but does not (yet) have a clear picture of the miracle or the goal and is unable to find exceptions, or if there is a power struggle between two or more clients, suggest that the client or clients "Do something else, preferably something unexpected, and note the difference it makes."

If the client in a customer-relationship does have a clear picture of the miracle or goal but is unable to find exceptions, the therapist can give the following homework suggestions:

- Pretend the miracle has happened. In the coming week, pretend for a day (or part of a day) that the miracle has happened and pay attention to the differences it makes;
- In the coming week, pretend for one day that you are 1 or 2 points higher on the scale and pay attention to the differences it makes. Pay special attention to the reactions of people who are important to you.

As a result, Positive CBT prevents unnecessary battles (referred to as "resistance" or "noncompliance" in problem-focused therapies) between the professional and the client. If a client hasn't done the agreed-upon homework, the problem-focused professional will talk to the client about the importance of doing the homework and will want to know why the client failed to do the homework. The Positive CBT therapist will be more inclined to say that he thinks it's fine that the client hasn't done the homework, as the client undoubtedly had a good reason not to; he probably did something that worked better and the therapist invites him to talk about that. In this way, cooperation with the client is improved.

In my 30 years of practicing as a CBT trainer and supervisor I have observed that one of the best ways to ruin the therapist-client alliance is when an ongoing visitor- or complainant-relationship is not addressed and the client is given further behavioral tasks to perform when he is not yet or no longer motivated to carry them out.

It is important that the suggestions that the client receives be doable and realistic. The key is to keep it simple. Offering one or at most two suggestions is sufficient. In order to remember what the suggestions are, the client may write them down before the end of the session. The homework suggestion is often concluded with the phrase "So that you can tell me what's going better next time" (with behavioral tasks for clients in a customer-relationship) or "So that you can tell me something about it next time" (with observational tasks for clients in a complainant-relationship). In other words, the therapist implies that the client will have something to relate at the next session.

Case 10.1

Her family doctor has sent a woman for CBT. The woman agrees with her doctor that she is not feeling well: she is showing symptoms of depression lately. The relationship with the client quickly turns into a customer-relationship, especially when the therapist acknowledges the fact that the family doctor has insisted on therapy, even when the client was not sure she needed it. As a suggestion for homework the client is asked what she herself would be willing to do in order to feel better but also what she thinks the family doctor would like to see different and what the latter thinks the client should do in order to feel well again. In this way, it is as if the family doctor is also present in the room. By carrying out her own ideas for improvement and the ideas she thinks the doctor has, she manages after a few sessions to get back on track.

Basic Homework Assignments

Walter and Peller (1992), mention four basic homework tasks. These tasks show some overlap with the general suggestions mentioned previously.

1. Observe for positives: "Between now and the next time that you come in, we would like you to notice what is going on in your life (marriage, family, work, etc.) that you would like to see continue."
2. Do more of the positives or exceptions when these are perceived as deliber-ate and within the client's control: "Keep up what you are doing that is helpful and take notice of what you are doing that is helpful so that you can tell us about it next time."
3. Find out how the spontaneous exceptions are happening: "We would like to suggest that on the odd-numbered days of the week you pretend to feel different and see what happens. We know that you might not always feel that way, in fact, you might feel the same old way. However, we think there is some potential in how you act and think differently when you do. So, every other day, pretend to feel different and on the even-numbered days just do as you normally do. Let us know what differences you notice."
4. Do some small piece of the hypothetical solution: "We would like to suggest that you might want to experiment with this new idea. Because you tend to be a giving person and being proactive might seem a bit awkward at first, you might want to do just a small piece of it to try it on for size."

Walter and Peller urge their clients to observe rather than to do something when they sense in the session that their clients may be feeling somewhat hesitant about change (e.g., there is a complainant-relationship with the client). The thought of doing something might seem too big of a step. The observational task might not seem as threatening. They might ask: "We would like to suggest that between now and the next time you come in you notice what you are doing or what is different when you are acting even the slightest bit more the way you want to act. Make mental notes, if not written ones, so you can tell us about it next time." This task assumes that clients are already doing some of what they want and does not require them to do anything in the areas where they might be fearful.

Since clients do not have the pressure to do anything different, they might be more likely to observe what they are already doing. By doing this, they will find more exceptions to enumerate in the next session. Also for clients who like to think about changes first before they take action, this observational task seems to be a good fit.

Case 10.2

In a Positive CBT therapy the therapist gives the client this suggestion: Between now and the next time we meet, I would like you to observe, so you can describe to me the next time we meet, what happens in your life (or in your relationship in the case of couples therapy) that you want to continue to have happen. This is the so-called "first formula task." This intervention is an attempt to define therapy as dealing with the present and the future, rather than the past. The therapist expects something worthwhile to happen and this is opposite to what clients expect to happen. From this perspective, the assignment lets the clients know that the therapist expects change and that he is confident that change will occur. This assignment is an easy task for clients to cooperate with, since it does not call for anything different. Only observations are required. This is something clients will do anyway, and the assignment attempts just to direct the focus of their observations.

Self-monitoring

As explained in Chapter 6, in traditional CBT self-monitoring of symptoms is used to gain a more accurate description of behaviors (rather than relying on recall) to help adapt the intervention in relation to client progress and to provide clients with feedback about their progress. It is a means of helping the client to become an active, collaborative participant in their own therapy by identifying and appraising how they react to events (in terms of their own physiological reactions, behaviors, cognitions, and feelings). Self-monitoring is often integrated into the therapy, both in the sessions and as part of homework assignments.

The difference between traditional CBT and Positive CBT is that the self-monitoring in Positive CBT is not (only) about clients' symptoms and problems but (also) about clients' strengths and about exceptions to the problem. When clients use this form of positive self-monitoring they may feel more competent and can choose to do more of what works to change their situation for the better.

If the self-monitoring pertains to frequency, it is concerned with how often the desired situation or behavior (or cognition or feeling) occurs. For instance, how often does the client manage to remain calm or even just a little bit calmer in stressful situations, which would otherwise elicit a panic attack? How does the client already manage to have (more) functional cognitions in these situations? This may be followed by additional competence questions, for example, "How did you succeed in doing that?" In other words, the objective is to find exceptions. If the self-monitoring concerns intensity, it asks the client to rate positive emotions associated with the desired situation or behavior/cognition instead of the negative emotion associated with the undesired behavior/cognition.

In the following section you will find a description of several ways of positive self-monitoring: self-monitoring of strengths, of exceptions to the problem, journaling of strengths, positive journaling, journaling gratitude, writing a letter from your future, and training optimism.

Self-monitoring of strengths

Set up a tracking system to monitor your experiences throughout the day. Track one or more of the strengths (see Chapter 4 for an overview of the 24 character strengths or do the VIA strengths test on the Internet) you are using hour by hour; you might need an alarm or another external cue to remind yourself to closely track the strengths you use.

Self-monitoring of exceptions

There are three ways of using self-monitoring in Positive CBT: 1. Using a "thought record"; 2. Observing positive changes; and 3. Monitoring exceptions to the problem (see Chapter 6). In monitoring exceptions, special attention should be paid to the ways in which these exceptions are different from problem times. Whereas in traditional CBT the therapist would explore the who, what, when, and where of client problems, the Positive CBT therapist is interested in exploring the who, what, when, and where of exceptions. Exceptions-finding questions are:

• When didn't you experience the problem after expecting that you would?
• What happens as the problem ends or starts to end?
• Could the problem be worse? How come it isn't worse?
• When was the problem less of a problem (even just a little bit)?
• What is better already?

Appendix H contains a journal for the monitoring of exceptions.

Exercise 10.1

Keep a diary for a week. Pay attention to the things in your life that you would like to keep the way they are because they are already working (these may be exceptions to the problem), and write them down. Pay yourself a compliment at the end of every day based on the things written in your diary, and write it down as well.

Journaling of strengths

Write about your strengths; explore them in this intra-personal way. For example, if you want to build upon your strength called prudence, consider a situation you are conflicted about, and write about the costs and benefits of both sides.

Positive journaling

Write down daily three good things that happened each day for a week. This is called the "three blessings exercise." These three things can be small in importance (I went to bed early tonight as I had planned) or big (The guy I've liked for months asked me out). Next to each positive event, write about one of the following: How come this good thing happened? What does this mean to me? How can I have more of this good thing in the future?

Journaling gratitude

Consider buying a handsome blank book to be your "gratitude journal." In it, describe the things for which you are grateful each day. Beyond simply listing good things in your life, one effective strategy is to describe why each good thing happened, in a few sentences. Doing so draws your eye to the precursors of good events.

Writing a letter from your future

Write a letter from your future self to your current self from X years from now (X stands for what is relevant in your situation: one year, two years, or even five or ten years).

Describe that you are doing fine, where you are, what you are doing, what you have gone through to get there, and so on. Tell yourself the crucial things you realized or did to get there. And finally give yourself some sage and compassionate advice from the future.

Training optimism

Seligman shifted his research from "learned helplessness" to "learned optimism." Clients can learn to have more optimistic thoughts, even when they are pessimistic (see Chapter 7). He battles with his own pessimistic outlook: "I am not a default optimist. I am a dyed-in-the-wool pessimist; I believe that only pessimists can write sober and sensible books about optimism, and I use the techniques that I wrote about in *Learned Optimism* every day. I take my own medicine, and it works for me" (Seligman, 2002, p. 24).

Every night before going to bed write down a sentence about the most pleasant event of that day, as if the event was brought about by something general, global, and within your control (because I am . . . or because I can . . .). As an example: Today my colleague offered to help me out, because I am also someone who would help another person if needed and he knows that.

Also write down a sentence about the most unpleasant event of that day, as if that event were brought about by something specific, temporary, and outside of your control (because X, then Y). As an example: Because the bus was delayed, I was not able to get to the appointment with my dentist on time.

Behavioral Experiments

There are three types of behavioral experiments, as described in Chapter 8:

1. Experimental manipulation of the environment. This necessitates doing something that is different to what the client would usually do in a particular situation ("do something else for a change").
2. Observational experiments, in that it is either not possible or not necessary to manipulate key variables. Instead clients set out to observe and gather evidence that is relevant to their specific negative thoughts or beliefs.
3. Discovery-oriented experiments, when clients have little or no idea what will happen when they undertake a behavioral experiment and need to collect data systematically in order to "build a theory."

De Shazer (1985) developed "skeleton keys," keys that fit different locks. The skeleton keys are based on these three types of behavior experiments. De Shazer's "formula tasks" (see later) are good examples of skeleton keys. Having a different key (solution) for each lock (the problem) is unnecessary, and there is no need for the lock to be analyzed first; interventions can initiate change even when the therapist does not know in detail what the problem is. The only thing the interventions need to ensure is that a new behavioral pattern can emerge. The key to building a new habit or "positive addiction" (see Chapter 8) is to practice the behavior, over and over. De Shazer provides the following examples of skeleton keys.

The write, read, and burn task

This task can be used if the client is plagued by obsessive or depressive thoughts. De Shazer described a client who was obsessed with her ex-partner months after breaking off the relationship. She felt guilty and kept asking herself what she had done wrong. The thoughts had even grown into nightmares. After normalizing the problem, De Shazer gave the client the following task in order for her to move on with her life. At the same time every day, she was to retire to a comfortable place for at least an hour and no more than an hour and a half. During that time, she had to focus and, on all odd-numbered days, write down all her good and bad memories of her ex-partner. She had to keep writing the entire time, even if it meant that she ended up writing some things down more than once. On even-numbered days, she had to read her notes from the previous day and then burn them. If the unwanted thoughts came to her at times other than during the scheduled hour, she had to tell herself, "I have other things to do now and I will think about it when the scheduled hour has arrived," or she had to make a note to remind herself to think about it at the scheduled time. After just a few days, the thoughts had largely disappeared.

The structured-fight task

This task can be used if clients complain that their arguments never lead anywhere. This task consists of three steps:

1. A coin is flipped to determine who gets to go first;
2. The winner may berate the other person for 10 minutes, without interruption;
3. The other person may do the same, also without interruption. Ten minutes of silence follow before the next round is begun with another coin toss.

The do-something-different task

This task can be used if the client complains about another person and claims to have "already tried everything." Solutions involve doing something that is different from what didn't work before. De Shazer offered the following example: A 10-year-old boy was apprehended for prowling around his school. He had broken in to get his homework, which he'd forgotten; however, he refused to answer the policeman's questions. Once the policeman had tried everything to get him to talk, he threatened to hold his own breath until the boy explained why he had broken into the school. This proved too much for the boy. He revealed that he had broken in to retrieve his homework so as not to get a failing grade.

The pay attention to what you do when you overcome the urge task

This task can be used to help the client find and use exceptions. It can be used as an alternative to the do-something-different task. Although the client will often say that the problematic behavior (e.g., drug use, gambling, nail-biting) always occurs, there are often circumstances under which the problematic behavior does not manifest itself. These are exceptions on which one can build, because they are already part of the client's repertoire. This task presupposes that the client definitely conquers the urge every now and then and that he may be doing something different in order to overcome the urge. The client's attention is directed to his behavior, not to any internal sensation. In some cases, it may also be useful to draw attention to what other people do in comparable situations.

The first session formula task

This task can be used to shift the client's attention from the past to the present and the future, and to increase the expectancy of change. This task implies that the professional has positive expectations. The professional says: "Between now and the next time we see each other, pay attention to what happens in your life (e.g., your family, marriage, relationship, work) that you would like to continue to see happening."

Pretend tasks

If a client has multiple options and is unable to choose, an observation task may be useful:

- Suggest that the client observes what happens that gives a clearer indication of what he should do so that you can talk about it together the next time.

- The client can flip a coin and pretend. Every night before going to sleep, the client flips a coin and the next day he or she carries out what has been agreed upon on the basis of the coin toss. Heads may mean that the client pretends to have made decision A, for example, to stay with his wife, and tails means he pretends to have made decision B, that is, to leave his wife. This may bring the client more clarity so that he can reach a decision. This task is a behavioral task.
- With problems of choice, projection into the future can be a useful technique: The client imagines how he or she will be doing in the future (in one year, five years, or ten years) if he or she decides to do A or B (or even C). The client can also look back from the future to the present and examine what helped him make a decision.

If a client has strong negative emotions that cause nothing to change, the therapist may propose the following to the client as an experiment:

- When you are angry/sad, just pretend you are not. Observe the difference and see what happens.
- Pretend you feel differently (e.g., on odd-numbered days).

These too are behavioral tasks, which require motivation to change on the client's part (i.e., the client must be in a customer-relationship).

Mindfulness exercise

Find a quiet place where you can sit comfortably without being disturbed. Rest your hands lightly on your lap, palms up. Close your eyes and take a few deep breaths and breathe normally. Just let it be, and just continue to observe your breath. The goal in attending to your breath is to practice being present, here and now. There is no need to suppress your thoughts, just let them be and become aware of them as they come and fade away again.

Mindfulness exercises can be used to cultivate loving-kindness (see Chapter 3). It is a bit like guided imagery in which you reflect on positive feelings for others around you. First reflect on a person (or animal) for whom you feel warm and compassionate feelings. Once these feelings take hold, creating positivity in you, gently let go of the image and simply hold the feeling. Then extend that feeling to yourself, cherish yourself as deeply and purely as you would cherish your own newborn child. Next, radiate your warm and compassionate feelings to others, first to someone you know well, then gradually calling to mind other friends and family members and then all people with whom you are connected, even remotely. Ultimately, extend your feelings of love and kindness to all people and creatures of the earth: may they all be happy (Fredrickson, 2009, p. 209).

Compassion exercise

An important way of compassionately engaging with different and problematic parts of the self is in imagery. When clients have practiced this a little, they can learn to focus their compassionate self. Suppose you are very anxious about something. Sit quietly and engage in your breathing and then imagine yourself as a compassionate person. When you can feel that expanding and growing inside you, then imagine you can see your anxious self in front of you. Look at his or her facial expression; note the feelings rushing through them. Just sit and feel compassion, and send compassionate feelings out to that anxious self. Try to surround that anxious self in compassion and understanding of the torment of anxiety. For now you are not trying to do anything other than experience compassion and acceptance for your anxiety. Imagine giving as much compassion and understanding as that anxious part needs. You may want to imagine what happens to the anxious part when it actually has all of the understanding and support it needs (Gilbert, 2010, p. 171).

Design yourself a beautiful day exercise

Next Saturday, set the day aside, and design yourself a beautiful day. Plan the enjoyable things which you will be doing that day, where you will be, and with whom.

Design the beautiful day or even beautiful half day in a way that uses your personal strengths and talents. If for example, one of your main strengths is your curiosity and love of learning, your day might include a trip to the museum or simply reading a book that you have been meaning to read. When your beautiful day arrives employ your savoring and mindfulness skills to enhance these pleasures.

Gratitude visit

Close your eyes. Call up the face of someone still alive who years ago did something or said something that changed your life for the better. Someone who you never properly thanked; someone you could meet face-to-face. Got a face? Write a letter of gratitude to this person and deliver it in person. The letter should be concrete and about three hundred words: be specific about what the person did for you and how it affected your life. Let this person know what you are doing now, and mention how you often remember what he did. Once you have written the testimonial, call the person and tell him you'd like to visit him, but be vague about the purpose of the meeting; this exercise is much more fun when it is a surprise. When you meet him, take your time reading your letter. Notice his reactions as well as yours. If he interrupts you as you read, say that you really want him to listen until you are done. After you have read the letter (every word), discuss the content and your feelings for each other. Research shows that you will be happier and less depressed one month from now.

Exercise 10.2

Here is a Positive CBT exercise for more gratitude in four steps. By doing this exercise you will experience more satisfaction and well-being. The four steps are as follows:

1. *Focus on some of your nongrateful thoughts;*
2. *Formulate some grateful thoughts instead;*
3. *Replace your nongrateful thoughts with your grateful thoughts;*
4. *Translate the inner positive feeling into action: do something with it.*

Research shows that performing an act of kindness produces the single most reliable momentary increase in well-being of any exercises tested. Find one wholly unexpected kind thing to do tomorrow and just do it. Notice what happens to your mood.

Research done by Lyubomirsky (2008) shows that performing five new acts of kindness in a single day contributes to feelings of happiness. So set yourself the goal of performing five new acts of kindness in a single day (however, don't do them every day, since this may become boring and less effective). Aim for actions that really make a difference and come at some cost to you, such as donating blood, helping your neighbor with her yard work, or figuring out a better way that your ailing father might manage his chronic pain. Be both creative and thoughtful and assess what those around you might need most. Make a point to carry them all out on a single day. At the end of the day notice the good feelings that come with increasing your kindness. For lasting impact, make your kindness day a recurring ritual and be creative each week. Find new ways to make a positive difference in the lives of others. Try it for a few months and see the difference it makes.

Learn and apply your strengths exercise

First take the online survey of your character strengths at the website www.authentichappiness.com. After completing the survey, you will receive a report that ranks the 24 strengths by the degree to which they characterize you. The report also features your top five strengths and encourages you to reflect on which ones truly resonate for you.

Another way of discovering your strengths is by contacting between 10 and 20 trusted people in your life and ask them to give you three detailed stories about the ways you add value and make important contributions. Once the feedback has arrived, you analyze it, looking for commonalities and themes. Your task is to pull those themes together in a "Reflected Best Self Portrait," a short essay that captures the wisdom within the narrative data you have gathered and studied. Once you have learned your strengths, redesign your job and life so you can use them every day (Fredrickson, 2009, p. 206).

Talk about your strengths exercise

Talk with others about your strengths, tell stories about how your strengths have helped you and were at play when you were at your best. Use your strengths while you are in conversation; for example, if you want to build upon your curiosity, ask questions with a sense of genuine interest.

Research on so-called "capitalization," telling others about positive events in one's life, shows that this generates additional affect, over and above positive affect associated with the event itself. There are several possible mechanisms for such an effect. First, sharing a positive event with others requires retelling the event, which creates an opportunity for reliving and re-experiencing the event. Furthermore, the communicative act may involve rehearsal and elaboration, both of which seem likely to prolong and enhance the experience by increasing its salience and accessibility in memory. In this way, capitalization builds personal and social resources (Gable, Reis, Impett, and Asher, 2004).

Finally, unlike in problem-focused therapies like traditional CBT, the Positive CBT therapist does not tell the client what he needs to do differently, nor does the client learn new techniques. Nonetheless, Positive CBT has an enormous impact because it demonstrates how a small difference can make a big difference. Therapists do examine with their clients how they can improve certain skills, but that is different from learning new skills that clients do not already possess. My suggestion is therefore not to use the word "learning" anymore and to opt instead for "becoming better at." The word "to learn," which is often used in CBT, assumes that the client has to start from ground zero and thus detracts from what the client has already accomplished, that is, the road already traveled (see Chapter 6).

Routine Outcome Measurement

The average treated client is better off than about 80% of the untreated sample (Duncan, Miller, Wampold, and Hubble, 2010). But unfortunately dropouts are a significant problem and although many of our clients profit from therapy, many do not. Another point of concern is the variability among therapists. Some therapists are much better in getting positive results than others (see Chapter 12). In fact, therapist effectiveness ranges from 20–70%. Moreover, even very effective clinicians seem to be poor at identifying deteriorating clients (Duncan, 2010). Hannan *et al.* (2005) found that although therapists knew the purpose of their study, were familiar with the outcome measures, and were informed that the base rate was likely to be 8%, they accurately predicted deterioration in only 1 out of 550 cases. In other words, therapists did not identify 39 out of the 40 clients who deteriorated!

Other findings were: therapists routinely overestimate their effectiveness; only about 3% of therapists routinely track their outcomes and therapists routinely fail to identify clients who are at risk of deteriorating, drop out, and negative outcome.

The answer to these problems is using feedback as a therapist's compass to successfully navigate a client's unique path to change, something Duncan (2010) calls "practice-based evidence": delivering what works. Therapy should, according to Duncan, be a discovery-oriented journey, anchored by feedback, to manage the uncertainty along the way.

To promote the monitoring of clients' progress the APA Presidential Task Force on Evidence-Based Practice (2006) state: "The application of research evidence to a given patient always involves probabilistic inferences. Therefore, ongoing monitoring of patient progress and adjustment to treatment as needed are essential" (p. 280).

Story 10.1: Brilliant Insights

During the 1950s and 1960s a series of intriguing experiments was conducted on the nature and effect of feedback on human activity. In one study, two participants were exposed to a series of pictures of either healthy or sick cells (Watzlawick, 1976). Neither person in this study could actually see the other and each was given the assignment to learn to distinguish between the two types of cells through a process of trial and error. Small lights marked "right" or "wrong" were the source of feedback they received about their choices.

There was just one "wrinkle" in the experiment, of which both participants were unaware. Only one of them received accurate feedback about their guesses. When the light indicated he had made the right choice, he had indeed guessed correctly. On the other hand, feedback for the second participant was not based on his own but rather on the guesses made by the first participant. Regardless of his choices, in other words, this person was told he was right if the other person had guessed correctly and wrong if the other had been incorrect. Data collected without their knowledge showed, at the conclusion of the experiment, that the first participant had learned to distinguish healthy from sick cells with an 80% rate of accuracy while the second continued to guess at no better than a chance rate.

The two types of feedback also had a distinct and interesting impact on the theories each participant developed over the course of the study to differentiate between healthy and sick cells. The participant who received accurate (reliable) feedback ended the experiment with a very simple, concrete, and parsimonious explanation. The second participant, however, developed a complicated, subtle, and elaborate theory. This person, it must be recalled, had no way of knowing the feedback he received was not contingent on his own responses. Sometimes his responses happened to coincide with the correct answer, sometimes not. Given the inconsistent (unreliable) feedback, this participant was prevented from learning anything about his own actions and choices.

Even these results may not seem all that surprising. Something more troubling occurred when the two participants shared their respective theories with each other. In contrast to what one might hope and expect, the first participant was actually impressed with the complicated, mysterious, and ultimately unreliable theoretical formulations of his co-participant. The second, on the other hand, dismissed the statistically accurate theory of the first as "naïve and simplistic." In subsequent retests during which both participants received accurate feedback about their own guesses, the second continued to guess at little better than a chance rate. The performance of the first participant, however, who was now attempting to put some of the "brilliant" insights of their co-participant into practice, significantly worsened!

Source: Adapted from Watzlawick (1976).

Duncan, Miller, and Sparks (2004) believe that feedback from our clients is essential and improves success. Therapists do not need to know in advance what approach to use for a given diagnosis but rather whether the current relationship is a good fit and is providing benefit, and, if not, they need to be able to adjust and accommodate early enough to maximize the chances of success.

O'Hanlon and Rowan (2003) add to this the importance of transforming the belief patterns of both therapist and client to encompass the possibility of change, thus drawing attention away from beliefs in the impossibility of change, and from ideas that blame, disempower, or invalidate clients, or that see clients as nonaccountable (see Chapter 7).

Until now in traditional psychotherapy – including CBT – the evaluation of progress is usually carried out only at the end of therapy. Progress is measured by a decrease in problematic behavior and it is usually the therapist who decides when to stop therapy. But session-by-session outcome monitoring appears to be essential. Therefore, in Positive CBT the evaluation of progress is done during every session by scaling progress and also at the end of every session. Progress is measured not only by a decrease of problems but also by an increase in the desired behavior or situation, and the Outcome Rating Scale (ORS) and the Session Rating Scale (SRS) are used to obtain feedback from the clients. And what's more, it is usually the client who decides when to stop therapy.

Kuyken, Padesky, and Dudley (2009) state that therapists often consider amelioration of client distress the most important therapy outcome. It is an outcome that CBT therapists generally view as primary, and they assume that their clients share this view. However, a large survey of people receiving mental health services revealed the most important outcomes for clients are: attaining positive mental health qualities such as optimism and self-confidence; a return to one's usual, normal self; a return to usual level of functioning; and relief from symptoms (Zimmerman, McGlinchey, Posternak, *et al.*, 2006).

Therefore, it is helpful to evaluate therapy outcome on both the decrease of problems and the increase of what is wanted instead:

- Amelioration of distress
- Building resilience
- Proactive movement toward positive personal goals.

In the ongoing discussion in psychotherapy between those who advocate empirically supported treatments and those who advocate the importance of common factors, monitoring outcomes may hopefully, in the end, provide a common ground for both.

Client-directed, outcome informed therapy

Miller, Hubble, and Duncan (1996) collected data from 40 years of outcome research in psychotherapy, which provide strong empirical evidence for privileging the client's role in the change process. Clients, not therapists, make therapy work. As a result, therapy should be organized around their resources, their perceptions, their experiences, and their ideas. There need be no a priori assumptions about client problems or solutions, no special questions that are best to ask, and no invariant methodology to follow in order to achieve success. Rather therapists need only take directions from clients: following their lead; adopting their language, worldview, goals, and ideas about the problem; and acknowledging their experiences with, and inclinations about, the change process. The most potent factor of successful outcome, the client and his own propensities for change, are left out of the medical model. It is the client who is the director of the change endeavor, not the therapist.

Traditionally, the effectiveness of treatment has been left up to the judgment of the provider of this treatment. But proof of effectiveness can emerge from the client's perception and experience as a full partner in the therapy process.

The client's theory of change offers ways of integrating many perspectives on therapy. Trusting the client's theory of change requires a focused effort to conduct therapy within the context of the client's unique ideas and circumstances. Research has shown that all model and technique factors only represent 15% of outcome variance at most. They may or may not be useful in the client's circumstances. Therefore theories should be de-emphasized and instead the focus should be on the clients' theories. Exploring their ideas has several advantages:

- It puts the clients center stage in the conversation;
- It enlists the clients' participation;
- It helps ensure the clients' positive experience of the professional;
- It structures the conversation and directs the change process.

According to research, it is the client that matters: his resources, participation, evaluation of the alliance, and his perceptions of the problem and the solutions. The therapist's techniques are only helpful if the client sees them as relevant and credible.

If for example it is the clients' theory of change that it is useful to talk at length about who is wrong and is to blame, the therapist may ask:

- How do you think this will be helpful?
- What are your ideas about the positive effects this will have on your preferred future?
- How may your relationship with the other(s) benefit from this?
- How will you know this will be helpful for you? What needs to be better the next time we meet, so we know this has been useful and we should do more of it?

Conventional wisdom suggests that competence engenders, if not equals, effectiveness. As a result there is a continuing education requirement, designed to ensure that therapists stay abreast of developments that enhance positive outcome of therapy. The vast majority of these trainings do not include any methods for evaluating the effectiveness of the approach. Emphasis is placed on learning skills or techniques of a particular brand or style of therapy.

But this emphasis on competence versus outcome decreases effectiveness and efficiency. Research has shown that there is no or little relationship between the experience level and effectiveness of professionals (Clement, 1994). The data indicate that increasing the amount and type of training and experience that most professionals receive may even lessen their effectiveness! Researchers distinguished successfully between least and most effective therapists (as determined by outcome, Hiatt and Hargrave, 1995). They found that therapists in the low-effectiveness group tended to have been in practice for more years that those in the high-effectiveness group. They also found that the ineffective therapists were unaware that they were ineffective. Even worse, they considered themselves to be as effective as the truly helpful therapists in the study!

Miller, Duncan, and Hubble (1997) state that using client feedback to inform the professional would invite clients to be full and equal partners in all aspects of therapy. Giving clients the perspective of the driver's seat instead of the back of the bus may also enable them to gain confidence that a positive outcome is just down the road. "Systematic assessment of the client's perceptions of progress and fit are important, so the clinician can empirically tailor the therapy to the client's needs and characteristics. Such a process of becoming outcome-informed fits well with how most therapists prefer to think of themselves: sensitive to client feedback and interested in results. Becoming outcome-informed not only amplifies the client's voice, but also offers the most viable, research-tested method to improve effectiveness" (Duncan, Miller, and Sparks, 2004, p. 16). They offer the following equation: Client resources and resilience + client theories of change + client feedback about the fit and benefit of service = client perceptions of preferred outcomes.

Building a culture of feedback

Apart from asking scaling questions about progress during the therapy sessions, in Positive CBT clients are given the Outcome Rating Scale (ORS) at the beginning of each session and the Session Rating Scale (SRS) at the end of each session. At the center of this system is the Outcome Questionnaire 45 (OQ 45), a 45 item measure of client functioning along three dimensions (symptom distress, interpersonal functioning, and social role functioning).

The ORS is a clinical tool, a general outcome instrument, and provides no specific content other than the broad individual, relational, social, and overall domains. The instruction is as follows: Looking back over the last week, including today, help us understand how you have been feeling by rating how well you have been doing in the following areas of your life, where marks to the left on a 10 cm line represent low levels and marks to the right indicate high levels. Administering the ORS at the beginning of each session sets the stage and invites the client into a collaborative partnership.

The SRS is a feedback instrument, divided into the three areas that decades of research have shown to be the qualities of change-producing relationships: 1. the relationship between therapist and client (the alliance), 2. the goals and topics, and 3. the approach or method (the allegiance). Clients are asked to place a mark on each 10 cm line, where low estimates are represented to the left and high to the right. The instruction is as follows: Please rate today's session by placing a mark on the line nearest to the description that best fits your experience.

Each line has a potential of 10, with a grand total possibility of 40. A centimeter ruler can be used to measure the mark of the client on each line and then you can add them up. There is no specific cut-off score between relationships that have "good" or "bad" change potential. Higher scores (above 30) reflect relationships that have better change potential, lower scores suggest the relationship may need some extra attention. In this case, it is the therapist who should ask: "What should I (in my work as a therapist) do differently next time so you (the client(s)) will give higher marks on the scale?" More information about the ORS and SRS can be found in Duncan (2010).

The SRS is an engagement instrument, it opens space for the client's voice about the alliance. There is no magic in the scale itself, it is aimed at starting a conversation with the client, which can be used by the therapist to improve the therapy for this particular client. Dropout rates will be higher if the SRS is forgotten. It is helpful to make a graphic of the results of the ORS and SRS over time (for free downloads and instructions see www. centerforclinicalexcellence.com). This paints a good picture and gives good feedback to the therapist. A small decrease (one point) is a signal that the therapist should discuss the relationship with his client.

"Monitoring progress is essential and dramatically improves the chances of success. You don't really need the perfect approach as much as you need to know whether your plan is working – and if it is not, how to quickly adjust your strategy to maximize the possibility of improvement" (Duncan, 2005, p. 183). An absence of early improvement may substantially decrease the chances of achieving what clients want to achieve with the current methods. Research showed that when no improvement occurred by the third visit, progress was not likely to occur over the entire course of treatment. Moreover, people who did not indicate that therapy was helping by the sixth session were very likely to receive no benefit, despite the length of the therapy. The diagnosis the person had and the type of therapy delivered were not as important in predicting success as knowing whether the treatment that was provided was actually working. Individuals whose therapists got feedback about their client's lack of progress were, at the conclusion of therapy, better off than 65% of those whose therapists did not receive any information. Just knowing that their clients were not benefiting from their therapy allowed these therapists to modify their approaches and promote change. Clients whose therapists had access to progress information, like the SRS, were less likely to get worse with treatment and were twice as likely to achieve a clinically significant change. Nothing else in the history of psychotherapy has been shown to increase effectiveness this much!

Becoming client-centered and outcome-informed is simple and straightforward. Unlike the product-oriented efforts the field has employed so far, outcome management results in significant improvements in effectiveness. Liberated from the traditional focus on models or techniques, therapists will be better able to achieve what they always claimed to have been in the business of doing: assisting change. In Appendix I you will find an example of the SRS.

Reflecting on the Session

The Positive CBT therapist may reflect on sessions in the case of a successful treatment and in the case of stagnation or failure of the treatment. What did work in these sessions and what would I do again next time in a comparable situation? What did not work and what would I do differently next time in a comparable situation? Every therapist does well in any case to reflect for a while on each session he conducts. Reflection may also take place in the company of colleagues, in the form of peer consultation or supervision.

The Positive CBT therapist will ask himself some questions at the end of each session. The questions help him reflect on his contribution to the session. They also help develop his Positive CBT skills. The questions from the interactional matrix (see Appendix F) can also be helpful in this respect. Some questions for the therapist about his professional performance are:

- Suppose I were to conduct this session again. What would I do differently or better next time?
- What would my client say I could do differently or better?
- What difference would that make for him?
- What difference would that make for me?
- Suppose I conduct sessions in the future with a client who has comparable problems. Which interventions would I use again and which wouldn't I?
- How satisfied do I think my client is with my performance (on a scale of 10 to 0)?
- What would he say about how I've managed to get to that number?
- What would it look like for him if I were one point higher on the scale?
- How satisfied am I myself with my performance (on a scale of 10 to 0)?
- How did I manage to get to that number?
- What would one point higher on the scale look like?
- What difference would that make for the treatment?
- What positive aspects of this treatment stand out?
- What useful information have I received from my client?
- Which of his strengths and competencies and features can I compliment him on?
- What does my client want to achieve in meeting with me?
- What strengths and competencies can my client utilize to solve the problem that brings him here and to reach his goal?
- What strengths and resources did I fail to capitalize on?
- What kind of resources from his environment can help my client? Which resources are already available?
- What do I see in my client (these partners/this family/this team) that tells me that he can reach his goal?

Berg and Steiner (2003) suggest the following questions for the therapist if there has been no progress:

- If I were to ask my client how my contribution has helped, even if only a little bit, what would he respond?
- What does my client consider to be a sign of a successful outcome?
- How realistic is that outcome?
- What do I myself consider to be a sign of success?
- If my client's and my views differ, what needs to be done so that we can work on the same goal?

- On a scale of 0 to 10, where would my client say he is right now?
- What needs to happen to bring my client one point closer to 10?

With the second and subsequent sessions, the same critical self-reflective process can be used to monitor our clinical thinking and therapeutic actions closely with each client we work with. A follow-up session a few months after the treatment has ended may provide information not only about the client's current situation but also about what has worked and what is going better since the last session. Moreover, clients generally experience this form of aftercare as solicitous and pleasant. A short follow-up session may also take place via telephone, Skype, or e-mail. In my opinion, such follow-up sessions should be conducted more frequently than has been customary.

11

Subsequent Sessions

Turn your face to the sun and the shadows will fall behind you

Anonymous

Introduction

In subsequent sessions the client and therapist carefully explore what has improved. The therapist asks for a detailed explanation of the positive exceptions, gives compliments, and emphasizes the client's personal input in finding solutions. At the end of every session the client is asked whether he feels another meeting is still necessary or useful and, if so, when he would like to return. In fact, in many cases the client feels it is not necessary to return or schedules an appointment further into the future than is typical in other forms of psychotherapy.

According to De Shazer (1994), the goal of the second and each subsequent session is:

- To ask questions about the time between the sessions in such a way that one can definitely discern some progress: If one looks carefully and creatively, one can (virtually) always find improvements;
- To see whether the client feels that what the professional and the client did in the previous session has been useful and has given him or her the sense that things are going better;
- To help the client find out what he or she is doing or what has happened that has led to improvements so that he or she will know what to do more of or more often;
- To help the client work out whether the improvements have caused things to go well enough that further sessions are not necessary;
- To ensure that the professional and the client will not do more of what doesn't work, if the client does not see any improvement, and to find a new approach.

Practicing Positive CBT: From Reducing Distress to Building Success, First Edition. Fredrike Bannink.
© 2012 John Wiley & Sons, Ltd. Published 2012 by John Wiley & Sons, Ltd.

Progress

The opening question in each subsequent session is a question about progress: "What is better?" The question implicitly suggests that something *is* going better and that one only needs to pay attention to *what* is going better. Therefore, the question is fundamentally different from "Is anything going better?", "How are you?", or "How have things been since our last session?" With this opening question about the client's progress, the Positive CBT therapist determines the answer he receives.

At the beginning of therapy clients usually react to the question with surprise because they don't expect it. Sometimes clients initially respond with "Nothing," because that is, in fact, what they experience from their point of view; they have not yet given any thought to anything better. In that case, the professional can ask questions about the recent past and look for times when the problem was absent or was less of a problem. Working on the assumption that one can always find exceptions if one only looks for them (see Chapter 4), the therapist asks questions not about *whether* there are exceptions but about *when* there are or have been exceptions.

It has been my experience that if the therapist opens every session with this question, clients begin to anticipate it and start to reflect on the answer prior to the session.

In each subsequent session one may also ask the four basic solution-focused questions presented in Chapter 4. They may pertain to each individual session (e.g., "What are your best hopes for this session?") or to the entire therapy, or even to the client's entire life.

De Jong and Berg (2002) developed the acronym "EARS" to distinguish the activities in subsequent sessions. E stands for "eliciting" (drawing out stories about progress and exceptions). A stands for "amplifying." First, the client is asked to describe in detail the differences between the moment when the exception takes place and problematic moments. Afterwards, one examines how the exception took place, especially what role the client played in it. R stands for "reinforcing." The therapist reinforces the successes and factors that have led to the exceptions through the meticulous exploration of the exceptions and by complimenting the client. S, finally, stands for "start again." The therapist goes on with the question: "What else is going better?"

Exercise 11.1

Start the next ten or twenty subsequent sessions with the question: "What is better?" Dare to ask that question! You will notice that your clients will start anticipating and prior to the next session will reflect on what has improved, so they can tell you about this. And if – unfortunately – the answer is that nothing is better or things are even worse, just acknowledge their disappointment, take a look at the possibilities that follow, and find out how you can stay on a positive track with your clients.

Clients can provide four different kinds of responses to the question as to what is better (Selekman, 1997; Bannink, 2007a, 2007b, 2009e, 2010a). How well clients are doing and whether the homework suits them determine whether the therapist should continue on the same path or should do something else. Therapists must always carefully tailor their questions and homework assignments to the relationship they have with the client (i.e., whether there is a visitor-, complainant-, or customer-relationship between the therapist and the client). It is important to keep in mind that clients want their problem solved, however pessimistic or skeptical they may be. For that reason, it is important to listen closely and to examine *how* clients want to change. In subsequent sessions, it is vital to optimize the relationship with the clients and to retain the progress already made and build on it. In addition, one needs to verify whether the homework has been useful and meaningful, and any possible regression must be caught. The four possible responses are: 1. things are better, 2. we disagree (if there is more than one client), 3. things are the same, and 4. things are worse.

When things are going better, one can generally tell by the client's appearance. He usually looks better and often identifies many things that have changed. The therapist does well to ask for details about the improvements, to emphasize the difference from how things were before, and to pay compliments. Questions for clients who report that things are better are:

- How did you make that happen?
- How do you manage to . . . ?
- How did you manage to take such a big step?
- How did you come up with that fine idea?
- What did you tell yourself to help you do it that way?
- What do you have to keep doing so that that will happen more often?
- How is that different for you?
- Suppose we see each other again in a month. What additional changes will you be able to tell me about then?
- How do I know that you have enough confidence to halt the sessions now?
- What ideas do you now have (e.g., about yourself) that are different from the ideas you had before?
- What would you have to do to go back to square one?
- Can you indicate on a scale of 10 to 0, where 10 means that things are fine the way they are, where you are today?
- How will you celebrate your victory over the problem?
- Who will you invite to this party?
- What will you say in the speech that you give at the party?

At the end of the every session, the therapist asks: "Is it necessary or would it be useful for you to come back?" If so: "When would you like to come back?" If the client does not have a preference, the professional can gradually increase the time between sessions, to indicate his confidence that the client will work things out him or herself.

Homework suggestions for clients who report that things are better are:

- Go on with what works;
- Do more of what works.

If there are multiple clients and they disagree about the progress they have made or are concerned that they have not made enough progress, it is wise to normalize matters. The therapist can make it clear that clients often make progress by taking three steps forward and then taking one or two steps back. In any case, it is a good idea to begin by taking a look, together with the clients, at what *is* going better, even if it is only going better to a very small degree. Those differences can be amplified and the therapist can pay compliments. Moreover, he can point out that small differences may lead to significant changes later on.

A useful question for clients who disagree is: "Suppose we see each other again in four weeks, what changes would you like to have achieved by then?" If any of the clients remain concerned, the therapist may ask competence questions (especially with complainants who often use "Yes, but" phrases):

- Could the situation be worse?
- How come things aren't worse?
- What steps have you taken to ensure that things don't get worse?
- What else helps to ensure that things don't get worse?
- What difference does that make?

The therapist can ask himself the following questions:

- Do I have a customer-, complainant-, or visitor-relationship with these clients?
- Is there a goal and has it been formulated well?
- What homework suggestions would suit these clients best?
- Can I present the clients with a number of homework suggestions to choose from?

Homework suggestions for clients who disagree are:

- If a client tries to undermine another client's attempts to achieve a desired behavior, the therapist can suggest an observation exercise. For a week or longer, each of the clients observes what desired behavior the other client displays and makes a note of it. Clients bring their notes to the next session. They are not allowed to go over the notes together before the session;
- If the homework suggestion was helpful, but if one or both of the clients did not find it a pleasant or useful exercise, the therapist can examine together with the clients how the suggestion may be improved;
- If more exceptions are needed, the therapist may propose the "surprise task," a playful way to challenge a person's fixed ideas. It is agreed with all clients that they will do something (either subtle or highly noticeable) to surprise

the other in a positive way. What that might be is left to each client. The other may then guess what the surprise was and talk about it at the next session. Children and adolescents in particular take great pleasure in these surprise tasks;

- If both clients are stuck in a pattern of negative interaction, the therapist may also propose the "do-something-different task." Here, too, clients themselves decide what they will do differently in the upcoming period. What they do is immaterial; the purpose is to break a fixed pattern. For example, during a course of family therapy, there has been frequent mention of serious arguments because the adolescent son and daughter did not follow the parents' rules. During the next argument, both parents lie down on the floor and stop speaking. The children were so shocked that they came along to subsequent sessions because they were worried about their parents;
- Another possibility is the "pretend-the-miracle-has-happened task." All clients are instructed to pretend for a day or two (or for a shorter period of time if that proves too ambitious, e.g., part of a day or an hour) that the miracle has happened. They are asked to pay attention to the difference that the task makes. Everyone may guess on what days the others chose to pretend that the miracle had happened. They keep their findings to themselves and do not share them until the next session with the professional. As it turns out, they may well guess the wrong day!
- The therapist may suggest the "prediction task": Every day, the clients predict what the following day will look like. This task is intended to supply information about what works. Afterwards, the clients examine whether the prediction has come true and what contributed to this. In a variant of this homework suggestion, the client may predict each morning whether or not he or she will be successful at fulfilling the prediction.

It is important to distinguish between behavioral tasks for clients in a customer-relationship and observational tasks for clients in a complainant-relationship. The "do-something-different task" and the "pretend-the-miracle-has-happened task" are behavioral tasks, whereas the "prediction task" is an observational task. In the latter instance, clients do not (yet) have to change their behavior.

The client may feel that things are the same and nothing about the situation has changed. In that case, it is useful to find out when small improvements in the situation have been noticeable nonetheless. The client can use every exception that is found by making that exception happen again. Sometimes remaining stable is a great result in itself; progress is not always attainable.

Questions for clients who report that things are the same are:

- How did you manage to remain stable?
- Suppose I were to ask someone who knows you well what is going a little better. What would that person say?
- On a scale of 10 to 0, how would you rate your current situation?
- What is needed for you to maintain that rating in the time to come?
- Who among the most important people in your life is most worried about you?
- On a scale of 10 and 0, how worried is that person?

It may be useful to expand the sessions to include an important person from the client's life to help find solutions to the problem. If the client stays negative and fails to name exceptions, one can ask more competence questions, such as: How do you cope? How do you manage to go on with these sessions?

The therapist may ask himself the following questions:

- Do I have a customer-, complainant-, or visitor-relationship with this client?
- Do we need to revisit the goal?

Homework suggestions for clients who report that things are the same are:

- If the do-something-different task has not yet been assigned, it can be introduced as an experiment, especially if the client is stuck in a rut;
- The pattern of interaction can be changed through the addition of a new element or through deliberate exaggeration of the pattern;
- If the client indicates that he or she cannot exert any control over the problem, he or she can be asked to *externalize* the problem (see Appendix E).

Clients who say that things are going worse often have a long history of failure or have contended with big problems for years. If the therapist is too optimistic, they will usually be unable to help them. These clients often need a lot of space to tell the story of the problem, including any (negative) experiences with previous professionals. In that case, the therapist may apply the "Greek chorus" technique (Papp, 1983). Anyone who has seen Woody Allen's 1995 film *Mighty Aphrodite* will remember that the Greek chorus warns of potential dangers between scenes. With the Greek chorus technique, the therapist always adopts an attitude in favor of change, whereas his team of colleagues adopt an attitude against change. If the therapist works alone, he can apply the technique by introducing a pessimistic supervisor. Clients are then invited to work with the therapist to prove the team or the supervisor wrong. The therapist may ask "pessimistic" questions of clients who report that things are going worse:

- How do you manage to go on under these circumstances?
- How come you haven't given up by now?
- How come things aren't worse than they are?
- What is the smallest thing you could do to make a minimal difference?
- How can you make the same thing happen to a very small extent right now?
- What can others do for you?
- What can you remember about what used to help that you could try again now?
- What would most help you climb back into the saddle and face these difficulties?
- How did you manage to get out of bed this morning and make it here?

It is useful to put these clients in an expert position and ask them, as *consultants*, what their treatment should look like. Questions for expert clients are:

- What did professionals you worked with previously miss?
- Of all the things that these professionals did, what did you find most disagreeable?
- How could I be of greater assistance?
- What qualities would your ideal professional have, and what would he or she do?
- What questions would your ideal professional ask you, and what, in your opinion, would be the best course for him or her to follow?
- If I worked with other clients who were in the same boat as you, what advice would you give me that would allow me to help them?
- What question can you think of, that would allow me to help you the most?

The therapist may ask himself the following questions:

- Do I have a customer-, complainant-, or visitor-relationship with this client?
- Do we need to revisit the goal?

Homework suggestions for clients who report that things are going worse:

- It may help to have the exceedingly pessimistic client predict in detail when and how the next crisis will take place. As a result, the crisis may fail to occur or the client may discover better ways to deal with it;
- The client can also be asked to exaggerate the problem. This is a paradoxical assignment: As a result, the gravity of the problem may immediately decreases, as the client does not feel like carrying out such an assignment. If the client does exaggerate the problem, he or she will likely experience more control than he or she first thought;
- The therapist may examine the client's earlier successes in solving problems to see what strategies he or she can try again.

With this group of clients one may deploy the same strategies as with clients who report that nothing is going better. If the therapist works alone, it may be useful to invite a colleague to sit in and give feedback. With this group of clients, the therapist might also apply the technique of externalizing the problem (see Appendix E). Lastly, the therapist may discharge himself in a final rescue attempt if all other strategies have failed. He can explain to the client that he apparently does not understand the client or does not have the expertise to help him. He might say it would be best for the client to enlist the help of another therapist, who may have fresh ideas. Client may agree with this proposition or they may begin to formulate more realistic expectations, after which cooperation may be possible. For a protocol of subsequent sessions see Appendix C.

Case 11.1

This is an example of the use of the Greek chorus. An 18-year-old client smokes a couple of joints every day. He says would like to break the habit, he cannot see himself finishing school if he doesn't, and he would like to pass his final examination. The therapist introduces a pessimistic colleague, who predicts that he will undoubtedly relapse if he stops smoking marijuana, because this has happened so many times before. This upsets the client: he explains to the therapist that he knows what he is getting into, and once he has made his decision he will certainly stick to it! At the next session he reports having barely touched a joint. The therapist offers compliments: he must be a truly determined person! The client blossoms as he shares, when asked, that this is not the first time in his life that he has shown such determination.

Behavior Maintenance

In traditional CBT "relapse prevention" is a standard intervention towards the end of therapy. But what are we suggesting or even predicting when we talk with our clients about possible relapses? Exactly: that they are bound to happen! Another question is whether it is always necessary for the therapist to bring this subject up, or is it only useful if the client thinks it is useful to talk about this topic? I think the answer to this question is just to ask your clients if they are interested or not in finding out how to maintain the changes they made in therapy. If they are not interested, there will be no commitment to cooperate with you on this topic, nor will they do the necessary things required in case of a setback.

Of course maintaining hard-won changes isn't always easy and clients have to work hard and show determination to do so. Therefore, instead of talking about relapses and how to prevent them, Positive CBT prefers to talk about the progress made and how to maintain these positive changes. In this vein "relapse prevention" becomes "behavior maintenance."

To create and sustain change, therapists have to embrace a "growth mindset" instead of a fixed one and instill it in their clients (Dweck, 2006). People (including us therapists) who have a fixed mindset believe that their abilities are basically static. They believe that they may get a little bit better or worse at different skills, but basically their abilities reflect the way they are wired. People with a fixed mindset tend to avoid challenges, because if they fail, they fear that others will see their failure as an indication of their true ability and see them as a loser. They feel threatened by negative feedback, because it seems as if the critics are saying they are better than them, positioning themselves at a level of natural ability higher than theirs. In contrast, people who have a growth mindset believe that abilities are like muscles – they can be built up with practice. People with a growth mindset tend to accept more challenges despite the risk of failure. They seek out more challenging assignments at work and are more inclined to accept criticism, because ultimately it makes them better. Dweck states that if you want to reach your full potential and be more successful at almost anything, you need a growth mindset.

If failure is a necessary part of change, then the way clients understand failure is critical. The paradox of the growth mindset is that, although it seems to draw attention to failure, and in fact encourages people to seek out failure, it is optimistic, because in the end people will succeed.

Research by Dweck shows that students who have a fixed mindset have stronger and more depressive complaints than students who have a growth mindset. The students with a fixed mindset stagnated when encountering their failures and in dealing with their mistakes, and the more depressed they became the more they gave up, making no further attempts to solve their problems. On the contrary, students with a growth mindset, suffering from depressive complaints, displayed different behavior. The more depressed they reported themselves as being, the more action they undertook to solve their problems, the harder they worked, and the more active they became in structuring their lives. To sum up: when people believe that their personal qualities can be further developed then, despite the pain of failure, people do not become pessimistic, because they are not being defined by their failures. Change and growth remain a possibility, opening up pathways to success.

Questions that may be used when asking about a growth mindset are:

- How did you do this?
- What did you do to make that happen?
- How is this different from how you used to do this?
- What could you do (even) better next time?
- What do you like about it?
- What do you already understand and what not (yet)?
- Could you give me some feedback on how I did this job?

According to Menninger (1959), anticipation is the best defense. But what should be anticipated? He surely was talking about anticipation of the danger of relapses and setbacks. But anticipation by using a positive focus is by analyzing and predicting what may go well and what clients should do to flourish and thrive, instead of using a negative focus on analyzing and predicting what may go wrong and what clients should do to avoid relapse, and cope and survive. By doing the latter, risks are that there will be an increase in negative cognitions and feelings, because this concerns an avoidance goal. Clients will focus on what they fear most, trying to keep the distance between their present situation and the feared outcome as large as possible. In contrast, in behavior maintenance – an approach goal – clients will notice an increase in positive cognitions and feelings. Clients will focus on what they want most, trying to make the distance between their present situation and their preferred future as small as possible.

During therapy clients are encouraged to think about ways to maintain the gains of the therapy, thereby contributing to the client's "mental road map." The therapist may ask clients to imagine a better future and consider how their strengths and resources can be used to make this future come true. Snyder's research (see Chapter 5) has shown that hopeful people are able to come up with more alternative routes than nonhopeful people if the original route is blocked. Discussing ways to tackle possible future obstacles serves as a means to develop alternative solutions before these difficulties present themselves. This builds coping strategies and enhances "pathway thinking," which further diminishes the risk of relapse or better: augments the chances of behavior maintenance.

Furman and Ahola (2007) developed "Kids' Skills" as a therapy method for children. One of the steps in their method is about the term "forgetting." They state that they replaced the concept of relapse or setback – or the return of the problem – with the concept "forgetting." The idea is that whenever we learn new skills, we typically experience moments when we temporarily lose the skill we are learning. This normal phenomenon does not need to be seen as a relapse or setback – it can equally well be seen simply as a temporary loss of the skill or an incident of "forgetting" the skill. There is an advantage of viewing moments of slipping into the old behavior as temporarily forgetting the skill that one is currently learning: deliberate use of the word "forgetting" paves the way for a discussion of how, in the event of forgetting the skill, the child should be reminded of the skill he is learning. So instead of asking the child: "So what shall we do with you when you do (the problem behavior) again?", you ask the child: "If you sometimes forget the skill (the preferred behavior), how would you want us to remind you of it?" The idea is to get the child involved in the decision making about how others are to react to these – inevitable – moments in the learning process. The 15 steps of Kids' Skills are described in Chapter 14.

If a setback occurs, the therapist does well to normalize it: progress often means taking three steps forward and one or two steps back (and it would be a shame to give up even a single step). The therapist may also give a positive slant to the setback; after all, a setback offers an opportunity to practice getting back on one's feet. As Erickson once said: "If you fall on your face, at least you are heading in the right direction" (in: O'Hanlon, 2000).

In Positive CBT it is not necessary to dwell on the cause of the relapse and its consequences. The therapist does well to offer acknowledgment by showing that he understands how frustrating the relapse is to the client. Following this, it is most important to explore how the client has managed on previous occasions to get back on the right track after a relapse. If the client remains disconcerted in the wake of the recent relapse, he and the professional can consider what steps he can take to get back on the right track.

The session can also deal with relapse in a lighter, more playful manner. The therapist may ask "What would it take for you to obtain a low rating on the scale or go back to square one as quickly as possible?" This immediately indicates what the wrong approach is and often lends the conversation a light-hearted tenor.

Consolidating questions

Selekman (1993) describes the use of "consolidating questions" at the conclusion of the sessions as an effective means to get clients to talk about differences.

A few of these questions, which can ensure that the achieved results become permanent, are:

- What would you have to do to go backward?
- What would you have to do to prevent a relapse?
- What do you have to keep doing to make sure that these changes keep happening?

Selekman (1993, p. 156) invites clients to use what he described as his "imaginary crystal ball" to tell him what changes they saw themselves making in the future. He expresses disbelief in the psychoanalytic hypothesis that clients are subject to a "flight from health" if they terminate treatment following rapid changes at the beginning of the therapy. He thinks that clients must determine not only the goal of the therapy but also when to end it: "As a solution-oriented therapist, I do not believe my job is to cure people, but instead, to help clients have more satisfactory life situations. If clients call to cancel future scheduled appointments because they feel things are better for the time being, I always let them know that I have an open door policy and if they need to schedule a future tune-up session, they may feel free to call me."

This touches upon my sense that the Positive CBT therapist has a task comparable to the family doctor's. Often the patient doesn't visit the family doctor for years; sometimes he visits a few times in a row. When clients re-enter therapy, a positive question is: "How did you succeed in staying away as long as you did?" It is not the family doctor's objective to make the patient healthy once and for all. Many professionals have a much loftier goal in mind than most clients do. If therapists are more in tune with the client's goal, treatments would become shorter and probably more successful. It is customary in problem-focused therapies to make several appointments for sessions concerning relapse prevention and follow-up sessions. It has been my experience that this is rarely necessary in Positive CBT. It quite often seems that the point of these sessions is to reassure the therapist rather than to meet a need on the client's part.

Rothman (2000) found that the decision criteria that lead people to initiate a change in their behavior are different from those that lead them to maintain that behavior. Decisions regarding behavioral initiation depend on favorable expectations regarding future outcomes. This can be conceptualized as an approach-based self-regulatory system in which people's progress toward their goals is indicated by a reduction in the discrepancy between their current state and a desired reference state. Decisions regarding behavioral maintenance depend on perceived satisfaction with received outcomes. This can be conceptualized as an avoidance-based self-regulatory system in which progress is indicated by a sustained discrepancy between a current state and an undesired reference state. Other research (Ross and Wilson, 2002) shows that recalling an old, pre-change self from the third-person perspective helps to deal with the challenge of maintaining personal change. Greater perceived change – as is the case when people adopt a third-person perspective – leads to greater satisfaction with one's efforts thus far and, therefore, to make it easier to summon the resources necessary to maintain one's efforts. Psychologically distancing oneself from negative past selves and remaining close to positive past selves promotes well-being. Questions that may be useful are:

- How did you succeed in making lasting changes in other parts of your life? Which of those strategies might be useful now?
- How satisfied are you with the positive changes you made on a scale from 10 to 0?
- How would a point higher on the scale look like?
- What can you do to get to one point higher on the scale?
- Predict what tomorrow will be like, find an explanation for why the day turned out the way it did tomorrow evening, and then make a new prediction for the following day. If your prediction was correct: how did you know? If your prediction wasn't: how come the prediction was incorrect?
- Find supporters to help you in maintaining these changes. Who will you invite? How will you keep them updated? How will you thank them for their help?
- If you look back to your past self, from an observer perspective before you made these changes, what would this observer say that is going better in your life right now?

Do you remember the song "Fifty Ways to Leave Your Lover" by Paul Simon? Inviting your clients to make long lists is always a fun and challenging task.

- Think of 50 good reasons to maintain the positive changes you made;
- Think of 50 ways to maintain these positive changes (or even 100 ways!);
- Think of 50 positive consequences (for yourself, for important others) of maintaining these positive changes.

Case 11.2

A client sighs heavily and says: "I don't know if I can keep up with everything that is going on in my life." The therapist invites her to write down 50 ways in which she is keeping up right now. "You mean I have to write down five ways of coping?" she asks wearily. "No, not five, I mean 50 ways" answers the therapist. Would you like to start here or would you prefer to do the task at home? The client looks at her therapist incredulously, but starts anyway. As she continues to find ways which are already working for her (going to bed early once every week; asking her sister to help with bringing the kids to their sports activities, and so on) her posture changes to a more active one. She manages to find 43 ways during the session and when she leaves she is quite confident she can find the other 7 ways as well. When giving feedback, she states: "This session has made me see that it is not a question of whether I can keep up, but how I can do it."

Recovery plan

Focusing on what the client (and others) has done to help recovery or prevention in past experiences may be useful (O'Hanlon and Rowan, 2003). When prevention plans fail or are not put into practice, you may map out a "recovery plan" – especially with clients who have severe mental problems, like psychosis, major depression, or suicidal thoughts. This can usually be derived from asking about what happened as the person regains equilibrium after a previous crisis. "What did you do when you started to feel better again?", "What usually happens when you begin to emerge from one of your depressive episodes?", or: "What did you learn from your previous hospitalizations that may be helpful in this situation?"

Failures

As explained in Chapter 10, the average treated client is better off than about 80% of the untreated sample (Duncan *et al.*, 2010). But unfortunately dropouts are a significant problem and although many of our clients profit from therapy, many do not. Sometimes our clients come back and tell us that things are worse instead of better, or nothing has changed. This may be discouraging for therapists and clients alike, especially when everybody has worked hard in therapy. Clients also may feel embarrassed or ashamed at having to report failure or setbacks. I will discuss the importance of saving face later in this chapter.

Another point of concern is the variability among therapists. Some therapists are much better in getting positive results than others (see Chapter 12). In fact, therapist effectiveness ranges from 20–70%. Moreover, even very effective clinicians seem to be poor at identifying deteriorating clients (Duncan, 2010).

In psychotherapy, failures often involve a breakdown of therapy involving an answer to the question: "How will we know when we can stop meeting like this?" (De Shazer, 1994). He states that clients and therapists often are willing to accept the absence of the problem as a good enough goal, but the absence of the problem can never be proved and, therefore, either clients or therapist cannot know success or failure. Unless clearly established beforehand, even the presence of positive changes is not enough to prove the absence of the conflict. Therefore questions like: "What are your best hopes?" and: "What difference will that make?" are considered essential for establishing a well-defined goal in psychotherapy.

Some failures can be seen as related to a difficulty in shifting from a problem-focused conversation into a solution-focused conversation. The fault here is situated neither on the therapist's side nor on the client's side: both are in it together. Most frequently the therapist has been unable to help the clients see exceptions to the problem as differences that can be made to make a difference and thus as precursors of the goal of the clients.

Therapists may also cause some failures. Oettingen (1999) and Oettingen, Hönig, and Gollwitzer (2000) elucidate the technique of "mental contrasting" to goal setting (see Chapter 6). Mental contrasting is an expectancy-based route and rests on mentally contrasting fantasies about a desired future with negative aspects as obstacles of the present reality, emphasizing a necessity to change the negative present reality to achieve the desired future. This necessity to act activates relevant expectations of success, which then informs goal commitment. Reversing this order (i.e., reverse mental contrasting) by first elaborating the negative reality followed by elaboration of the desired future – as is usually done in traditional CBT – fails to elicit goal commitment congruent with expectations of success (Oettingen *et al.*, 2001).

Case 11.3

Clients who want to change their behavior (lose weight, stop smoking, exercise more) are invited to participate in an "if-then" training, based on mental contrasting. They write down three "IF-THEN" assumptions:

- One to overcome an obstacle: IF I feel exhausted after work, THEN I will put on my running shoes and go for a jog in the neighborhood;
- One to prevent the obstacle: IF I hear the clock chime five, THEN I will pack my things and leave the office to go for a run;
- One to identify a good opportunity to act: IF the sun is shining, THEN I will go for a 30 minute jog in the park).

Gollwitzer (1999) found that people can delegate the initiation of goal-directed behavior to environmental stimuli by forming so-called implementation intentions ("if-then plans" of the format: "If situation x is encountered, then I will perform behavior y"). Forming implementation intentions facilitates detecting, attending to, and recalling the critical situation. Moreover, in the presence of the critical situation, the initiation of the specified goal-directed behavior is immediate, efficient, and does not need a conscious intent.

Exercise 11.2

Ask your clients questions about their desired future: "How will you know you don't have to come here anymore?" Or: "How will we know we can stop meeting like this?" Then, as a follow-up question, ask: "How confident are you that you are on track to getting what you want?" The responses to these questions will give you some hints about the next step. Are your clients saying they are on track? What personal strengths and solutions do they use? What else may be helpful to overcome the obstacles down the road?

Pathways to impossibility

Duncan, Hubble, and Miller (1997) describe four pathways to impossibility. The first pathway arises in the anticipation of impossibility. Historically, impossibility has been located in the client. In a well-known experiment, Rosenhan (1973) recruited and trained a group of normal confederates (one of them was Martin Seligman, cofounder of Positive Psychology) to obtain psychiatric hospitalization. To gain admission, they falsified a single psychotic symptom (hearing voices). The clinicians diagnosed the pretend patients as mentally ill and admitted them for stays ranging from 7 to 52 days. During their hospitalizations, the pseudopatients showed no signs of psychosis, yet the original diagnosis remained in place. Rosenhan also demonstrated how the clinician's initial expectations came to serve as confirmatory biases. In one instance, staff took truthful historical information provided by a pseudopatient and made it conform to prevailing theoretical notions about schizophrenia. Therefore, the therapist's expectation of impossibility will probably distort new information to conform to his expectations.

The second pathway to impossibility is the professional's traditions or conventions. Therapists are often eager to corroborate their theory with each client, and their theory is often over-applied. Remember the story of the man who bought a hammer and then found that everything needed to be nailed?

Clients have their own theories about their lives and their problems, and when their points of view are ignored or dismissed by the therapist's theory, noncompliance or resistance is a predictable outcome. To the therapist, the client begins to look, feel, and act impossible; to the client the therapist comes across as uncaring or disinterested. The therapy changes from a helping relationship to a clash of cultures with noone the winner. Client-directed, outcome-informed therapy, as described in Chapter 10, may be an answer to this second pathway to impossibility.

The third pathway to impossibility is persisting in an approach that is not working. Watzlawick, Weakland, and Fisch (1974) reasoned that unmanageable problems, those that are often called "chronic," couldn't be sufficiently explained on the basis of innate characteristics of the client. Rather, they concluded that the unyielding or impossible nature of a problem arises in the very efforts to solve it. For a difficulty to turn into a problem, only two conditions need to be fulfilled. First, the difficulty is mishandled; the attempted solutions do not work. And second, when the difficulty proves refractory, more of the same ineffective solutions are applied and the original difficulties will deteriorate. Over time, a vicious downward spiraling cycle ensues with the original difficulty growing into an impasse, immense in size and importance.

Therapists doing more of the same are sometimes convinced that persistence will eventually win the day, even when all the evidence suggests that the strategy is ineffectual. All theoretical models and strategies are inherently limited and will generate their share of impossibility when repetitively applied. Wampold (2001) found that when there is no improvement after the third session, the chances are 75% that the therapy with fail. This percentage is 90% when no improvement is found after the sixth session. Research by Lambert *et al.* (2002) indicates that treatment should be brief when little or no progress is being made in the early sessions: then it should be as short in duration as possible. Therapy should not be used for the purpose of just sustaining or maintaining clients. As long as clients are making documentable progress and are interested in continuing, however, treatment should be extended.

Research (Piper *et al.*, 1999) showed that dropouts could be predicted by treatment process variables, not by client variables. In other words, only what happened in the sessions predicted whether the client failed to return, not who the client was and what the client brought to the process. The Outcome Rating

Scale and Session Rating Scale, as described in more detail in Chapter 10, are great tools for measuring the desired progress and change.

The fourth and last pathway to impossibility is created when the therapist neglects the client's motivation. There is no such individual as an unmotivated client. Clients may not share the ideas and goal of the therapist, but they hold strong motivations of their own. An unproductive therapy can come about by mistaking or overlooking what the clients want to accomplish, misapprehending the client's readiness for change, or pursuing a personal motivation. Research has established that the critical process-outcome in psychotherapy is the quality of the client's participation in a positive working alliance (see Chapter 5). The motivation of the clients not only for sitting at the therapist's office, but also for achieving their own goal, has to be understood, respected, and actively incorporated into the therapy. To do less or to impose agendas motivated by theoretical perogatives, personal bias, and perhaps some sense of what would be good for the clients, invites impossibility.

Case 11.4

Is it to be expected that clients will get worse before they get better? Of course not! Considerable clinical lore has built up around the idea that deterioration of the client's situation comes before the situation gets better. This is rarely the road to recovery and, in fact, is an indicator that portends a final negative outcome. This idea also allows therapists to ignore, to some degree, client worsening (Lambert and Ogles, 2004).

Top performers review the details of their performance, identifying specific actions and alternate strategies for reaching their goals. Where unsuccessful people attribute failure to external and uncontrollable factors ("I just had a bad day"), experts know exactly what they do and more often cite controllable factors ("I should have done this instead of that"). Average therapists are far more likely to spend time hypothesizing about failed strategies – believing perhaps that understanding the reasons why an approach did not work will lead to better outcomes – and less time thinking about strategies that might be more effective. Walter and Peller (1992) offer some questions in situations where there seems to be no progress:

- Who is the client (who is in a customer-relationship) and wants to change?
- What is the client's goal?
- Do you have a goal and not a wish? Is the goal well-defined and within the control of the clients?
- Are you and the clients looking for too much too fast? Try looking for a smaller change;

- Do clients not do tasks while you have been expecting them to do something? You can provide some feedback to think about rather than an action-oriented task;
- If you have gone through all of these steps, is there anything you need to do differently? Sometimes we are too close to the trees to see the forest and may not recognize a nonproductive pattern between the clients and us. A team or consultant can be helpful to provide a more detached frame of reference.

Case 11.5

Mr and Mrs Brown are sitting in the therapist's office. Mr Brown says: "I do not think that this therapy will succeed; the former therapist has also not helped us much. We did make a plan to change things in our relationship, but the implementation of what was agreed has never come off the ground. It has only led to more arguments between us." The (overoptimistic) therapist ignores this remark and before long therapy reaches a deadlock.

The therapist would have done better to validate the doubts of Mr Brown by acknowledging them and by asking scaling questions with respect to his confidence and hope. Then there may have been an opening to increase his confidence and hope. "Suppose you would have a bit more hope, what difference would that make?" Also the therapist could have asked: "How, despite your previous experience, do you manage to sit here in a therapist's office?"

Saving face

Duncan *et al.* (2010) state that the place of saving face should be considered. When clients feel overwhelmed and stuck, they are apt to experience their problems as impossible. Seeking help offers the prospect of something better. Simultaneously, it may also signify their failure to resolve the problem on their own. In fact, their feelings of failure may be so acute that they crowd out any favorable self-evaluation. In these circumstances, going to therapy can represent just one more unpleasant reminder of how badly they have managed their difficulties. Humiliation is added to insult. If a therapist then suggests or implies that the client's point of view is wrong, or somehow invalidates or upstages the client, resistance may appear. After all, even if not already demoralized, who wants to be reminded of failure, criticized, judged, or made to feel that you have to follow orders? What we come to call "resistance" may sometimes reflect the client's attempt to salvage a small portion of self-respect. As such, some cases become impossible simply because the treatment allows the client no way of saving face or upholding dignity. This is probably what Erickson had in mind when he suggested that the art of therapy revolves around helping clients to "bow out of their symptoms gracefully." (In Duncan, Hubble, and Miller, 1997,

p. 12.) He recognized that clients simultaneously hold a desire to change and a natural tendency to protect themselves if change (for worse or for better) compromises personal dignity.

Story 11.1: Ten Million Dollars Lost

In the 1960s, an executive at IBM made a decision that ended up losing the company 10 million US dollars. The CEO of IBM, Tom Watson, summoned the offending executive to his office at corporate headquarters. A journalist described what happened next: As the executive cowered, Watson asked, "Do you know why I've asked you here?" The man replied, "I assume I'm here so you can fire me." Watson looked surprised. "Fire you?" he asked. "Of course not. I just spent 10 million dollars educating you."

Source: Heath and Heath (2010)

Exercise 11.3

During sessions, continue to pay attention to what is going better or what is different and how your clients make that happen. In the next sessions, give your clients at least three compliments in each session and ask them competence questions such as: "How did you do that?", "How were you able to do that?", and "How did you decide to do that?" Take note of the difference this makes for your clients (and for you as their therapist).

Concluding Therapy

De Shazer (1991) states that if the therapist accepts the client's statement of his problem at the beginning of treatment, by the same logic the therapist should also accept the client's declaration that he has sufficiently improved as a reason to end the treatment.

There is no limit to the number of sessions a client attends Positive CBT. The sessions are discontinued if the client achieves his treatment goal (to a sufficient degree). After the second session, the time interval between sessions usually increases. One week between the first and the second session is generally a good amount of time (but it can be more if the clients so wishes). In principle, each session is viewed as the last session and just one session may even be enough if the client's goal has become clear. In a chapter titled "How Can We Know When to Stop Meeting Like This?" De Shazer (1991) described how the client's goal comes into view if, during the sessions, the client and the professional have been attentive to:

- The occurrence of exceptions and the presence of parts of the client's preferred future (the goal), which indicate that desired changes are taking place;
- The client's vision and description of a new life;
- The confirmation that change is taking place and that the client's new life has, in fact, begun.

Contrary to what happens in problem-focused psychotherapies, discussion of ending the client's contact with the therapist occurs as soon as the therapy starts. This is evident from the questions clients receive about goal formulation: "What needs to change in your life in order for you to say that these sessions have been worthwhile?" or "What would indicate to you that you're doing well enough that you no longer have to come here?" What the therapist wishes to elicit here is a description of what clients would consider a successful result, in concrete and measurable behavioral terms. A recorded description of the preferred future situation can be of great help: "What do you do differently in that recording that tells me that that's the situation you would prefer?"

Discussing the desired outcome from the very beginning of the sessions creates an atmosphere of optimism and gives clients hope that their problem can be solved (to a sufficient degree). That is why the importance of adequate goal formulation cannot be stressed enough. The therapist should feel free to set aside a fair amount of time for it, for it has been my experience that when the goal has been formulated well, half the work is often already done and clients usually know precisely what they need to do to get closer to their goal. This relates to the image of the therapist as a tugboat or, better yet, a push tug: as soon as clients are released from the shoal, they can sail on unaided. It is often unnecessary for the therapist to travel farther along with their clients.

The moment when the sessions can be concluded can also be revealed by means of scaling questions. After goal formulation, the therapist can ask clients where they currently are on a scale of 10 to 0, and at what number they need to be in order not to have to come and visit anymore. Experience shows that most clients are happy with a 7 or 8 and don't need to reach a 9 or 10 before they're content and able to finish the treatment. Sometimes the treatment can be concluded at a low rating, because clients have enough confidence that they can go alone from there, toward the number where they would like to end up. In any case, it should be clear that in Positive CBT the client decides when the treatment can be concluded, in close cooperation with the therapist. Bannink (2010a) offers many creative ideas for concluding the treatment: making certificates, celebrating successes, using drawings and letters, designing symbols, and inviting clients to share their expertise.

Spacing sessions

I would like to add a final word about spacing therapy sessions. Traditional psychotherapy models, like CBT, usually schedule one or more sessions regularly every week or every two weeks. In Positive CBT each session is scheduled according to:

- Time needed for the performance of some homework assignment;
- Promotion of confidence in the solutions;
- Promotion of independence from therapy;
- The client's responsibility for therapy.

Some homework suggestions take more time to do or to perceive a meaningful difference for the clients. Spacing out the sessions enables clients to have a longer perspective on their construction of solutions and to put setbacks in perspective. The spacing of sessions over longer periods of time, from two weeks to three to six, can also promote confidence in solving the problems since some clients think that their changing is dependent on therapy and that the therapist is responsible for the change. The spacing of sessions is determined by the clients and not by the therapist by asking questions like: "Do you think it is useful to schedule another session?" and if so: "When would you like to return?" Clients are responsible for their therapy and the Positive CBT therapist determines with his clients the amount of time they should be spending on a homework suggestion or the length of time between the current and the subsequent session, based on the confidence the clients have in their own strengths and solutions.

12

Role of the Positive CBT Therapist

Water the flowers, not the weeds

Fletcher Peacock (2001)

Introduction

In general, traditional problem-focused psychotherapies share the property of being difficult to do, no fun at all, and difficult to incorporate into clients' life. Pope and Tabachnick (1994) found that 61% of their sample of about 500 psychologists reported at least one episode of depression during their career, 29% had experienced suicidal feelings, and 4% had actually attempted suicide. In 2006, the American Psychological Association's Board of Professional Affairs' Advisory Committee on Colleague Assistance (ACCA) issued a report on distress and impairment in psychologists. The report pointed out that depending on how depression is measured, its lifetime prevalence in psychologists ranges from 11% to 61%. In addition to depression, mental health practitioners are exposed to high levels of stress, burnout, substance abuse, and vicarious traumatization. Seligman (2011, p. 1) states: "While we do more than our bit to increase the well-being of our clients, psychology-as-usual typically does not do much for the well-being of its practitioners. If anything changes in the practitioner, it is a personality shift toward depression." Therefore, it is about time to take better care of ourselves as therapists by adopting a more positive stance to psychotherapy by paying attention to what we want to see expand in our clients and in ourselves. The "least burden principle" applies not only to our clients but also to ourselves as therapists.

Watering the Flowers

Both Solution-Focused Brief Therapy and Positive Psychology ensure that therapists will have a lighter workload and, ultimately, less stress. This is done by

Practicing Positive CBT: From Reducing Distress to Building Success, First Edition. Fredrike Bannink.
© 2012 John Wiley & Sons, Ltd. Published 2012 by John Wiley & Sons, Ltd.

placing attention on what they want to see expand. Peacock (2001, p. 39), author of *Water the flowers, not the weeds,* tells the following story: "After a seminar that I gave to 250 managers, half of them bought a watering can. They put them, different sizes and different styles, in plain sight in their offices to remind themselves that they were gardeners and that their job was to water what was working well in their organisations and in their personal life. 'Energize' what is positive and what works!"

Erickson (in Rossi, 1980) states that if we place the emphasis on what is positive, on the little movements that take place in a good direction, we are going to amplify these improvements and this in turn will create more cooperation with other persons (with our partners, parents, children, colleagues, and with our clients).

Three specific types of therapist behavior result in clients being four times more likely to speak about solutions, change, and resources:

1. Eliciting questions such as "What would you like instead of the problem?"
2. Questions about details such as "How did you do that? What exactly did you do differently?"
3. Verbal rewards: giving compliments ("Wow, that is a great achievement") and asking competence questions such as "How did you manage to do that? Where did you get that good idea?"

Seligman (2011, p. 53) takes watering the flowers even more literally: "I am a rose gardener. I spend a lot of time clearing away underbrush and then weeding. Weeds get in the way of roses; weeds are a disabling condition. But if you want to have roses, it is not nearly enough to clear and weed. You have to amend the soil with peat moss, plant a good rose, water it, and feed it nutrients. You have to supply the enabling conditions for flourishing."

Role of the Positive CBT Therapist

In Positive CBT the attitude of the therapist is different from the attitude of the traditional therapist. This attitude can be described as: "leading from one step behind" and "not-knowing."

Positive CBT therapists work in ways that allow clients to be the co-experts about their own experiences and what these mean. From a solution-focused point of view the best way to lead clients is the way of "leading from one step behind." In this the therapist, metaphorically speaking, stands behind the clients and taps them on the shoulder with solution-focused questions, inviting them to look at their preferred future and, in order to achieve this goal, to envisage a wide horizon of personal possibilities.

Therapists adopt a posture of "not-knowing" and develop interviewing skills that allow clients to provide information about themselves and their situation. He allows himself to be informed by the client, whose own life context will determine in what way solutions are devised. They do not pull or push, they are not leading or advising. Clients are considered to be the experts of their own lives and the therapists ask questions to invite clients to inform him and to come up with their own solutions to their problems. This attitude promotes client trust, confidence, and hopefulness about the future. From a Positive Psychology point of view the therapist remains more of an expert: his role is one of an advisor (see chapter on homework assignments), telling clients what they might do to feel better (e.g., proposing a gratitude visit if the client feels depressed or setting a "strengths date" if a couple is having relational problems).

Problems are primarily determined by how people respond to each other. Leary (1957) developed a practical model to categorize social relationships: Leary's Rose. He distinguished two main dimensions: on the one hand on the vertical axis, power and influence ("above") or the lack thereof ("below") and, on the other hand on the horizontal axis, personal proximity and sympathy ("together") or distance ("opposed"). These two dimensions govern how people interact with each other. People with a great need for power position themselves above others. They are quick to engage in battle and tell others what they have to do. People at the other end of the power spectrum take a subservient or dependent position. If the division of influence is equal, the relationship is symmetrical. If it is unequal, the relationship is complementary. Some people only feel happy if they can work with others. Cooperative behavior, such as providing support and help, suits them. People at the other end of the spectrum are associated with behavior that creates distance and implies opposition.

On the basis of these dimensions, Leary came up with four communication positions: "below and together," "above and together," "below and opposed," and "above and opposed." The client and therapist often assume a preferred position within one of these four quadrants. There may also be a varying preference for two (or more) quadrants. The communication position taken by one person prompts in the other person a supplemental (complementary) or an opposite (symmetrical) interactional position: Above elicits below, down elicits below, together invites opposed, and opposed provokes together. Communication behavior and, hence, interactional disruptions proceed according to these rules. The therapist quickly identifies this behavior on the basis of his or her own reactions and on the interactional position that is, as it were, forced upon him or her. He can also help the client change positions, for example, from "below and together" to "above and together," by means of the solution-focused stance of "not-knowing" and by regarding the client as competent and as an expert. The four main positions are:

1. Above and together: I adopt a position of leadership and solidarity and command cordial docility from the other person;
2. Below and together: I adopt a dependent and cordial position in relation to the other person and command him or her to benevolently take the initiative;
3. Below and opposed: I adopt a dependent and suspicious position in relation to the other person and command him or her to ignore me (contrary and complaining);
4. Above and opposed: I adopt a superior and oppositional position in relation to the other person and command him or her to stand in awe of me.

In the medical model, the therapist usually adopts the "above and together" position (he is the expert), which automatically puts the client in the "below and together" (or opposed) position. In solution-focused sessions, the therapist takes the "below and together" position as much as possible (the stance of "leading from one step behind" and "not- knowing"), which causes the client to move, seemingly automatically, to the "above and together" position, in which the client is the co-expert. The therapist enhances cooperation, commitment, and motivation of clients by paying attention to their preferred position and by shifting from his own position "above and together" to "below and together." Inquiring about clients' ideas and competencies produces equal cooperation between the therapist and clients as well.

A client with whom there is a customer-relationship (see Chapter 5) is in the together position, and a client with whom there is a complainant-relationship is in the opposed position as far as behavior change is concerned. If the therapist notices himself becoming irritated, insecure, or discouraged, there is negative countertransference, that is, a negative reaction by the therapist to the client's behavior. In practice, this usually occurs because there is a visitor- or complainant-relationship, but the therapist – mistakenly – considers the client to be in a customer-relationship.

To sum up: Positive CBT therapists may choose which position fits them best: one being that of expert-advisor or being that of interviewer to elicit clients' expertise.

Supertherapists

It is obvious that not every therapist is equally successful. Wampold (2001) notes that as some lawyers have better results, some artists create more remarkable works of art, and students perform better with some teachers than others, some psychotherapists also will achieve better results than others. Therefore most of us, when we recommend a mediator, lawyer, doctor, or psychotherapist to a friend or relative, we rely more on the competence and expertise of this person than on his theoretical background.

Miller, Hubble, and Duncan (2007) found that recent studies show solid empirical evidence for what distinguishes highly effective therapists (that they call "Supershrinks") from other therapists. The data show that clients of the best clinicians achieve 50% or more improvement and 50% or fewer dropouts than those seen by average therapists. Surprisingly, training, certification, supervision, years of experience, and even use of evidence-based practices do not contribute to superior performance. Research conducted over the last 30 years documents that the effectiveness rates of most clinicians plateaus very early in training, despite the fact that most professionals believe they improve with time and experience.

Despite the important role played by the psychotherapist, it is clear from the research that our knowledge exhibits major gaps. We still know surprisingly little about the variables and qualities that are the characteristics of a competent and effective supertherapist and about the interaction of these variables with different approaches in therapy or mediation. We know even less about the interaction with clients or client variables.

Wampold gives an overview of research in psychotherapy. One chapter in his book is about "allegiance": the faith the therapist has in his own treatment model. The faith one has in the treatment and the capacity of that treatment to help clients change is an important quality of a competent therapist. When the therapist does not invest sufficiently in his treatment, this may endanger the treatment outcome. Allegiance towards a treatment is based on the idea that if a therapist is favorably disposed towards a treatment and experiences the positive effects of that treatment, he will execute this treatment with more perseverance, enthusiasm, hope, and competence.

Research on the impact of variables of therapist's characteristics shows that competent, creative, committed therapists can often smooth out any restriction on their age, gender, or color of skin (Beutler, Malik, Alimohamed, *et al.*, 2004). There is a consistent relationship between a positive and friendly attitude of the therapist and a positive outcome. A critical and hostile attitude has the opposite effect. A supertherapist seeks, obtains, and maintains more consumer engagement. Another consistent outcome of research is that it is important that therapists are sufficiently active and directive to ensure that their clients do not simply repeat their dysfunctional patterns and that they structure the sessions sufficiently to stimulate clients to face up to their cognitions and behavior.

Miller, Hubble, and Duncan (2007) show that good therapists are much more likely to ask for and receive negative feedback about the quality of their work and their contribution to the alliance. The best clinicians, those falling in the top 25% of treatment outcomes, consistently achieve lower scores on standardized alliance measures at the outset of therapy – perhaps because they are more persistent or are more believable when assuring clients that they want honest answers – enabling them to address potential problems in the working relationship. Median therapists, by contrast, commonly receive negative feedback later in treatment, at a time when clients have already disengaged and are at heightened risk for dropping out. So supertherapists are exceptionally alert to the risk of dropping out and treatment failure.

Most aspects of the style of the therapist are strongly dependent on whether the therapist adjusts to the preferences, hopes, and characteristics of his clients. He should give fewer directives if the client does not comply and he should adjust his style to hold a moderate arousal (not too much and not too little), because a moderate arousal promotes change. Flexibility and building rapport are therefore essential qualities for a therapist. Which specific responses from the therapist are responsible for a positive "alliance" varies from client to client. Good therapists are sensitive to the reactions of their clients and can adjust their interactions on the basis of this feedback (Duncan, Miller, and Sparks, 2004).

Norcross (2002) and Wampold and Bhati (2004) found that the personality of the therapist and the alliance with his client are far more powerful determinants of the outcome of the meetings than the choice of methodology. The therapist's degree of comfort with closeness in interpersonal relationships, low hostility, and high social support predicted clients' ratings of the alliance early in treatment. Additionally, they found that therapist experience was not predictive of the strength of any aspect of the therapeutic relationship.

In sum, the therapist is in many ways intertwined with change. In most models of change the therapist is central and it depends on the therapist whether and how change mechanisms operate in the therapeutic process. The expectation is that this research into the role of the therapist also applies to other professionals such as doctors, lawyers, and mediators (Bannink, 2010b).

Exercise 12.1

Make your own Certificate of Competence *(see website John Wheeler). This certificate is a self-coaching tool for optimizing professional practice.*

1. *When I do my work I take my inspiration from the following people:*
2. *These people have taught me that when I do my work it is most important to remember the following:*
3. *These are the people who encourage me to do the work I do:*
4. *They encouraged me to do this work because they noticed the following about me:*
5. *When I do my work, the people I deal with are likely to appreciate that I have the following qualities and abilities:*
6. *These are the people in my support network who know I have these qualities and abilities:*
7. *If I am under pressure at work and can only remember one quality or ability it should be this:*

Easy and Fun

If the therapist works harder than the client, if he thinks therapy is a difficult endeavor, or if he never laughs during sessions with his clients, he should probably stop and do something else. Maybe he should lean back more and start asking more questions. Maybe he wants to reach the goal more than the client does, or maybe the goal of the client is not clear yet. Maybe there is a complainant-relationship with the client, whereas he assumes that the client is motivated to change. Maybe he has a higher or other goal than the client. Or maybe he should make a joke now and then or ask about his client's strengths and resources. In these cases – and in many others – the therapist can go back to square one and use one of the protocols for the first session (see Appendix A). If a traditional therapist is too tired and stressed at the end of a working day to do anything fun, while his clients still can, Positive CBT may be a good alternative!

As we know, the responsibility for a good alliance not only rests with the clients but equally with us, therapists. If no progress is being made, we can ask ourselves:

- If I would ask the clients how my contribution has helped so far, even though it may only be a little bit, how would they respond?
- What do the clients see as sign(s) of a successful result?
- How realistic is this result?

- What do I see as sign(s) of success?
- If my ideas and those of my clients differ, what needs to be done in order for me to work towards their goal?
- Where on the scale of 10 to 0 would the clients say that they are right now?
- What should happen for them to be able to achieve a score closer to 10?
- How much motivation, hope, or confidence do I have as a therapist that this therapy will be successful? Suppose I would have more motivation, hope, or confidence, what would I then be doing differently? And what difference would that make to my clients?

If we are no longer motivated, confident, or hopeful that we can help our clients reach their preferred future, we should examine what needs to be done to regain motivation, confidence, or hope. If we are ourselves in a complainant-relationship with a client (we become irritated or discouraged because there is no progress and we think the client has to do something first before we will be motivated to do anything) and if we are no longer motivated to re-establish a more positive cooperation with our clients, it is advisable that we reassign the therapy to a colleague.

Case 12.1

So far the client makes little or no progress. The therapist feels somewhat irritated, he is working hard, while the client is saying "yes, but . . . " to almost all his explanations and the advice he is giving. The therapist realizes that he has the inclination to stop doing anything for this client anymore, since the client is not doing anything to change his behavior.

Instead, he plans to pay the client at least three compliments in every session. This means he really has to look hard at what the client is doing to see where he can be complimented. As he focuses on the client's strengths and what works, it appears that paying three compliments is easier than he thought. And as a bonus, the alliance improves dramatically, resulting in the client making progress.

Exercise 12.2

Examine which three strengths have brought you to where you currently are in your profession. You may discuss this with a colleague and ask him or her which three strengths of yours he or she would name. You can then switch roles.

The Alliance Revisited

Clinical researchers have been focusing on the one aspect of psychotherapy that seems to make little difference, that is, the type of therapy delivered. Psychologist contributions to outcomes overwhelm treatment differences. The most researched common factor – the alliance between the psychologist and the client – has been found to be a robust predictor of outcome, even when measured early in therapy (Wampold, 2001). Regardless of theoretical orientation or professional discipline, the strength of the relationship between the therapist and the client is consistently associated with effective treatment outcome. In particular this is true for the client's assessment of the relationship, not the professional's assessment. Their ratings of the alliance have a stronger correlation with outcome than the ratings of therapists. Moreover, ratings at early stages of treatment are more predictive of outcome than ratings taken later in the process.

Nevertheless, only a few psychotherapy studies have been designed to assess psychological effects, despite the fact that ignoring them biases the results. The evidence-based treatment movement places emphasis on treatments when it has been found that the type of treatment accounts for very little of the variability in outcomes; aspects of treatment that are valued by psychologists and clients and that have been shown to account for variability in outcomes, have been ignored.

Research shows that alliance is particularly predictive of outcome when measured early in treatment and poor early alliance predicts client dropout. The implication is that attention must be paid to the alliance as soon as therapy begins.

Microanalysis

Bavelas, Coates, and Johnson (2000) state that "Communication is the tool of therapy just as physical instruments are the tools of surgery, and it is incumbent on us to treat therapeutic communication equally carefully and precisely". Microanalysis of dialog aims for a detailed and replicable examination of observable communication sequences between therapists and clients as they proceed, moment by moment, in a dialog, with an emphasis on the function of these sequences within the dialog. Two tools are being observed when analyzing video recordings of the dialogs: analysis of formulations and analysis of questions. Formulations are a way for therapists to display their understanding of what a client has said:

- The client presents information ("I don't know what to do anymore")
- The therapist displays his understanding with a formulation ("Do you mean you are at your wits end?")
- The client acknowledges, explicitly or implicitly, that the formulation is a correct understanding (or not) ("Yes, that's right")

Another tool is the analysis of how questions function (intentionally or not) as therapeutic interventions. The impact of a question begins with its (often implicit) presuppositions, assumptions that form the background of the question. Questions from different therapeutic approaches demonstrate how the therapist's story shapes these presuppositions. In a problem-focused (CBT) conversation the question might be: "Could you please tell me more about the problem you want to address today?", whereas in a solution-focused conversation the question might be: "What would be the best result of our meeting today?"

The content of each question or formulation could be positive, negative, or neutral.

Tomori and Bavelas (2007) used microanalysis to analyze expert sessions on Solution-Focused Brief Therapy and Client Centered Therapy (De Shazer and Berg for SFBT; Rogers and Raskin for CCT). Results showed that the solution-focused and client-centered experts differed in how they structured the sessions: the client-centered therapists used formulations almost exclusively, that is, they responded to client's contributions. Solution- focused experts used both formulations and questions, that is, they both initiated and responded to client contributions. They also differed in the tenor of their contributions: the solution-focused therapists' questions and formulations were primarily positive, whereas those of the client-centered therapists were primarily negative and rarely neutral or positive.

Positive therapist content includes question, statements, formulations, or suggestions by the therapist that focus the client on some positive aspect of the client's life (e.g., a relationship, trait, or experience in the past, present, or future). Positive client content includes questions, statements, formulations, or suggestions by the client that focus on some positive aspect of life (e.g., a relationship, trait, or experience in the past, present, or future). Negative therapist or client content is the opposite of positive content.

Another finding is that when the therapist's utterance is positive, clients are more likely to say something positive, whereas when the therapist's utterance is negative, clients are more likely to say something negative.

Smock, Froerer, and Bavelas (article forthcoming) compare positive versus negative content in three Solution-Focused Brief Therapy and three Cognitive Behavioral Therapy expert sessions (one of the CBT therapists is Meichenbaum). The content of the SFBT therapists was significantly more positive and less negative than that of the CBT sessions. Across all of the therapists, the clients responded in kind, that is, positive talk led to more positive talk, and negative talk led to more negative talk. Thus, a therapist's use of positive content seems to contribute to the co-construction of an overall positive session, whereas negative content would do the reverse. The third finding was that, as a group, the SFBT experts were all consistently more positive than negative, whereas the CBT experts differed widely among themselves (Franklin *et al.*, 2012). This finding is consistent with my remark in Chapter 1 that there is no single form of CBT, but it is rather a class of treatments, which have the same features in common and also differ in important respects.

Exercise 12.3

Think about what opening sentence you usually start a first session with. You may opt for a problem-focused question: "What is the problem?" or "What is bothering you?" You may choose a neutral question: "What brings you here?" You may opt for a question that implies that you will work hard: "What can I do for you?" Or you may choose a solution-focused question about the goal of the session: "What is the purpose of your visit?" / "What needs to be accomplished by the end of this session (or this therapy) so that you can say that coming to see me was useful?" / "What would you like to see different in your life, so that you don't have to come here anymore?" / "What would you like to see instead of the problem?" Or you may ask the "miracle question": "Suppose that while you're asleep tonight a miracle happens. The miracle is that the problem that brought you here has been solved (to a sufficient degree). When you wake up, you are unaware that the miracle has occurred because you were asleep. How would you first notice tomorrow morning that this miracle has happened? What would be different and what would you be doing differently? What else? After you, who would be the first to notice that the miracle has happened? How would that person react differently? And how would you in turn react? How else would you notice over the course of the day that the miracle has happened (work, relationships, etc.)?" Or you may ask: "What are your best hopes?" "And what difference will that make?"

Try out all the possibilities and note the differences in your clients' reactions and the differences in the mood of the sessions.

The importance of language

As mentioned previously, microanalysis can complement outcome research by providing evidence about what therapists do in their sessions and how the co-constructive nature of language is important in dialogs. Co-constructing a dialog may even be compared to a dance or a duet between therapist and client.

Some useful ideas for paying more attention to language are:

- Change "if" into "when": "If I get out of this depression, I will be able to do what I want" into "When I get out of this depression, I will be able to do what I want."
- Change "can't" into "not yet": "I can't lose weight" into "I haven't lost weight yet"
- Move problems from internal to external: "I am depressed" to "Depression has been visiting me for a while." Or: "I am a negative person" into "Negativity speaks to me regularly and mostly I listen to what it says."
- Use the past tense when talking about problems and the future tense when talking about what clients want different in their lives: "So until now you have not been able to have a steady relationship." "How will your life look like when you have a girlfriend?"

Benefits for Therapists

"While we do more than our bit to increase the well-being of our clients, psychology-as-usual typically does not do much for the well-being of its practitioners. If anything changes in the practitioner, it is a personality shift toward depression" (Seligman, 2011, p. 1).

At the beginning of this chapter I already mentioned research showing that the lifetime prevalence in psychologists of depression ranges from 11–61%. In addition to depression, mental health practitioners are exposed to high levels of stress, burnout, substance abuse, and vicarious traumatization. Anyone in the health or mental health community inherently knows about "compassion fatigue," also known as secondary traumatic stress disorder. It is a condition characterized by a gradual lessening of compassion over time with symptoms such as hopelessness, a decrease in experiences of pleasure, an increase in stress and anxiety and a pervasive negative attitude. In turn this may lead to a decrease in productivity, an inability to focus, and the development of feelings of incompetence and self-doubt. In the medical professions this condition is often called "burnout."

Research on microanalysis (see previously) shows that positive talk leads to more positive talk, and negative talk leads to more negative talk. Thus, a therapist's use of positive content seems to contribute to the co-construction of an overall positive session, whereas negative content does the reverse.

Therefore, it is about time to take better care of ourselves as therapists by adopting a more positive stance to psychotherapy and by paying attention to what we want to see expand in our clients and in ourselves.

Seligman describes the impact Positive Psychology has on its practitioners (2011, p. 2). "Positive Psychology makes people happier. Teaching positive psychology, researching positive psychology, using positive psychology in practice as a coach or therapist, giving positive psychology exercises to tenth graders in a classroom, parenting little kids with positive psychology, teaching drill sergeants how to teach about post-traumatic growth, meeting with other positive psychologists, and just reading about positive psychology all make people happier. The people who work in positive psychology are the people with the highest well-being I have ever known."

De Jong and Berg (2002, p. 322) describe the impact of Solution-Focused Brief Therapy on its practitioners. They quote practitioners who are working with domestic violence groups, groups for adolescent substance abuse offenders, and parents of adolescents who were on probation, but also with the entire range of clients in a community mental health clinic. "Using solution-focused practice has made a tremendous difference for us as practitioners. When we used to do problem-focused work, it seemed we were tired all the time. We never seemed to know when a client was done with therapy, and often felt that we were doing all the work, and had to be the 'expert' and figure out how to 'fix' or 'cure' the client. We spent hour upon hour listening to people's stories about what was wrong with their lives, and felt that in order to be effective, we needed to ask more and more questions about what was wrong. Solution-focused therapy was a breath of fresh air. All of a sudden, it was the client who determined when they were done with therapy. There were clear behavioural indicators when the goal was reached. We no longer had the burden of being 'an expert', but worked in collaboration with the client to figure out together what would be helpful. We no longer listened to months of problems but were listening to strengths, and competencies, and abilities. We no longer saw clients as diagnostic labels but as incredible beings full of possibilities. Work became fun and felt empowering and our life outside of work was affected as well. What a difference it makes when you are looking for what is positive, and recognise that it is your own behaviour that determines the quality of your life. We discovered that current reality gets created through the use of language in conversation with others, not by what happened to you in the past. We found we were living life in the present and were definitively having more fun."

Professional growth

Many therapists grow weary and begin to wonder why they enlisted in this difficult job in the first place. So what keeps us from succumbing to burnout or getting a job that is more fun? Orlinsky and Ronnestad (2005) did a 15-year, multinational study of nearly 5000 therapists and found that therapists stay in the profession, not because of material rewards or the prospect of professional advancement, but because, above all, they value connecting deeply with clients and helping them to improve. On top of that, clinicians consistently report a strong desire to continue learning about their profession, regardless of how long they have been practicing. They found that professional growth is a strong incentive and a major buffer for burnout. What therapists seek in their professional careers and the satisfaction they receive from the work they do is called the "healing involvement." This concept describes us at our best: it is about therapists' reported experiences of being personally engaged, communicating a high level of empathy, and feeling effective and able to deal constructively with difficulties. This healing involvement emerges from therapists' cumulative career development, as they improve their clinical skills and increase their mastery, but an even more powerful factor promoting healing involvement is the therapists' sense of currently experienced growth, the feeling that we are learning from our day-to-day clinical work, deepening and enhancing our understanding in every session. This growth is fundamental to maintaining our positive work morale and clinical passion. Having a sense of currently experienced growth remoralizes therapists and it is our greatest ally against burnout.

Duncan (2011) states that achieving a sense of healing involvement requires a continual evaluation of where we are compared with where we have been. Research literature offers strong evidence that not all therapists perform equally well and that most therapists are poor judges of client deterioration. They are no good judges of their own performance either. Sapyta, Riemer, and Bickman (2005) asked clinicians of all types to rate their job performance from A+ to F. About 66% ranked himself A or Better. Not one therapist rated himself as being below average! If you remember how the Bell Curve works, you know that this isn't logically possible.

Therefore, some quantitative standard as a reference point is essential. Taking the time to measure outcomes, using the Outcome Rating Scale (ORS) and the

Session Rating Scale (SRS), described in Chapter 10, relates both to having an awareness of our mastery over time and experiencing a sense of current professional growth. In this sense it is clear that not only our clients benefit from the use of feedback forms, but so do we. In the largest randomized clinical trial of couples therapy ever done Anker, Duncan, and Sparks (2009) found that clients who gave their therapists feedback about the benefit and fit of services on the ORS and SRS reached clinically significant change nearly four times more than nonfeedback couples did. Tracking outcomes also improved the results of 9 out of 10 therapists. This finding implies that many of us therapists can become "supertherapists" if we are proactive about tracking our own and our clients' development.

Part III
More Applications

13

Positive CBT with Couples and Groups

The art of being wise is the art of knowing what to overlook

William James

Introduction

When asked what, in two words or fewer, Positive Psychology is about, Christopher Peterson, one of its founders, replied, "Other people," because very little of what is positive in life is solitary. Is there someone in your life whom you would feel comfortable phoning at four in the morning to tell your troubles to? If your answer is yes, you will likely live longer than someone whose answer is no. Isaacowitz, Vaillant, and Seligman (2003) discovered this fact in the so-called "Grant study" (see Chapter 4): the master strength is the capacity to be loved. They found that the capacity to love and be loved was the single strength most clearly associated with subjective well-being at age eighty.

Most people want to make connections and want to avoid loneliness. In this quest, approach and avoidance motives and goals are linked to different social outcomes (see also Chapter 6). Approach social goals are strongly associated with outcomes defined by the presence of social rewards, such as affiliation and intimacy. For individuals who are largely approach-oriented (to make connections) or find themselves in a reward-rich environment, pleasing interactions and relationships are defined as those which provide such rewards as companionship and understanding; painful relationships are those that fail to provide these rewards. Avoidance social goals are strongly associated with outcomes defined by the presence of punishment, such as rejection and conflict. For individuals who are primarily avoidance-oriented (to avoid loneliness) or find themselves in a threat-rich environment, pleasing interactions and relationships are defined as those that lack uncertainty, disagreements, and anxiety; painful relationships are those that possess these negative qualities. These social outcomes (e.g., intimacy, conflict) are predicted to combine and form global feelings about social bonds and relationship quality.

Practicing Positive CBT: From Reducing Distress to Building Success, First Edition. Fredrike Bannink.
© 2012 John Wiley & Sons, Ltd. Published 2012 by John Wiley & Sons, Ltd.

Approach goals are generally associated with better results and more well-being than avoidance goals, although both approach and avoidance goals are necessary for successful adaptation. Whereas approach motivation facilitates growth and flourishing, avoidance motivation facilitates protection and survival.

Gable (2006) found that persons with strong approach motives were more likely to adopt short-term approach social goals (e.g., make new friends; be considerate) and those with strong avoidance motives were more likely to adopt short-term avoidance social goals (e.g., to not be lonely; avoid conflict with my partner). Moreover, these motives and goals were associated with different social outcomes. Specifically, approach motives and goals were associated with positive social attitudes and more satisfaction with social bonds. Avoidance motives and goals were associated with more negative social attitudes and relationship insecurity.

Positive CBT with Couples

Links between approach and avoidance motives and outcomes have also been examined in romantic relationships (Impett, Gable, and Peplau, 2005). Romantic couples' motives for everyday relationship sacrifices (enacting a behavior that is not preferred, such as accompanying a partner to a dull work function, not spending time with friends, having sex when not in the mood) were studied in a daily experience study that included a longitudinal component. The results showed that on days persons sacrificed for approach motives (e.g., to promote intimacy), they reported greater positive affect and relationship satisfaction. But, on days when they enacted the same behaviors for avoidance motives (e.g., to avoid conflict), they reported greater negative affect, lower relationship satisfaction, and more conflict. Sacrificing for avoidance motives was particularly harmful to the maintenance of relationships over time: the more individuals sacrificed for avoidance motives over the course of the study, the less satisfied they were with their relationships 6 weeks later and the more likely they were to have broken up. These results remained when controlling for initial levels of satisfaction.

Much research emphasizes the value of positive, approach-oriented emotions for "broadening" awareness and "building" social networks (Fredrickson, 1998).

Research with couples indicates that stable relationships tend to have partners expressing five times as many positive approach emotions towards each other as negative emotions, including both anger and avoidant emotions (Gottman, 1994). Gottman computed the positivity ratio of a marriage. He found that among "flourishing" marriages positivity ratios were about 5 to 1. By sharp contrast, languishing and failed marriages had positivity ratios lower than 1 to 1 (see Chapter 9 for more details).

In line with the research mentioned previously, Gable *et al.* (2004) demonstrated that how you celebrate is more predictive of strong relationships than how you fight. Our partners may tell us about a victory, a triumph, or good things that happen to them. How we respond can either build our relationship or undermine it. There are four basic ways of responding:

1. Active and constructive: Verbal: "That's great, congratulations! I know how important this is to you." Nonverbal: maintaining eye contact, displays of positive emotions such as smiling or laughing;
2. Passive and constructive: Verbal: "That's good news." Nonverbal: little to no emotional expression;
3. Active and destructive: Verbal: "That sounds like a lot of responsibility to take on. Are you going to spend even fewer nights at home now?" Nonverbal: displays of negative emotions such as frowning or crying;
4. Passive and destructive: Verbal: "What's for dinner?" Nonverbal: little to no eye contact, turning away, leaving the room.

Only the first way helps in building positive relationships. Every time someone you care about tells you about something good that happened to them, listen carefully and respond actively and constructively. Ask these persons to relive the event with you: the more time they spend reliving, the better. Seligman (2011, p. 51): "Once you start doing it, other people like you better, they spend more time with you, and they share more of the intimate details of their lives. You feel better about yourself, and all this strengthens the skill of active, constructive responding."

In the same vein, research on "capitalization," telling others about positive events in one's life, whereby the other responds in an active and positive way, shows that this generates additional affect, over and above positive affect associated with the event itself (see Chapter 10). Furthermore, the communicative act may involve rehearsal and elaboration, both of which prolong and enhance the experience by increasing its salience and accessibility in memory. In this way, capitalization builds personal and social resources.

Exercise 13.1

This is an exercise for active-constructive responding: respond in a manner of genuine happiness, excitement, and active questioning to someone who shares an event of good news. This allows the other person to re-experience the pleasure of the event and builds a stronger, more positive relationship between the speaker and the listener.

Practice of Positive CBT with couples

Start by building a positive alliance with both partners, ensuring that you start with the person who is more likely to be there involuntarily. Sometimes a partner is brought in for therapy, because the other partner wants him or her to change. Ask them questions about strengths and resources. "What is the other person good at?" "What do you appreciate in the other person?" "What do you like about him or her?" "What are you proud of? "Which positive aspects do you find in your relationship?" This process of clients complimenting each other by describing each other's strengths is useful because it generates hopefulness and goodwill, which usually makes the rest of the session proceed more quickly and in a more positive tone.

Needless to say, couples therapy is a balancing act for therapists: each person should have equal time to tell their story and express their wishes and ideas for a better future.

Then go on asking both partners what they want different in their lives and in their relationship (their goal in coming to therapy). It invites clients to move away from past problems and frustrations in their relationship to something more productive and satisfying. Work toward a common goal: What would you like to see different in your relationship? What difference will it make if the other person changes in the direction you want him or her to change? What will be different between the two of you?

Walter and Peller (2000) state that clients often speak of what they do not want or what they want to eliminate from their lives. In interactional situations, clients often speak of what they want the other person *not* to do. Their only course of action at that time has been to try to get the other person to stop doing what they consider to be problematic behavior. The other person is also in a strange position, in that the options are either to defend the present behavior or to stop what the other finds so problematic. He/she is still in the dark as to what the client does want to happen. Sometimes, talking about what the client does want opens up the conversation in a more positive direction.

Then ask questions about exceptions and scaling questions: When was there a moment or a time when things were better, even just a little bit? If clients cannot find these exceptions, ask them to observe these moments between the sessions to come. Where are you on the scale from 10 to 0, where 10 means the best situation possible and 0 means the worst situation possible? And where on the scale would you like to be in order to be able to stop therapy?

Case 13.1

In a couple's therapy both partners share a common goal; they wish to restore their relationship. The Positive CBT therapist asks "relationship questions," in which other perspectives are invited into the conversation (see Chapter 7).

Some of the questions to the husband are: "How would your wife be able to tell that as a couple you are starting to get on the right track?" "What would your wife say you are doing differently then?" "How do you think your wife would react?"

The therapist asks the wife: "How would your husband be able to tell that as a couple you are on the right track again?" "What would your husband say you are doing differently then?" "What would your husband say is helpful to make that happen?"

The therapist asks both husband and wife: "How do you think your two children would be able to tell that things are going better between you?" "What will they see you doing differently together?"

The Positive CBT therapist also invites the couple to both fill out the VIA test (see Chapter 4) and set a "strengths date" every two weeks, using their top five character strengths during the date (see later). Because husband and wife share "curiosity" as one of their top five strengths, they decide to spend time during their date visiting some new museums together.

Exercise 13.2

Planning a "strengths date" is a great way to enhance your relationship and to increase positive emotions for yourself and your significant other through understanding, recognizing, and celebrating one another's character strengths. In order to plan a strengths date, first complete the VIA Inventory of Character Strengths (see Chapter 4) so you know each other's top five strengths from this measure. Take as many of your top strengths as you see fit and sculpt an activity together that taps into the individual strengths for both you and your loved one.

Story 13.1: The Norway Feedback Project

The effects of providing treatment progress and alliance information to both clients and therapists were investigated during couple therapy in Norway. Outpatients at a community family counseling clinic were randomly assigned to treatment as usual (TAU) or feedback (using the ORS and SRS, see Chapter 10). Couples in the feedback condition demonstrated significantly greater improvement that those in the TAU condition at post-treatment, achieved nearly 4 times the rate of clinically significant change, and maintained a significant advantage on the primary measure at 6-month follow-up while attaining a significantly lower rate of separation or divorce (Anker, Duncan, and Sparks, 2009).

A second study, by Anker et al. (2010), supports both the feasibility and the importance of the feedback intervention. The alliance significantly predicted outcome over and above early change, demonstrating that the alliance is not merely an artifact of client improvement, but rather a force for change in and of itself. The study also found that those couples whose alliance scores ascended attained significantly better outcomes than those whose alliances scores did not improve. Together these findings suggest that therapists should not leave the alliance to chance but rather routinely assess it and discuss it with clients in each session.

Beck (1988, p. 5) suggests that distressed couples need help with "correcting their misinterpretations, untying the knots that twisted their communication, and tuning up their abilities to see and hear their partners' signals accurately."

From a Positive CBT point of view, distressed couples may need help in observing which interpretations are already right, which don't have to change, and do more of those. Instead of untying the knots that twist their communication, they may observe which parts in their communication are still sound and focus more on those, and maybe focus more on tolerance instead of on their communication (see later). Finally, they may observe which abilities they already possess (and may indeed tune up) with regard to seeing and hearing their partners' positive signals instead of the negative ones.

Murray, Holmes, and Griffin (2003) did a set of studies on good marriage. They carefully measured what people think about their spouse: how handsome, how kind, how funny, how devoted, and how smart he/she is. They posed the very same questions about the spouse to the closest friends of the other spouse, and they derived a discrepancy score: if someone thinks more of his/her spouse than the friends do, the discrepancy is positive. If someone sees his/her spouse exactly as the friends do, the discrepancy is zero. If the spouse is more pessimistic about him/her than the friends, the discrepancy is negative.

The strength of the marriage is directly a function of how positive the discrepancy is. Spouses with very strong benign illusions about their mates have much better marriages. The mechanism is likely that the spouse knows about these illusions, and tries to live up to them. Their conclusion is that optimism helps love, and pessimism hurts.

For years, difficulties in relationships have been attributed to poor communication. In response, professionals have focused their efforts on improving communication between partners, especially about problems and the expression of emotion. While effective communication has been linked to marital satisfaction in the research literature, Gordon, Baucom, Epstein, Burnett, and Rankin (1999) suggest a sometimes more effective alternative: teaching tolerance. In particular, partners can be helped to become more tolerant (and probably more forgiving) when they adjust their expectations to the type of communication pattern they have. For example, avoidance of discussing problems and sharing emotions had less relation to marital satisfaction and happiness in couples that preferred more emotional and psychological space and less conjoined decision making.

Bannink (2010a, 2010b) offers many tips and questions for couples with difficulties or conflicts; just to name a few:

- If there is a power struggle between two clients, suggest that they do something else, preferably something unexpected, and note the difference it makes;
- If there are arguments, ask your clients what they do agree on;
- If there are arguments, ask your clients if the situation could be worse. If so, how come it is not worse?
- If there is a conflict, ask both partners what the other partner could do to encourage them to adopt a different attitude;
- If there is a conflict, ask both partners what small signs they have detected that give them hope that the conflict can be resolved?

combine this exercise with their VIA Survey results to get a clear picture of their character strengths in action, as well as seeing how closely the strengths they perceive they have lines up with the strengths others perceive they have.

Note that 20 people may sound like a daunting number, but think of the impact this might have. You would be having meaningful conversations with 20 people in your life; you would be soliciting positive, engaging comments from these people; you would probably be connecting with people across numerous domains of your life – personal, social, work, spiritual, and so on. Consider how transformative this could be for you, for the others, and for these relationships.

Reteaming

Furman and Ahola (2007) describe a method called "reteaming," consisting of 12 consecutive, logical steps intended to help individuals as well as groups to change for the better by facilitating setting of goals, and increasing motivation and enhancing cooperation needed to achieve them. Reteaming generates hope and optimism, builds motivation, and enhances creativity and cooperation between people. In reteaming change is seen as a collective process, something done together with others. Individuals, in order to change, need in most cases help, support, and encouragement from others. The 12 steps are: 1. Describe your dream; 2. Identify a goal; 3. Recruit supporters; 4. Highlight the benefit of the goal; 5. Recognize progress already made; 6. Picture forthcoming progress; 7. Acknowledge the challenge; 8. Find grounds for confidence; 9. Make your promise; 10. Follow up your progress; 11. Prepare for possible setbacks; and 12. Celebrate success and acknowledge your supporters. For more information about the reteaming process see www.reteaming.com.

Exercise 13.5

Invite group members to sit in a circle. Ask everyone to write down their name on a sheet of paper and pass this sheet of paper round to each other. Everyone will write down which strengths he attributes to the person whose name is on the paper and will then pass the paper to his neighbor. The paper, now filled with compliments, will finally end up with the first participant. The paper can be folded concertina style to prevent anyone from reading the previous remarks.

Homework suggestions for a group

Metcalf (1998) describes how she helps group members develop a homework task. If the goals of all the clients in the group have been identified, the therapist can encourage them to work toward their goals in between group sessions. For instance, he might say: "You all have good ideas about the moments when the problem is less of a burden to you. Now let's talk about what you could do until the next meeting to keep the problem under control." If the goal is not yet clear, the therapist can motivate the clients to make good use of the time between sessions: they are invited to closely observe their daily activities until the next group session and to pay attention to when the problem does not bother them quite as much. The goal is for the clients to keep track of exceptions to the problem, so that they can describe them during the next group session. At the end of the first group session, Metcalf asks the following questions:

- If a 10 means that you have control over your life and a 1 means that the problem has control over you, where on that scale would you say you are today?
- Where on the scale would you like to be when our group reconvenes?
- What did you learn about yourself today that can help you reach that number?
- Does anyone have a suggestion for anyone else?

As a homework suggestion clients then keep track of times when they have more control over their lives.

Exercise 13.6

The therapist may invite clients to make a "compliment box" during therapy with couples, children, families, or groups. At the end of the session, each person puts a note with a compliment for each of the other persons into the box. These notes are read aloud during the next session. The compliments may be given anonymously or signed.

A variant on the compliment box is the "success box," which may be used in group therapy. First, the group members make or buy a beautiful box together. All group members are asked to anonymously submit three separate notes with solutions that have helped them successfully face or solve their problems. Examples of solutions are: talking to a friend, taking long walks, or keeping a positive data log. When all notes have been placed in the box, they are removed and placed on a table. All group members can pick up one of two of these notes with solutions that are new to them (or which they want to try again), and try them out in a behavioral experiment.

Feedback

Building a culture of feedback is essential in psychotherapy, also when working with groups. You can find more information about the use of the Outcome Rating Scale (ORS) and the Session Rating Scale (SRS) in Chapter 10.

The Group Session Rating Scale (GSRS) is one of the feedback instruments developed for working with a group. Feedback is given by the group members on the same three topics: relationship with the leader and/or the group; goals and topics; approach or method. Overall feedback covering all the topics is also given. For more information see: www.centerforclinicalexcellence.com.

14

Positive CBT with Children and Families

Growth comes from activity, not from intellectual understanding

Maria Montessori

Introduction

De Jong and Berg (2002) give some advice regarding working with families. They state that when you first meet with a family it is easy to forget that they care about each other, because they seem so angry, hurt, and disappointed with each other. It can help to remember that the other side of anger, hurt, and disappointment with the other person is the wish to be cared about, respected, valued, and loved by that person. It is always helpful to be aware of both sides of emotions, not just the side that is showing. Remember that when people truly do not care about another person, they do not get stirred up about the other but cooly walk away from developing conflict. The reason clients become so upset with one another is because they care deeply about these other persons. Staying aware of both sides makes it easier for you to ask the questions that invite clients to construct something more satisfying. The task for therapists is to foster and highlight the signs of caring and goodwill between clients to promote hope for the relationship. Inviting families to talk about their past successes, their strengths, and where they want to be when therapy is not needed anymore empowers them to create their own positive "self-fulfilling prophecies."

Even when one member of the family refuses to come to therapy, the Positive CBT therapist and the other client(s) can still work on the relationship. It is useful to ask so-called "relationship questions" to bring the missing person into the room. For example, if you are meeting with two parents of an adolescent son or daughter who refuses to come to therapy, you may ask the parents:

- What do you think your son/daughter would say if we asked him/her what he/she would like to see different between you and him/her?

Practicing Positive CBT: From Reducing Distress to Building Success, First Edition. Fredrike Bannink.
© 2012 John Wiley & Sons, Ltd. Published 2012 by John Wiley & Sons, Ltd.

• Suppose he/she were here, knowing him/her as well as you do, what do you think he/she would say if I were to ask him/her how his/her preferred future would look?

Positive CBT with Children

Children who see a therapist are essentially in an involuntary situation or have even been mandated. The adults in their lives define their successes and problems. By the time children are sent to a therapist, many concerned adults have already tried many things to help them, usually without success. Understandably, these adults are often frustrated or angry and anxious to have their child change. The children are also often frustrated and discouraged because of all the negative messages they have been getting and the conflicts that have arisen between them and important adults.

To some degree, conflict is an unavoidable part of maturation. Children and adolescents change roles and test the boundaries of relationships with authority figures and peers as they grow and master new skills. Approach emotions will motivate limit-testing behavior, whereas avoidance emotions will de-escalate conflict and promote periods of stability where the status quo of relationships and authority are maintained. Although parents, teachers, and sometimes youths will seek therapy for these sorts of developmental conflicts, typically these do not represent psychopathology or emotion dysfunction so much as the inevitable bumps of growing up.

A nice way to start therapy with children (and their parents) is to ask the child how they would like to celebrate when they have reached their goal and do not have to come to therapy any longer. Children in particular find this highly enjoyable, but parents also like this question, because it generates hope that things can change for the better and that there will be a celebration at the end of therapy.

Optimism

Seligman, Reivich, Jaycox, and Gilham (1995) concluded that optimistic children fare better at school work and in sport than pessimistic children. They also conclude that optimistic adolescents are less angry and less likely to indulge in drug and alcohol abuse. Seligman and colleagues distinguish four factors, which influence the development of optimism in children:

1. The genetic definition;
2. The child's immediate environment where the parents have a strong influence on the child's level of optimism. There is in particular a strong relation between the way the mother deals with events (her interpretations and expectations) and the way her child deals with them. If the mother is optimistic then the likely outcome is that her child will be too. Children see their parents as role models and imitate their behavior. There also appears to be a correlation between pessimistic mothers and pessimistic children. Indeed, the same applies to the development of the child's capacity for demonstrating gratitude;

3. The influence of the wider environment: the educational input of both teachers and parents. There is more depression and pessimism amongst children whose mothers granted them less autonomy. The exertion of control does not lead to more optimism in children. Criticism from parents, teachers, coaches, and other adults will also play a part. If an adult criticizes a child's proficiency, for example by saying "you will never learn that," the chances are that the child will start to think in a pessimistic way. With the child's increasing maturity, there is a decline in the importance of the role played by his upbringing on his well-being. The influence of friends and peers will take on greater importance. However, even then a degree of structure and space for autonomy provided by parents remains important;

4. The events the child will experience: they either present a feeling of control or an experience of helplessness. Seligman and colleagues state that optimism has its limits. Children must be able to look at themselves realistically if they are to take on life's challenges.

Hope

Hope is an important construct if one wants to understand how children deal with stressful events, how to prevent them from developing problematic behavior, and how they can use past events to lead their lives in a good and effective way. Hope and intelligence are not related: the majority of children have the intellectual capacity to think hopefully and purposefully. Children's capacity for hope has a bearing on their performance at school. Boys and girls equally demonstrate hopefulness. A child's idea of the future is often slightly too positive. However this is a plus because this ensures that their thoughts develop in a positive way and they can retain them, even if these are not, under the circumstances, realistic.

Research shows that hopeful children cope better with stressful events. The degree of hope children possess is positively linked to self-reporting competence. Hopeful children have higher self-esteem and are less prone to depression. Besides, self-esteem in children is connected to the development of hope. Research into children with sickle-cell disease, a serious genetic form of anemia, showed a positive connection between hope and adaptation within a group of these children. On the other hand it demonstrated a negative connection between hope and fear. Adolescents, who as children suffered serious burns, took part in a questionnaire to assess their level of hopefulness – it being a good predictor of the definitive occurrence of behavioral problems. More hope, fewer behavioral problems. On top of that it showed that hope combined with social support contributed to a more substantial feeling of self-worth. Research into hope and the level at which adolescents were exposed to violence, whereby they thought they would become victims themselves of this violence, proved that they were able to maintain a high level of hope so long as they were only witnessing the violence and were not directly involved themselves. For that reason researchers plead for children to be told hopeful stories at school. After reading these stories discussions will take place with the children on how hope can be brought into their lives. In this way children experience increasing feelings of hopefulness.

Story 14.1: Little Squid

Once upon a time there was a little squid who lived in warm shallow water, close to the coast. He swam across coral reefs and between beautiful colorful fish. One day, while he was swimming, he noticed a strange object. It was the bottom of a large ship with an anchor. The little squid embraced the anchor with his tentacles so as to feel secure in the dark unknown water. While he fearfully clung to the anchor, the anchor started to sink deeper and deeper, the water becoming colder and darker. The little squid could feel the pressure of the water increasing but he was not sure what to do: let go of the anchor or continue to cling to it. Finally the anchor reached the bottom of the sea with a loud thud. The little squid clung onto the anchor even tighter because now he was very scared and in a state of despair. Then, out of the darkness, a fish appeared. The little squid softly called out for help. The fish heard him and said: I can help you but you will have to let go of the anchor, only then can I show you how to get out of here. I do not know how the little squid was able to let go of the anchor, maybe one tentacle at a time, or maybe he let go all at once. The friendly fish waited patiently and encouraged the little squid every step of the way. As soon as the little squid was free from the anchor the fish said: just follow me. The fish started to swim from side to side and slowly upwards. The journey up took quite a lot longer than the little squid had hoped for. He knew that it was really dangerous to go up too fast. But this way the little squid learned how to go up safely from deep deep down. He even started to think of it as a great adventure! The further up they swam the warmer and clearer the water became. The gloom and despair disappeared leaving that dark ocean behind him. He caught up with the fish and together they swam up. Not long after the fish said: you do not need me anymore, you can go on by yourself. You have learned how to get where you want to be. The little squid thanked the fish profusely and swam further up. Something had changed, not just around him but also within him. He was so happy to have left the anchor and the deep ocean behind him. And while the little squid rested and enjoyed all the beautiful things around him, his thoughts went back to everything he had learned. He felt strong, happy, and enjoyed life to the full.

Source: Anonymous

Resilience

Grotberg carried out research in 14 countries, with the International Resilience Project, into the interaction between children and the wider social context in relation to resilience. According to her it is important in working with children to implement a focus on resilience. She states that: *"With resilience, children can triumph over trauma; without it, trauma (adversity) triumphs."* (1995, p. 6).

The population consisted of 589 children and their families or caregivers. Overall, only 38% of adult responses had high resilience promoting scores. Adults promote more resilience than children, and older children promote more resilience than younger children. These findings suggest that the promotion of resilience depends more on the behavior of parents and adults for children age 6 and under, while children 9 to 11 do as much to promote their own resilience as do their parents and other adults. When well over half of the responses show little or no resilience promotion, the case for such promotion becomes more important. It may well be true that resilience in children is dependent on adult contributions to its promotion. Resilience does not develop in a vacuum; it is within a context. As children become older they appear to assume a larger role in the promotion of their own resilience, still in the context of their supports, their acquired skills, and their enhanced inner strengths. The challenge, then, is how to help younger children be more able to promote resilience, how to help adults contribute to this more effectively, and how to help all adults and children become more resilient.

Until recently, research into child development and treatment of disorders in children focused on pathology and risk factors. These days increasing attention is paid to protective and resilience factors of children and their environment (Kuiper and Bannink, article forthcoming), as well as the normal development of children and how they can "flourish."

The children from the participating countries appeared to use the same common factors, which can be divided into three categories (I Have; I Am; I Can), which can, when combined, lead to resilience. Every category can be divided into five factors, which are of importance to each category.

I Have: factors in this category are all situated externally and involve resources and support from outside:

1. I Have trusting relationships;
2. role models;
3. access to health, education, welfare, and security services;
4. encouragement to be autonomous;
5. structure and rules at home.

I Am: factors in this category address the child's internal and personal capabilities:

1. I Am lovable and my temperament is appealing;
2. autonomous and responsible;
3. filled with hope, faith, and trus;
4. loving, empathic, and altruisti;
5. proud of myself.

I Can: factors in this category address the child's social and interpersonal skills:

1. I Can communicate;
2. manage my feelings and impulses;
3. gauge the temperament of myself and others;
4. problem solve;
5. seek trusting relationships.

In Positive CBT children and their families are invited to talk about which of these strengths they already possess and, if necessary, which strengths should be further enhanced.

Well-being

Many factors play a role in well-being: physical and mental health as well as spiritual and social aspects. In research with adults well-being has been defined as "quality of life." Little research has been carried out with children in this field. It is important to establish, when using questionnaires in research about well-being in children, just who is the right person to answer the questions, the child himself, the parents, the teacher, or the carer. The emphasis should be on what is right not on what is wrong. It would be more beneficial to phrase the items in these questionnaires in positive terms rather than in the usual negative terms (in the past week did your child suffer from . . .). The early upbringing and especially the bonding between mother and child is contributory for the mental health, the well-being of the child, and subsequent development of psychological problems. Behind every happy child you will find loving parents. Research shows that an adult's well-being is linked in particular to the concern and familiarity expressed by their mothers during their childhood. The outcome was the same for both sons and daughters. The adaptation of the environment plays an important role in the well-being of children; how could, for instance, the hospital environment be adapted in such a way as to help seriously ill children to feel as well as they possibly could; how can doctors and nurses be trained in such a way as to help them to focus on the needs of children and how can these children be more involved and have more control over their medical treatment.

Focus on strengths and possibilities

In Positive CBT with children the same base principles apply as in conversations with adults; the main emphasis being on their strengths and possibilities rather than on their weaknesses and impossibilities. Therefore it is important to differentiate between problems and disabilities. A solution can be found with problems, with disabilities (for example autism of intellectual disabilities) the child and his environment have to learn how to adapt, but there is no solution for disorders. One should try to limit "problem talk" to an even greater degree than when dealing with adults – parents are often so frustrated that it cannot be ignored and the therapist must first acknowledge their frustration – but move on as quickly as possible to "strengths and solution talk" to bring out the best in children.

The *VIA Strength Survey for Children* contains a list of 198 questions with statements to describe children who are 8 to 17 years old. The test explores the same 24 character strengths in children as in the test for adults. The survey can be found at www.authentichappiness.com.

The Penn Resiliency Project

The Penn Resiliency Project (PRP) is a group intervention for late elementary and middle school students who are at risk of depression. The curriculum teaches cognitive-behavioral and social problem-solving skills and is based in part on cognitive-behavioral theories of depression by Beck, Ellis, and Seligman.

Central to PRP is Ellis' ABC model, the notion that our beliefs about events mediate their impact on our emotions and behavior. Through this model, students learn to detect inaccurate thoughts, to evaluate the accuracy of those thoughts, and to challenge negative beliefs by considering alternative interpretations. PRP also teaches a variety of strategies that can be used for solving problems and coping with difficult situations and emotions. Students learn techniques for assertiveness, negotiation, decision making, social problem-solving, and relaxation. The skills taught in the program can be applied to many contexts of life, including relationships with peers and family members as well as achievement in academics or other activities. Within each lesson, resilience concepts and skills are presented and practiced in a variety of ways. So far the interventions of the Penn project are based on traditional CBT, using the problem-solving paradigm. Hopefully the project will change to the solution-building paradigm of Positive CBT in the near future.

Exercise 14.1

Ask the child which animal he would compare himself with and which animal he would like to be in the future. Ask the child to draw a comic strip with six drawings, first drawing the animal he wants to become (drawing 6) and then drawing the animal he is now (drawing 1). Then the child can draw the other pictures (drawings 2–5) in any order he wishes. Finally ask the child which strengths of the animal in the first drawing he wants to take with him as he transforms into the preferred animal. The therapist can discuss these drawings with the child (and his parents) and "translate" the drawings to his life as a child.

Kids' Skills

Furman and Ahola (2007) developed Kids' Skills in the 1990s in Finland. It is a solution-focused method for helping children overcome emotional and behavioral problems, using a 15 step-by-step procedure, with the help of parents, friends, and other people close to the child. Kids' Skills can be regarded as a Positive CBT method for working with children and their families. The main advantage of Kids' Skills is that inasmuch as children shy away from talking about problems, they enjoy learning skills (or becoming better at them), which is something that can be done in a way that is enjoyable and rewarding for children. In addition, Kids' Skills fosters cooperation with parents by regarding them as partners who are willing and capable of supporting their children in developing these skills.

The 15 steps in Kids' Skills are:

1. Convert problems into skills to be learned or to become better at;
2. Agree about the skill with the child;
3. Give a name to the skill;

4. Explore the benefits of the skill;
5. Ask the child to choose a "power creature" (animal, cartoon character) that can help him learning the skill;
6. Recruit supporters (family, siblings, friends);
7. Build confidence;
8. Plan the celebration;
9. Demonstrate the skill (in a role play, in real-life situations);
10. Go public;
11. Practice: act out the skill time and again;
12. Use the term "forgetting" instead of relapse or setback (see Chapter 11);
13. Celebration and thanking;
14. Teaching the skill to someone else;
15. Next skill (if necessary).

Case 14.1

Two concerned parents bring their 15-year-old daughter to the Positive CBT therapist. They are very worried about her weight: she weighs 88 pounds and is continuing to lose weight. The family doctor has spoken to them about hospitalization. The father surreptitiously butters her sandwiches to smuggle in some fat. They are at their wits' end: "Please do something about this!" The daughter, however, feels that she does not weigh too little at all, that she is still too heavy in fact. The therapist has a complainant-relationship with the parents (see Chapter 6) because they want their daughter to change and they want the therapist to make sure this happens. The therapist has a visitor-relationship with the daughter: she is not experiencing her weight and her eating as a problem. The therapist compliments them all on showing up, especially the daughter; she can undoubtedly think of something more fun to do than spend time with a therapist and her worried parents! When she is asked about her goal (since she came to the therapist anyway), she says she would like for her parents to leave her alone more. The therapist asks what she thinks would need to be different about her behavior and situation in order for her parents to be able to take a step back and to be somewhat more reassured. "If I were to go to school more often," she replies. The therapist asks questions about the positive consequences (functional behavior analysis (FBA) of the preferred behavior). As a result, she turns out to be willing to attend school more often to get a bit more freedom, and, as far as this goal is concerned, there is now a customer-relationship between the therapist and the daughter. The therapist also asks about the positive consequences (FBA) this will have in the relationship with her parents. Then the daughter is complimented on her willingness to go to school again, thus helping her parents to relax a little. Only at a later stage in therapy did it become possible to discuss her weight.

Exercise 14.2

In this balloon game every child gets two minutes to write down (or draw) what he is good at. Then pairs are formed and each pair blows up one balloon. The rules of the game are:

1. *You play until one of you scores five points;*
2. *You can hit the balloon with your hands and only after you say what you are good at (e.g., "I am good at playing chess");*
3. *The balloon must stay up in the air. You score points when your partner misses the balloon and the balloon hits the floor or when he can't say what he is good at;*
4. *You can check your partner twice during the game. Say CHECK and ask your partner to give you proof of what he has said.*

This is a nice exercise for children, because usually they come up with far more things they are good at than when they made the list at the beginning of the game. This exercise is also useful for adults with low self-esteem.

Homework suggestions for children (and families)

Berg and Steiner (2003) list a number of homework suggestions for children and families that can be divided into two categories: "do-more-of-what-works" tasks, which are the more prevalent, and "do-something-different" tasks, which are suggested only under extreme circumstances, especially where adolescents are concerned. Proposing a homework assignment or experiment carries the therapy into the client's (the child's and possibly his or her parents') real life outside the therapy room. They provide guidelines and principles for suggesting homework:

- The experiment must be related to what the client wants, as discussed during the first session;
- The experiment must be doable and should usually involve a small step toward the client's goal. It is important to take things slowly;
- The main purpose of the experiment is to elicit different reactions from those who play an important role in the child's life. The experiment or the homework alone rarely makes a difference; what matters are other people's responses to the child's execution of the experiment. If solely the child knows the child's new behavior, it has but a limited effect. It is important to generate a ripple effect that involves the observations and reactions of the people who are important to the child;
- If the therapist cannot think of an idea for an experiment, he should not force himself to come up with one; often a mere compliment is sufficient to bring about new behavior;
- Most experiments fall into the category of "doing more of what works";
- The number of "do-something-different" tasks that the child is asked to carry out should be extremely small. These exercises are useful for breaking a chronic pattern that has everyone frustrated.

Behavior experiments that Berg and Steiner propose are:

- Flipping a coin. When the child wakes up, he flips a coin. If the child throws tails, he engages in a secret new activity. If the child throws heads, it will be an ordinary day and the child does nothing different. The parents then have to guess which way the coin landed each morning, but the child has to keep this information secret. At the next session with the therapist, the parents can compare notes with each other and with the child;
- Surprise task. Together with the child, the therapist finds out what the child could do that would really surprise the parents (making breakfast, cleaning his room), which then becomes a surprise the child can carry out himself. The child is asked to pay attention to the others' reactions. A surprise task is sometimes referred to as a technique of pattern disruption. Parents who claim that they have "already tried everything" often make progress by carrying out a surprise task. The predictable way in which parents react to their child's behavior can be disrupted if the parents do something different, for example, give a surprise kiss or do something kind instead of becoming angry.

  The surprise can also come out of a "wonder bag." The child and the parents each write down five wishes, each on a separate piece of paper. The child's wishes and the parents' wishes are placed in separate bags and the bags are exchanged. Each week each family member pulls a wish from the bag he received in the exchange, and each individual has a week to make the wish come true. What we have here, then, are (fulfillable) wishes – for example, for the parents to read the child a story, for one of the parents to go along to a sports activity, for the child to clean his or her desk – rather than assignments;
- Pretend the miracle has happened. After there is a clear description of what the miracle looks like, the child is asked to choose a day or part of a day for the miracle to occur. On that day the child is to pretend that the miracle has occurred. The child then pays attention to who has noticed that he is acting as if the miracle has happened and what he is doing differently;
- General observation task. This task can be assigned to the child and parents. The therapist may tell the child: "Pay attention to the expression on your mom's face each time you start your homework without having to be told to." He may tell the parents: "Pay attention to the times when things are going well at home" or "Observe the times when things are going well and do not need to change."

Exercise 14.3

Invite the parents and the child to make a list of things that the child can do that are agreeable or impressive. Every time the child carries out a task assigned by the parents or the child engages in a desired behavior, the parents put a marble in a glass jar. In the evening the parents and the child briefly discuss what each marble signifies and what went well that day. When the jar is full, the child receives a reward.

Doing something fun with the child is a nice way to positively reinforce the desired behavior. Berg and Steiner describe three additional activities. For the first activity, called "magic five minutes," parents spend five minutes with the child every day, regardless of how the child has behaved. The child gets to determine how the five minutes are spent. The second activity that they suggest is horsing around with the child every day, and for the third, the parents ask the child to take on a "big responsibility," for example, preparing meals or running errands. This allows the child to feel important and make a positive contribution to family life.

Berg and Steiner believe that parents and teachers have a "treasure box" full of tricks at their disposal, even if they are often unaware of this. It is often enough, therefore, to "do more of what works." They also suggest a few techniques derived from hypnotherapy that parents and children can use:

- The hand-on-your-hand technique is a hypnotic form of cue conditioning, whereby the child carries a positive feeling from a previous situation into a situation where that positive emotion is needed. A connection is established between that positive feeling and a touch of the child's wrist. The parent demonstrates this to the child by touching the child's hand with his or her own. The goal is for the child to be able to conjure that positive emotion by himself in the future by briefly touching his or her own wrist;
- Concentration techniques, such as rubbing thumb and index finger together or placing one's hands on one's head, can be used by children to pay attention in class, for example;
- Imagining a safe place with the child is a technique that offers the child a feeling of security. It can be an existing or dreamed-up place that the child can visit in his or her mind whenever he or she needs to feel safe and relax.

I would suggest making a compliment box for the aforementioned techniques. To make a "compliment box," each day all members of the family put a note with a compliment for each of the other family members into a box. This encourages them to take a positive view of each other. At dinner, the family members remove the compliments from the box and read them to each other. It is my experience that if not every member of the family is motivated to change yet (there is a customer-relationship between the therapist and client), even those who initially do not want to play along often will later on when they notice how it improves the atmosphere among the others.

Positive reinforcement

Positive reinforcement is one of the most important tools that parents, teachers, and caregivers have at their disposal in dealing with children (and adults). It has a very positive effect on everybody irrespective of status, position, or nature of the problem. Positive reinforcement helps in solving problems but also helps in developing someone's possibilities to feel better and to maintain agreeable relationships. Material reinforcement such as sweets or an outing can be used, but also social reinforcement such as a smile, eye contact, company, compliments, or a pat on the shoulder. This social reinforcement is particularly effective but unfortunately underutilized. In all kinds of social situations the golden rule applies: 5 to 1 is the most effective, in other words five compliments, confirmations, and so on, against one disapproval, criticism, or negative remark (Flora, 2000).

However, there is a difference between positive reinforcement and positive approach. One does not reinforce the person, only the behavior of that person. A positive approach to the person is also very useful and produces favorable effects, for instance on the well-being of this person. Reinforcement of behavior must closely follow that behavior if it is to be at all effective and what for one is reinforcement is not so for another. It is not expensive, is inexhaustible, and it works, so long as there is enough variation.

Many things can be positive reinforcers, including consumables (for example, food or drinks), activities (for example, a favorite game), objects that can be manipulated, things we can possess, and social reinforcers which range from being with someone to physical affection. Some reinforcers, such as food and warmth, which are naturally desirable, are called primary reinforcers. Other things, such as money, are called conditioned reinforcers, because they come to function as reinforcers themselves when they have been paired with a primary reinforcer. An event or object can be said to be a positive reinforcer, however, only if we see that the behavior immediately preceding it has actually strengthened – increased in frequency, rate, duration, or intensity.

Effective approaches to parenting, teaching, and other guidance tend to emphasize systematic use of positive consequences – positive reinforcement – to shape new and more adaptive behavior. Positive reinforcement is the "magic" that leads to healthier, happier lives (Plaud, 2001).

In the upbringing of children and at schools there should be more awareness of the potential for the empowerment of the child and for the development of his competencies by making use of the previously-mentioned positive reinforcement. This contrasts with schools where the focus is mainly on achievement and where insufficient motivation or achievement is punished. Csikszentmihalyi, one of the founders of Positive Psychology, discovered that the principles and the practice of the Montessori method offered many possibilities for "flow." After research he confirmed that this was indeed the case in the Montessori education, for example, by over-learning subject matter. This means that when a child masters the subject perfectly, he will still continue repeating it several times. According to Csikszentmihalyi it is challenges such as these, which provide flow.

Exercise 14.4

Invite a small group of children in the classroom to become "happiness detectives." Their mission is to track down all the things they see others doing which lead to the class becoming a place with more happiness and well-being. All the ideas, which fulfill this mission, are first listed. After a week the small group get together again and share their discoveries. Subsequently there are regular monthly gatherings at which the group discuss what they have seen in the class that promotes well-being. Such a group can also be formed as support for a certain child or student who has difficulties or it can simply be started up without any specific reason. The groups can swap around from time to time.

Teachers who launched these "happy detectives" at school found that the children who spend some time being "happiness detectives" acquired better social skills and more self-confidence and showed more cooperative behavior in the class. "Happiness detectives" can of course also be introduced to group therapy, life-groups, and to groups at the workplace.

Positive assumptions

Berg (www.brief-therapy.org), one of the founders of SFBT, lists a number of positive working assumptions about children and about parents. These assumptions are helpful for therapists in maintaining a positive focus when doing therapy with children and their families. These assumptions are:

Until proven otherwise, we believe that all children want to:

- have their parents be proud of them;
- please their parents and other adults;
- be accepted as a part of a social group;
- be active and involved in activities with others;
- learn new things;
- be surprised and surprise others;
- voice their opinion and choices;
- make choices when given an opportunity.

Until proven otherwise, we believe that all parents want to:

- be proud of their child;
- have a positive influence on their child;
- hear good news about their child and what their child is good at;
- give their child a good education and a good chance of success in life (however they define it);
- see that their child's future is better than theirs;
- have a good relationship with their child;
- be hopeful about their child;
- feel that they are good parents.

Feedback

Building a culture of feedback is essential in psychotherapy, also when working with groups. You can find more information about the use of the Outcome Rating Scale (ORS) and the Session Rating Scale (SRS) in Chapter 10.

The Child Outcome Rating Scale (CORS) and Child Session Rating Scale (CSRS) are developed for working with children. The Young Child Outcome Rating Scale and Young Child Session Rating Scale do not use words, but emoticons (smileys). For more information see: www.centerforclinicalexcellence.com.

Positive CBT with Families

Positive genograms

A genogram is a pictorial display of a person's family relationships and (medical) history. It goes beyond a traditional "family tree" by allowing the users to visualize hereditary patterns and psychological factors. In a problem-focused way it is used to identify negative repetitive patterns of behavior and to recognize hereditary tendencies. In a problem-focused family therapy, genograms are used to study and record relationship patterns between family members and the individual characteristics that make up these patterns that occur. A genogram will help family therapists to make an appropriate assessment of the relationship patterns and where intervention may be needed to assist the family to reduce their dysfunction and/or problematic situation that brought them into therapy.

In a Positive CBT family therapy, the genogram or family tree may be used to study and record existing positive relationship patterns and positive hereditary tendencies and the strengths used to create and maintain them. All family members involved can be asked what they think the strengths and resources of their family are and, if they think it is useful, how to use them more often. Also, ask family members which positive "life mottos" exist in this family (such as: "we will survive" or "no matter what happens, we always have each other").

Exercise 14.5

This is an exercise for very pessimistic or anxious clients. If you are expecting a visit or are planning a holiday with family, which you are dreading, pretend you are the director of a movie in which your family members are playing their usual parts (the ones that drive you or others crazy) and that your job is to get them to deliver their lines or do their usual behaviors to perfection. Imagine some "worst case scenarios" before the visit/holiday and then compare what actually happens to those scenarios to see if they can even come close.

Homework suggestions for families

Selekman (1993) describes a number of sometimes paradoxical homework suggestions for families:

- Solution enhancement task. This task is comparable to the "pay attention to what you do when you overcome the urge" task (see Chapter 10). The client writes down helpful solutions on cards and he carries these "solution cards" around with him in order to read them in difficult times;
- Coin flip task. At the start of the day, parents flip a coin to determine who will be in charge of the children's education for the day. This task can help parents who disagree about how their children should be raised or punished.

This technique can also be used in a team if the team members have conflicting views;

- Habit control ritual. This task works well with families that have experienced problems over a long period of time. The task is based on a technique from narrative therapy called "externalizing the problem" (see Appendix E). Every day, family members observe what they do to face the problem and make sure that the problem does not take control. They can also pay attention to the times when the problem gets the better of them. In the evening, the family discusses how the day went and can design strategies for improvement. One variation is the symbolic externalization ritual: family members choose a symbol for the problem, describe their relationship to that symbol, what they would like to say to the symbol, and what they want to do with it once they have conquered it;

- Writing letters. It can be useful, especially in a school context, to write a letter. Selekman offers the example of a conflict between a teacher and a student. He helped the mother write a letter to the teacher in which she complimented him on his patience with, and concern for, her son and expressed her hope that things would go better for her son at school. She wrote to the teacher that she had given her son a task: He was to pay attention to the things he liked about the teacher, write them down, and tell her about them after school. This dramatically changed the relationship between the teacher and the student;

- Assigning ordeals. Erickson (in: Rossi, 1980) developed this therapeutic strategy as a last resort in order to make it as uncomfortable as possible for the client to maintain his problem. Selekman uses this strategy when the client reports that nothing is going better or that things are going worse. It involves the assignment of a very arduous task; for example, Erickson had a depressed client carry around a few pounds of bricks in a shopping bag for a while as a symbol of the heavy burden of her depression;

- Predicting the next crisis. Selekman suggests this for exceedingly pessimistic clients and families who are often in crisis. The therapist asks for many details about the next crisis: Who will be involved, where will it take place, what effect will it have on others? This may help break a pattern, as the therapist and clients can look for ways to withstand the crisis: How did they solve a previous crisis, what worked before, what could be useful again?

- Exaggerating the problem. When clients exaggerate the problem, it sometimes becomes apparent that they can exert more control over it than they suspected. This task may offer a starting point for change.

Parenting groups

Selekman (1993) describes a therapy for groups of parents of adolescents. The adolescents themselves do not attend these groups, because they are for parents only. The parenting group convenes six times, the time intervals between sessions progressively increasing as a sign of the therapist's confidence in the group. Numerous questions are asked during these parenting groups. At the end of each session, the following homework suggestions are given to the parents:

- First session. Parents are invited to pay attention to what is going well (at home, in the relationship with the adolescent, in the adolescent's behavior) and should remain the way it is;
- Second session. Parents are invited to observe what steps they can take to reach their goals. The parents are also asked to observe how their child responds to this so that they can talk about it during the next session;
- Third session. Parents are invited to do more of what works;
- Fourth session. Parents are invited to do something different if it doesn't work, and to pay attention to what works and do more of it;
- Fifth session. Parents are invited to do more of what works or, for parents who do not report any progress, to pretend the miracle has happened, and pay attention to how the child reacts to this;
- At the sixth and final session, there's a celebration: there are snacks and drinks and the parents receive certificates declaring them to be "Solution-Focused Parents," the parents all give a brief speech in which they talk about how they've grown as parents, and they are invited to join the "Solution-Oriented Parents' Alumni Association," through which they can be invited to act as consultants to future parenting groups.

Seating arrangements

Topographic interventions are interventions in which the therapist is the director who gives suggestions to his clients as where to sit. They require that the therapist does not see the seating arrangement as coincidental and unimportant but that he wonders whether the seat each person takes is functional for the therapy process. Erickson (in Rossi, 1980) often used topographic interventions. For example, he asked the child to leave the room for a while, so the mother could take his place: when the mother took the seat of her child, she could think more clearly about him and his point of view.

Also the therapist himself should not be too strongly tied to his own seat. When he is supportive, he can move his chair a bit closer to the client. By sliding his chair a bit backwards, he can indicate that he does not want to participate in the conversation. Each seating arrangement has its own effect. The way in which the clients are seated in relation to each other and the therapist, is a major structural intervention: it makes clear, in a nonverbal way, what is expected of the clients and how they are supposed to behave in front of each other and the therapist. It can stress the status and authority of the therapist and the way communication is supposed to happen.

The therapist may change the seating arrangements at the beginning or during the session or can invite his clients to go to a different room altogether. Selekman (1997, p. 57) even has two rooms: a problem-focused room and a solution-focused room. "Sometimes we go into a completely different room when beginning this part of the assessment session. I say: 'Now we can talk about solutions and change – where you want to be when we have a successful outcome here.'" Not every therapist will be so fortunate as to have a "problem room" and a "solutions room" and that is not necessary of course.

Metcalf (1998) provides a variation. In group therapy she uses a combination of topographic interventions and "projection in time," called the "three-chairs technique." The first chair represents life five years ago, the second chair stands for the present, and the third chair signifies life in five years' time. The intervals can be decreased or increased. The group members are all invited to take a seat in the three chairs and talk about themselves as if the time indicated by the chair is now. The other group members may ask the following questions:

- Are you happy?
- What was your greatest fear?
- In which chair did you feel less fear or more happiness?
- How did you manage to solve your problems in the past?
- What advice would have helped you then?

A "reflecting team" is a form of indirect learning and this often has more impact than direct instructions. It is a very helpful setting, especially for families with adolescents.

The rules of the reflecting team are simple. There are two or more persons (for example, the mother and a teacher) talking about a client who sits in the room (at some distance from the table at which the others and the therapist are sitting).

- The client is asked to carefully follow the conversation and take notes about new aspects he hears and new ideas that come to mind; he does not participate in the conversation.
- The conversation about the client includes:
  — The strengths of the client;
  — What went well in the past weeks;
  — Where improvements were observed;
  — Where on the scale the client is seen if 10 stands for the wished goal;
  — What the others would observe the client do differently, when he is one step up the scale;
  — Which of the existing strengths and competences the client might use to get one step up.

After about 20–30 minutes the therapist moves over to the client and asks about which new aspects he heard and which new ideas might have come up. Now the others follow the conversation and may take notes. Then the therapist turns back to the table and there is a last round of respectful comments about the things the client has said. There is a strict rule that the statements should be positive and respectful.

Feedback

Building a culture of feedback is essential in psychotherapy, also when working with families. Each member of the family fills out his own Session Rating Scale (SRS).

You can find more information about the use of the Outcome Rating Scale (ORS) and the Session Rating Scale (SRS) in Chapter 10. For more information see: www.centerforclinicalexcellence.com.

Transcultural Positive CBT

Cognitive behavioral therapy (CBT) emerged from the work of Beck and Ellis. However, it has been extended well beyond the borders of the research groups of these two founders, to all over the world. The question, taking into account the unprecedented expansion of cognitive-behavioral therapy, is whether current CBT is still a coherent and homogeneous approach. Therefore, the major representatives (presidents and/or board members) of major cognitive-behavioral psychotherapy organizations in Asia, Europe, South America, and the USA were interviewed. Interestingly, both at a theoretical and practical level, the perspectives are quite coherent, suggesting that the cognitive-behavioral approach is a robust approach with cultural adaptations that do not affect the main architecture of the theory and practice of CBT (David, 2007).

However, traditional CBT is based on western concepts and illness models. The focus is on the individual and on treating the individual. This may form a challenge, especially because some people view themselves in the context of their immediate and wider family and/or in the context of their community. Critics of CBT argue that by focusing on the individual, the larger familial, community, and societal issues and problems are ignored or left unspoken and unaddressed.

In my work as a trainer for the Mental Health Team of Doctors Without Borders I have the privilege of visiting many countries around the world, where I train counselors and other professionals such as doctors and midwives, working in areas of unrest and conflict about topics such as general psychiatry, posttraumatic stress, and staffcare. I am always very impressed with their resilience and hopefulness to survive and sometimes even thrive under very difficult circumstances. My training methods are based on Positive CBT; the courses are goal-driven ("What will be the best result of this training for you as participants?") and are focused on finding and using their strengths and competences, and applying their solutions and successes to confront their huge problems. At the end of every training session the trainees are invited to give feedback, using the Group SRS (see Chapter 13).

15

Positive CBT in the Workplace

Be the change you want to see in your team/organization
Fredrike Bannink (2012) (modified quote from Gandhi)

Introduction

We spend about a third of our lives at work, therefore there is no better reason to ensure that the workplace is as healthy as possible. When referring to a healthy working environment we think as much about physical as mental well-being. Job satisfaction, commitment, and employee perception of the organization are important aspects. There is a clear connection between well-being at work and good health. Well-being at work is indirectly influential on the level of contentment in all areas of life and is not exclusive to the workplace. A positive psychological development can be derived from a job where a high level of control and social support are possible to meet certain of the job's inherent requirements. Formerly in the workplace little or no control could be exerted by the employees (think conveyor belt).

Turner, Spencer, and Stone (2005) state that the best way to improve the workplace is to create jobs whereby employees are encouraged to be active both in their tasks and their environment. Autonomy, challenging work, and the possibility of social contact all contribute to the employee's feeling of competency. They describe the "Job Characteristics model" in which three elements are important:

- To experience work is useful;
- To feel responsible;
- To receive information about results.

Individuals commonly report that what they like about work is the sense of meaning and purpose it gives them, that is, serving a goal larger than themselves.

Practicing Positive CBT: From Reducing Distress to Building Success, First Edition. Fredrike Bannink.
© 2012 John Wiley & Sons, Ltd. Published 2012 by John Wiley & Sons, Ltd.

Finding ways to keep staff connected to a sense of purpose can be motivating and encourage more positive feelings. This can be done by having a strong vision or mission and talking about this more at meetings. Finding ways to tell inspiring stories about how staff's work affects clients is another useful way to do this.

Positive CBT in a Team

Well-being

Working in a team can provide individual well-being: it provides a social network where one can find support and the idea of belonging. High levels of clarity within the team of expectations of its goals and motivation in reaching these goals will provide for increased well-being of the team. Team members with clear perceptions of the task to be performed report better psychological health than lone workers or team members lacking such clarity. The social context in the workplace is therefore important. Team members with high levels of team motivation proved to be more motivated to contribute to the organization as a whole. There was also a positive connection between feeling good about the organization and an increased feeling of well-being (Turner , Spencer, and Stone, 2005).

There is a clear positive link between enjoying one's work and achievements, and between a positive attitude and well-being. Well-being therefore yields better results. A positive attitude delivers more pleasant and better work creating an upward spiral of positivity.

Exercise 15.1

Interview your colleague, using the following questions:

- *Ask your colleague to choose a situation at work when he was successful;*
- *Explore in detail how he did it: how, what, when, where, with whom;*
- *What else was important?*
- *Which of his competences and strengths were helpful?*
- *What would his client say he did that was helpful?*
- *On a scale from 10 to 0 how confident is he that this will happen again?*
- *What does he have to focus on to increase the chance that it will happen again?*

Resilience

Resilience means bouncing back from adversity. But instead of bouncing back, which suggests a quick and effortless recovery from adversity, I would prefer to use the term "coming back," because it often involves a struggle and lots of hard work.

Over the last few years the interest in resilience has centered not only on individuals but also on teams. Initially resilience is not reflected in the team results or in the quality of each individual employee. Resilient teams are teams wherein the team members inter-react and cooperate with each other in a defined way. Characteristics of employees in resilient teams are:

- Helping each other to excel;
- Openly sharing mutual evaluations;
- Listening attentively to a colleague's advice;
- Permitting and accepting critical comments;
- Having fun and enjoying humor at work;
- Supporting colleagues through difficulties;
- Constantly seeking solutions;
- Not to be disinclined to re-align their opinions;
- Not avoiding conflicts but constructively using them to attain deep dialog;
- To permit each other sufficient space to allow creativity and success;
- Being modest enough to learn from each other.

The resilience of a team is greater than the sum of the resilience of each individual member. It is concealed within the quality of the interactions between the members, which is being described in the example of the geese in the next story.

Story 15.1: We Can Learn From Geese

As each goose flaps its wings it creates an uplift for the bird following, by flying in a V- formation; the whole flock has 71% greater flying range than if the bird flew alone. Many of us recognize that there is a lot I can do by myself, there is a lot I can do with a colleague or partner, but the power of what I can get done with a group is quantum. The lesson from this fact – people who share a common direction and sense of community can get where they are going quicker and easier because they are traveling on the thrust of one another.

Whenever a goose falls out of formation, it suddenly feels the drag and resistance of trying to fly alone and quickly gets back into formation to take advantage of the lifting power of the bird immediately in front. Lesson from this fact – if we have as much sense as a goose, we will stay in formation with those who are headed where we want to go and be willing to accept their help, as well as give ours to others who are looking for support.

When the lead goose gets tired, it rotates back into the formation and another goose flies at the point position – an invaluable lesson for us to apply to all our group work. It pays to take turns doing the hard tasks and sharing the leadership. With people, as with geese, we are interdependent on each other's skills and capabilities and unique arrangements of power and resources; no one person is right to lead in all circumstances and at all times. Leaders need to learn to let

(continued)

go at times, and others must feel comfortable in stepping forward – no false modesty – no greed for power and position for its own sake.

When a goose becomes ill or wounded or shot down, two geese move out of the formation and follow it down to help protect it. They stay with it until it is able to fly again or dies, then they launch out together with another formation or they catch up with their flock. Lesson – if we have as much sense as geese, we, too, will stand by each other in difficult times as well as when we are strong.

The geese in formation honk from behind to encourage those up front to keep up their speed. Lesson – we need to make sure our honking from behind is encouragement and not something else! In groups where there is great encouragement against great odds, the production is much greater by the power of encouragement. The word "courage" means to stand by one's heart, to stand by one's core, to encourage someone else's core, to encourage someone else's heart – that's the quality of honking.

Source: Anonymous

Exercise 15.2

Reduce negativity in your team and enhance an upward spiral of positivity by ending negative gossip and by replacing this with "positive gossip." Positive gossip leads to the discussion of someone's attributes and successes. By painting a positive picture of your colleague you will, in an implicit way, exercise influence on the relationship of your colleagues with others. You may think of your colleagues in a positive way: what in their qualities do you value? Which strengths do you attribute to them? How do they contribute to your team? Speak about your colleague in a positive way to others, with or without your colleague being present. Remember that when you point your finger at another person (both in positive and negative gossip), there are three fingers pointing back at yourself!

Positive emotions

What are the strengths and resources of this team?

Gottman (1994) states that in relationships, for every negative or disapproving remark or signal there must be five positive remarks or signals if a relationship is to remain pleasant. Fredrickson carried out research, in cooperation with Losada, in order to develop a mathematical model on the foundation of her broaden-and-build theory of positive emotions. For years Losada was engaged in studying highly functioning teams. According to his mathematical calculations the magical positivity ratio is 2.9013 to 1, rounded up to 3 to 1 (Fredrickson and Losada, 2005). In addition, a lot of research has been done into the differences between flourishing teams and teams that fare less well or not at all well. In highly functioning teams we even see a ratio of 5 to 1 or 6 to 1 (Losada and Heaphy, 2004).

Glass (2009, p. 39) compares the broaden-and-build theory of positive emotions (Fredrickson, see Chapter 9) with Solution Focus and found many similarities. It appears to be the case that positive emotions are generated by asking questions in an open and positive way in combination with imagination, memory, and resources; this builds a wider thought/action repertoire. Thereby these people not only find more solutions for themselves but also generate more curiosity, openness, and acceptance to the thoughts of others. In this way better team cooperation is achieved and the organization's results improve: "Fredrickson's theory not only supports the power of Solution Focus in bringing the fruits of positive psychology to the workplace, but adds food for thought regarding the use and direction of SF in organisations and the aspects of SF we should focus on as practitioners in order to maximise what works."

Exercise 15.3

The following four recommendations will help to build up high quality relationships at your workplace. Cooperation in one or more of the following ways will create greater positivity. Practice this throughout the day at every opportunity. Take note of how this differs from ignoring others or gossiping about them. Also pay attention to how others react and what difference this makes to your relationships.

- *Respect the other person, make sure you are there for them and pay attention to them;*
- *Support the other person whenever you can;*
- *Trust the other person and let them know that you trust them to help you;*
- *Be playful together and have fun without a specific goal.*

"Yes, but" and "yes, and"

The use of "yes, but" is extraordinarily common. In fact, few people actually recognize the subtle negative influence of using "but." It is a worthwhile exercise to become more comfortable with the ability to switch from "yes, but" to "yes, and." The main reason to use "yes, and" instead of "yes, but" is that it positively influences dialog. When using "and" instead of "but," there is a sense of inclusion and acceptance, instead of exclusion and negation.

"Yes, but . . . " is frequently heard within teams and organizations. In reality "yes, but . . . " is simply a form of "no, because . . . ," it is merely not expressed in a direct way. "Yes, but . . . I see that in a different way," "Of course you are

Table 15.1 Differences between "Yes, but" and "Yes, and".

"Yes, but"	*"Yes, and"*
Excludes or dismisses what precedes it	Expands and includes what precedes it
Negates, discounts, or cancels what precedes it	Acknowledges what precedes it
Is often perceived as pejorative	Is often perceived as neutral or positive
Suggests the first issue is subordinate to the second	Suggests there are two equal issues to be addressed

© Fredrike Bannink

right, but . . . " With "yes, but . . . ," you always nibble a little bit off whatever was said before. In a conversation or meeting a "yes, but . . . " makes for negative emotions in no time at all and the conversation will lead nowhere. There ensues a downward spiral of negativity. Therefore it is more beneficial to use "yes, and . . . " to generate positive emotions. Now new possibilities emerge and an upward spiral of positivity is created. It stimulates cooperation with others and resilience within the team. Invite your team to practice "yes, and . . . " whilst avoiding "yes, but . . . " as much as possible. For instance: during meetings place a sign in the middle of the table with the words "YES, BUT . . . " as a reminder.

Positive coaching

There exist many forms of team coaching, previously all problem-focused, however they have in recent years increasingly found favor with Positive Psychology and Solution-focused Brief Therapy. Thereby strengths and solutions become the starting point, not the problem itself. Talking about problems creates problems, talking about solutions creates solutions. Positive coaching of teams and the individual is a goal and competency orientated form of coaching. It generates optimism and hope, increases self-efficacy, and contributes to more self-respect and a better functioning team even in the case of conflicts (Bannink, 2006b, 2008c, 2009bcd, 2010b, 2011).

Encouraging a growth mindset in the team is important. People with a growth mindset believe that ability can improve and develop with hard work and effort (see Chapter 11). They tend to do better than those of equal or superior intelligence but who have a belief that intelligence is fixed and unchangeable: a fixed mindset. It might be a good idea to prime the environment to reinforce a growth mindset, by using pictures representing growth (flowers etc.). When giving feedback to team members, use positive formulations instead of negative ones (e.g., "I think you could become even better at . . . ").

Following you will find some positive exercises for further use in coaching a team.

Exercise 15.4

Invite your team members to interview each other about a "sparkling moment" at work:

1. *Think of a time when you were at your best, when you felt yourself sparkling. Describe it briefly;*
2. *What was it in particular about that moment which caused it to stand out for you?*
3. *What are you most pleased to remember about yourself at that moment?*
4. *What might others have made of you at that moment had they noticed?*
5. *What else were you pleased to notice? What else? And what else?*
6. *If these qualities were to play an even bigger part in your life who would be the first to notice? What would they see? What difference would that make?*

Exercise 15.5

Challenging negative cognitions may be useful in a team. This exercise is about contradicting negative thoughts in your team as quickly as possible. Ask your team members to write down their typical negative thoughts about the team that pop up in their mind sometimes, such as "This team never accomplishes anything worthwhile" or "We don't seem to be able to work together." The idea is to write these thoughts on index cards. After they have written the cards with some of their regular negative thoughts, pick one up at random and read it out loud. Then together rapidly dispute the negative beliefs with every argument everyone can come up with. This is called "Rapid Fire Facts" – everyone rapidly fires contradicting positive facts at the negative sentence. When you run out of facts, pick another card and repeat the positive rapid fire facts. Coming up with contradictory facts will get easier and easier with each card. With this tool your team learns to become quick at contradicting their negative thoughts. This exercise can also be done with an individual client.

Positive CBT in an Organization

The desired future

Beckhard and Harris (1987) developed a model of planned change in organizations:

Current state → Transition state → Desired future state

This model helps to develop a deeper understanding of the process and the phases of planned change. The first step for those involved is to envision a desired future state (also see Chapter 6 about goals). This helps to establish a goal for the change and serves the purpose of beginning the process of unfreezing, as well as being open to something different. Research shows that starting with what people desire in the future generates energy, enthusiasm, motivation, and commitment to the plan and its implementation (Lindaman and Lippitt, 1979). Once this is undertaken, the next step is to move backwards and assess the current state of the organization, its current capabilities, capacities, and so forth. With the envisioned future, and assessment of the current state, the next phase is to create a transition state. This is based, in part, on the gaps between the current state and the desired future state. These gaps create tension, which serve as a motivating force in the transition state. The transition state is a way for a system to balance or modulate its own need for stability with its need for change. Although this model is most often used in large, complex organizational change, the concepts are applicable on both the individual and small-group levels.

Furman (1988), a solution-focused psychiatrist and trainer, asks the "dream team question": "How will your team function in the future when it works together like a dream team?" He proceeds to inquire about goal formulation and what the benefits of reaching the goal will be, in part to increase motivation. He encourages clients to view the path toward the goal as a stepwise process and asks them what actions are needed tomorrow, next week, and next month. He also looks at the strengths and resources within and outside the organization and asks staff members to look for exceptions. Instead of using the term "exceptions," he refers to "times when progress toward the stated goal took place" during another project. Questions are:

- "Who contributed to that?"
- "What about recent progress? Who or what made a difference?"
- "How did you do that?"

During a follow-up meeting an assessment is done to find out what progress has been made and who deserves credit for it.

Another way of inviting the team members to design their preferred future and the pathways towards it is to ask: "Suppose we would meet at the airport and you would tell me that you have won the first prize in a contest for the best team. Your team is about to catch the plane to retrieve the prize. Of course there must be a speech. What are you going to tell the public about how you succeeded in becoming the best team? And whom are you going to thank for their help?"

Appreciative inquiry

Appreciative inquiry (AI), developed by Cooperrider and Whitney (2005) shares much common ground with Positive Psychology and Solution Focus. AI is a method to realize positive change in organizations, searching for the best in people, their organizations, and the relevant world around them. It involves systematic discovery of what gives life to a living system when it is most alive, most effective, and most constructively capable in economic, ecological, and human terms. It involves the art and practice of asking questions that strengthen a system's capacity to apprehend, anticipate, and heighten positive potential. Instead of negation, criticism, and spiraling diagnosis, there is discovery, dream, and design. AI assumes that every living system has many untapped and rich and inspiring accounts of the positive. Contrary to the problem-solving model with its focus on problems, AI focuses on the already positive elements within the organization. In addition there is an essential difference that through AI every employee is involved at the onset of the necessary change. Thereby big changes can be realized in a very short space of time, since the fundamentals have been maximized. If, for example, an organization encounters dissatisfied clients, the question AI poses is not: "What are we doing wrong whereby our clients are dissatisfied" but: "At which point were our clients really satisfied with our organization." A team is not asked: "Tell us why you have so much conflict" but: "Tell us about your team at its best."

Exercise 15.6

The "appreciation wall" is an exercise, which you can do in about 30 minutes with a team. It helps people to get a clear view of what they and their colleagues do that works, creates energy, and strengthens relationships and trust. Hang a flip-over sheet on the wall with the names of all team members on it. Write on the top of the sheet: WHAT WE APPRECIATE IN EACH OTHER.

Then invite everyone to take a marker pen and write what he appreciates about what others do, right under their names. When, after 15 minutes, everyone is ready, look with the team at what has been written. It may be interesting to talk a bit about some of the appreciative statements. The team leader may ask questions: "Who wrote this compliment?", "How did you notice this person has this strength?", "What do you appreciate about it?", "What makes it valuable for you to have a colleague who does this?" Often the responses are enthusiastic. Complimenting people directly and accepting compliments can sometimes be awkward, but with this exercise this usually is very easy and pleasant.

Story 15.2: Swarm Intelligence

In line with the story about geese, mentioned earlier in this chapter, Stam and Bannink (2008) and Bannink (2010c) use the algorithm of a swarm of birds with their description of a positive organization. The human mind (and therefore also its intelligence) is a social phenomenon that arises through interaction in a social world. Human intelligence therefore results from human communication. This happens through evaluating, imitating, and drawing comparison with others' behavior and by learning from their experiences and successful solutions. This is sometimes referred to as "swarm intelligence." It explains how, for example, a swarm of birds can demonstrate very intelligent and complex behavior

(continued)

despite their scant individual brain capacity. A swarm is therefore a system of social processes. Swarm behavior in humans can manifest itself by way of ideas, religious conviction, attitudes, behavior, and everything else to do with the mind. And this is relevant to both teams and organizations. A computer model was developed to simulate this swarm behavior, whereby it was discovered that only three rules were needed to make the program work:

- *Retreat before you collide with the other;*
- *Try to fly as fast as the bird next to you in the swarm;*
- *Aim to fly at the center of the swarm as from your own perspective.*

In considering these rules it is clear that every rule links the lone bird with the other. They entwine the individuals into a system (a team or organization). By observing only these three simple rules the spots on the screen behaved as a swarm, just as with birds, fish, and bees. Migration could be explained by the birds' ability to combine a mutual goal (for example, a meadow in the south of France) with an acute sensitivity to magnetic fields. A team's or organization's sensitivity is not tuned to magnetic fields but to communication, whereby the following solution-focused rules apply:

- *If it works (better), do more of it;*
- *If it does not work, do something else;*
- *If it works, learn from each other and teach it to each other.*

Everyone in a team or organization is co-responsible for the quality of his own personal interactions. Gandhi once said: "Be the change you want to see in the world." With teams this statement can be adapted to: "Be the change you want to see in your team."

Positive leadership

Organizations, which employ the principles with positive leadership, achieve better results and enjoy more prolonged success than average organizations. These improved results are apparent not only through higher profits but also through prosperous growth, expansion, and the optimizing of human resources. This is not due to the qualities of the leader but the quality of the leadership. Instead of only solving problems, removing obstacles, increasing competition, or even improving efficiency – in order to achieve exceptional positive results – positive leaders concentrate on the flourishing of their organization and on the motivation of their people. This approach is always relevant and not limited to difficult circumstances. The key is in emphasizing the positive. People are more inclined to pay attention to negative rather than positive developments. This results in an inclination to concentrate on negativity – a tendency to which managers are particularly prone since they are more likely to be confronted with problems. Managers mostly think that they have been appointed to the role of problem solvers. Research into the usage of language in American business papers shows that positive terms (like virtue, empathy, care, or kindness) were rarely used, whereas within just in a few years the usage of negative terms quadrupled with words such as defeat, fighting, and competition. Positive leaders continue to assert the positive, even at times when there is less justification for positivity. When managers stimulate empathy amongst their employees, accept mistakes, and express gratitude, it benefits productivity, profitability, quality, innovation, and customer satisfaction. Additionally, personnel turnover decreases (Cameron, 2008).

Haidt (2006) suggests the metaphor of a rider on an elephant. The rider is our conscious thoughts (and emotions). The elephant is our unconscious emotions (and thoughts). The rider is the conscious, analytic part of our mind. It is extremely limited in capacity, requires significant effort, and is error prone. The elephant is much better at analyzing, organizing, prioritizing, and weighing multiple factors to reach a decision. The conscious mind is better at precise calculations and following rules. However, it also is subject to stereotyping and other framing errors, likely to be a way of managing its limited data handling capacity. It is also, however, capable of communicating with other riders, setting goals, and planning.

Fredrickson's broaden-and-build theory of positive emotions (see Chapter 9) suggests that we experience positive emotions when the rider and elephant are in sync and working well together. If, however, the elephant becomes out of sync with the rider, the rider is in trouble.

According to Haidt, changes regularly fail because the rider is unable to keep the elephant on course long enough, which is why it is sensible to push changes through gradually. There is no such difference in positive leadership: the importance in management is that rider and elephant stay in harmony, thereby increasing the possibilities of attaining successful leadership. It is important for managers to realize that their co-workers are both riders and elephants too. How harmonious are they? What is your organization doing to promote that harmony? Are the team members tapping into their elephant abilities?

Positive leadership contains the following elements:

- Begin by formulating some personal values like integrity, responsibility, honesty, and hope. Communicate these values to your co-workers and behave in accordance with these values;
- Set goals via, for instance, the PDCA-circle: Plan, Do, Check, Act (Deming 1986). Connect these goals to your personal values. As an example, the personal value "honesty" was premised by a manager when he was obliged to close one his departments and his co-workers had to be transferred to different departments;
- Formulate concrete goals;
- Employ your personal strengths to reach these goals. To draw out your strengths you can do the VIA Strengths test (see Chapter 4);
- Check the progress of these goals and regularly question your faith in your ability to reach these goals;

- Ensure that these goals are important and feasible. According to the Hope Theory (see Chapter 5), goals that are too difficult or too easily attainable discourage the application of effort;
- If a chosen project's goal is no longer obtainable then strike a balance between attempting to continue or discontinue the project;
- Be "realistically optimistic" by working on positive self-fulfilling prophecies and giving co-workers positive feedback;
- Display resilience in the face of obstacles and seek out alternative routes if the chosen path to the goal is impassable (Hope theory contends that hopeful people are faster than people lacking hope at finding more alternative routes to their chosen goal in the face of obstacles).

Building on the existing ideas of heroic leadership and servant leadership McKergow (2009) mentions the metaphor of "leader as host." We can look at hero and servant as opposing ends of a spectrum of hierarchical leadership. Host lies above this spectrum; it is a flexible and context-dependent role, which sometimes necessitates hero behavior, sometimes servant, and many in-between possibilities.

We are all familiar with the act of hosting. Who has not given a dinner party, invited people for drinks, and celebrated their birthday? We all know this role. And who has not attended a party as a guest, or stayed in someone's house for a weekend? So we all also know the counterpart to host: guest. These are both roles we know, and both come with norms and expectations. Indeed, one cannot be a host without guests. The creation of space for others and activity within it are the essential points of the style of leadership as host. As advantages of the solution-focused host metaphor, McKergow mentions that it is an everyday image; host and guest are co-defining; hosting is an activity, rather than a defining characteristic of a person; hosting gives a definite feel of some responsibility for the success of the event; and the role of host can involve behaving as total hero or absolute servant.

Story 15.3: What You Give is What You Get

New immigrants in the USA in the 1850s received free grants of land if they were prepared to do the necessary work to make them liveable. A family, living on the East coast, undertook the long trip of several months, finally arriving in the middle of the continent, in Kansas. They stopped near a stream to feed their animals and children and met an old farmer who had been living in the area for many years. They asked him: "What is it like in this region? Is it a good place to plant our seeds, to build our farm, and to raise our children? How are the people here? Are they good? Are they cooperative?"

The farmer replied: "What were the people like in the East where you came from?" The head of the family replied: "Oh, they were awful, and not at all cooperative!" The old farmer said: "I am sorry to inform you that it is exactly like that here. It would be better to continue your voyage and look elsewhere for your new home."

Then another family arrived and they had also traveled a long time coming from the East. By chance they stopped at the same stream, fed their animals and children, and met the same old farmer.

Like the first family they asked: "What is it like in this area? Is it a good place to plant our seeds, build our farm, and raise our children? How are the people here?" The farmer replied: "What were the people like in the East? And this family replied: "Oh, they were very kind, very helpful, and cooperative." The old farmer replied: "It is exactly like that here. My dear neighbors, welcome to your new land!"

From: Adapted from Peacock (2001)

Positive meetings and positive supervision/peer consultation

More information about how to conduct positive meetings in the workplace and about positive supervision and peer consultation can be found in Bannink (2010a, 2010c). An example of both how to conduct a positive meeting and a positive peer consultation follow.

Exercise 15.7

Begin a meeting, team discussion, or peer consultation by forming groups of four to five people and spend 5 minutes dealing with the question: What are you pleased about? (In your private life or in your working life). Or ask some members to briefly outline any of their successes in the past week. By beginning the meeting in a positive way you increase the chances of the meeting continuing in a positive vein. Also, a variation of the "three good things" exercise (see Chapters 7 and 9) can be used at the beginning of meetings with everyone saying what has gone well since they last met.

16

Positive CBT and the Future

The only real voyage of discovery consists not in seeking new landscapes but in having new eyes

Marcel Proust

Introduction

"Human beings are more often drawn by the future than they are driven by the past, and so a science that measures and builds expectations, planning and conscious choice will be more potent than a science of habits, drives and circumstances. That we are drawn by the future rather than just driven by the past is extremely important and directly contrary to the heritage of social science and the history of psychology. It is, nevertheless, a basic and implicit premise of Positive Psychology." (Seligman, 2011, p. 106). Whether it is about prevention or treatment, to further develop the science of human flourishing, and to achieve the goal of complete mental health, scientists must diagnose and study the etiology and treatments associated with mental health, and develop a science of mental health.

Research

Prevention

Unfortunately, the medical model did not move us much closer to the prevention of serious problems. Most prevention models have been developed from a perspective of building competences, not correcting weaknesses. Research discovered that human strengths such as courage, optimism, interpersonal skills, faith, hope, honesty, perseverance, flow, and insight act as buffers against mental illness. Therefore, a science of human strengths should be created to help

Practicing Positive CBT: From Reducing Distress to Building Success, First Edition. Fredrike Bannink.
© 2012 John Wiley & Sons, Ltd. Published 2012 by John Wiley & Sons, Ltd.

understand and learn how to foster these virtues in young people. Working on personal weakness and on damaged brains has rendered science poorly equipped to do effective prevention. "We need to ask practitioners to recognise that much of the best work they already do in the consulting room is to amplify strengths rather than repair the weaknesses of their clients" (Seligman and Csikszentmihalyi, 2000, p. 6).

Treatment

The model of Positive CBT is new. This is the first book about this promising approach, combining the best of three approaches: traditional CBT, Positive Psychology, and Solution-Focused Brief Therapy. This implies that so far no research has been done. Of course this model needs to be empirically tested and objectively evaluated. What criteria should be used to judge this model? How can we know whether this model leads to better therapy outcomes? Which mechanisms of change are operating with Positive CBT and its outcomes? How is Positive CBT different from traditional CBT and from other approaches, such as Solution-Focused Brief Therapy, Client Centered Therapy, and psychodynamic psychotherapy?

Research should be done on specific elements in Positive CBT and how these may help certain populations or problems under specific conditions or help therapists thrive in their profession instead of merely survive.

Microanalysis of conversations in Positive CBT (see Chapter 12) will be useful for this purpose, because at this moment we don't know yet if communication in Positive CBT is consistent with its model and differs from other models.

Pilot studies and larger studies with randomized control trials (RCT) are needed, since this is the best way to determine the effectiveness of a given approach. These studies will help to develop the evidence base of Positive CBT as an effective approach and to expand Positive CBT beyond psychotherapy to other areas such as education, social services, coaching, organizations, and governments.

Further research will hopefully help to increase the number of clients who benefit from traditional (CBT) approaches. Cost-efficiency considerations along with social and technological changes can make Positive CBT by telephone, Skype, or the Internet the preferred approach for the future, particularly because Positive CBT uses protocols, which easily lend themselves to social media applications.

Training

Positive focus

Until recently the primary emphasis in the training of both psychologists and psychiatrists focused on human weakness. In this way they became, as Seligman stated on TED.com, "victimologists and pathologizers." Slowly but surely, traditional CBT is experiencing a shift towards a more positive focus (see Chapter 3). With this book I would like to pursue the elements of this change.

In future training we would have to find a balance between a focus on pathology and a focus on the strengths of our clients and their environment. In training CBT, there should be a greater emphasis on using a positive lens, as used in Positive CBT, in addition to the negative lens, as used in traditional CBT. Ultimately the aim is to create a large group of Positive CBT therapists who in turn can teach others. Ideally, in the future, every CBT therapist should be competent to use both forms of CBT, since they are two sides of the same coin. They may even let their clients decide which form they prefer. Here one of the basic principles of Solution Focus applies: if it works, do more of it; if it does not work, do something else. It is important to keep in mind that whenever a problem-focused intervention works better than a solution-focused one, you are still working in a solution-focused way.

In training CBT there should also be a greater emphasis on outcome measurement. Conventional wisdom suggests that competence engenders, if not equals, effectiveness. As a result there is a continuing education requirement, designed to ensure that therapists stay abreast of developments that enhance positive outcome of therapy. The vast majority of these trainings do not include any methods for evaluating the effectiveness of the approach. Emphasis is placed on learning skills or techniques of a particular brand or style of therapy. But this emphasis on competence versus outcome decreases effectiveness and efficiency. Research has shown that there is no or little relationship between the experience level and effectiveness of therapists (Clement, 1994). Unlike the product-oriented efforts the field has employed so far, outcome management results in significant improvements in effectiveness. Liberated from the traditional focus on models or techniques, therapists will be better able to achieve what they always claimed to have been in the business of doing: assisting change.

Focus on clients' well-being

Our clients create meanings or definitions of reality through their use of words and talking to one another. Clients' capacity to change is connected to their ability to see things differently. De Jong and Berg (2002, p. 349) state: "These shifts in client perceptions and definitions of reality, which are a part of clients' solution building, occur most readily in conversations about alternative futures and useful exceptions. Solutions depend more on clients' capacity to develop and expand their definitions of what they want and how to make that happen than on scientific problem definition, technical assessment, and professional intervention . . . . By using your skills to sustain purposeful conversations, you allow clients to develop the expanded perceptions and definitions they need to live more satisfying and productive lives. Strictly speaking, practitioners do not empower clients or construct alternative meanings for them. Only clients can do that for themselves. However, practitioners can assume and respect clients' competencies and artfully converse with clients so they can create more of what they want in their lives."

Therefore, a focus on the art of psychotherapy may be added to the focus on techniques in traditional CBT, and a focus on mental health may be added to the focus on mental illness. Reducing distress by making miserable people less miserable is just one side of our job, whereas building success by helping them to flourish is the other side (hence the subtitle of this book).

"If science continues to show that one of the most important components of well-being is the ability to love and be loved, to care and to be caring, then our psychological therapies, interventions and training will become increasingly focused on that, be this in our clinics, schools or workplaces."(Gilbert, 2010, p. 197).

Focus on therapists' well-being

Remember the research described in Chapter 1, showing that between 11% and 61% of psychologists have at least one depressive episode in their lives. Positive CBT may reduce the strain placed on therapists and help them to have more lighthearted conversations, which may in turn result in less stress, depression, burnout, and secondary traumatization among therapists. The "least burden principle," described in Chapter 3, not only applies to clients, but also to us therapists.

Seligman (2011, p. 2) states: "Positive Psychology makes people happier. Teaching positive psychology, researching positive psychology, using positive psychology in practice as a coach or therapist, giving positive psychology exercises to tenth graders in a classroom, parenting little kids with positive psychology, teaching drill sergeants how to teach about post-traumatic growth, meeting with other positive psychologists, and just reading about positive psychology all make people happier. The people who work in positive psychology are the people with the highest well-being I have ever known."

"Over the last 45 years I've taught almost every topic in psychology. But I have never had so much fun teaching, nor have my teaching ratings ever been so high as when I have taught positive psychology. When I taught abnormal psychology for 25 years, I could not assign my students meaningful, experiental homework: they couldn't become schizophrenic for a weekend! It was all book learning, and they could never know craziness itself. But in teaching positive psychology, I can assign my students to make a gratitude visit or to do the what-went-well exercise" (Seligman, 2011, p. 34).

Professionals working within the Solution Focus model (psychotherapists, coaches, mediators, teachers) report the same experience: the positive focus in their work enhances their personal well-being. Most professionals and trainers in Solution Focus also believe that adequate skills can be achieved with less training time and experience than is the case for other psychological therapies.

I would like to highlight two more advantages of Positive CBT. One is the use of positive supervision and peer consultation models, as described by Bannink (2010a). With these models, far more cases can be reviewed using less time, with a focus on strengths and successes of our colleagues instead of on their weaknesses and failures, leading to better results. The second advantage is that expertise in short-term, goal-focused and strengths-based therapies, as seen in Positive CBT, will, in these times of economic recession, render its therapists highly marketable.

In Chapter 3 I described the possibilities of Positive CBT and my ideas about the preferred future of CBT.

Building bridges

Until now the fields of traditional CBT, Positive Psychology, and Solution-Focused Brief Therapy have been far apart. As a matter of fact: they know very little about each other. Maybe it is because I live in the Netherlands where we have to build bridges to survive (and flourish: we are one of the happiest nations in the world), and certainly because it is my mission to make this world a better one (even if only in some small way), my aim is to build bridges between different fields within psychotherapy and beyond psychotherapy. In my profession as a mediator, I often use the saying: "The wider the gap, the more beautiful the bridge."

With Positive CBT I want to build bridges between the fields of traditional CBT, Positive Psychology, and Solution-Focused Brief Therapy, so that they can benefit from each other and cooperate in making this world a better one for our clients and ourselves.

By way of introduction we, in the Dutch Association of Behavioural and Cognitive Therapy (VGCt), founded, in 2006, the highly successful Solution-Focused Cognitive Behaviour Therapy Section. By way of result, one out of ten Dutch CBT therapists are now working in a positive and solution-focused way. Our hope is that this effect will spread to other countries as well. The landscape remains the same, but with new eyes there is a real voyage of discovery waiting for you!

17

FAQ

The wise man is not the man who provides the right answers, but the one who asks the right questions

Claude Levi-Strauss

Introduction

Frequently Asked Questions (FAQ) are listed questions and answers, all supposed to be commonly asked in some context, and pertaining to a particular topic. Following you will find my answers to 20 frequently asked questions about Positive CBT. I would welcome your own inspiring answers and would like to invite you to email your suggestions to: solutions@fredrikebannink.com.

20 Questions and Answers

Question 1: *What if my client cannot find any strengths?*

- Help your client to explore areas of his life that are going relatively well, expressing curiosity for all of the client's life, not just problem areas;
- Ask your client what happens in his life that he would like to continue to happen and link that to his strengths;
- Link these areas to therapy goals (see "competence transference" in Chapter 6);
- Ask coping and competence questions: "How do you manage?" "How do you cope with this situation?" "How come the situation is not worse?";
- Invite your client to fill out the VIA strengths test on the Internet;
- Use the third-person perspective (see Chapter 7): "Suppose you had a twin brother/sister sitting right behind you, what would he/she say your strengths are?"

Practicing Positive CBT: From Reducing Distress to Building Success, First Edition. Fredrike Bannink.
© 2012 John Wiley & Sons, Ltd. Published 2012 by John Wiley & Sons, Ltd.

Question 2: *What if my client cannot find exceptions to his problem?*

- Do you have a complainant-relationship with your client (see Chapter 5)? Then only use observational homework suggestions. Don't give behavioral experiments. Examples of observational homework are:
- Ask your client to pay attention to what is going well and should stay the same or pay attention to what happens in his life that he would like to continue to happen;
- Ask your client to observe the positive moments in his life so that he can talk about them next time you meet;
- Ask your client to pay attention to the times when things are going better so that he can talk about them next time;
- Ask scaling questions: "Observe when you are one point higher on the scale and what you and/or (significant) others are doing differently then";
- Ask your client to pay attention to what gives him hope that his problem can be solved;
- Use prediction homework: "Predict what tomorrow will be like, find an explanation for why the day turned out the way it did tomorrow evening, and then make a new prediction for the following day";
- Ask your client to pay attention to exactly what happens when an exception manifests itself so that he can tell you more about it: "What is different then, and what are (significant) others doing differently?";
- With a client in a complainant-relationship, who thinks the other person is the problem and needs to change: "Pay attention to the times when the other person does more of what you want, to what is different then, and to what he/she sees you do then that is helpful to him/her";
- Ask your client to pay attention to what the other person does that is useful or pleasant and to the difference it makes so that you can talk about it next time;
- Ask other people around your client which exceptions they see;
- Ask your client: "Suppose you could find an exception, what difference will that make?"
- See Appendix B for finding exceptions pertaining to the goal and/or pertaining to the problem.

Question 3: *What is the role of diagnosis in Positive CBT?*

- The role of diagnosis is important, but diagnosis should not only be about disorders (DSM-IV-TR) and what is wrong with your client but should also be about strengths (VIA) and resources and what is right with him (see Chapter 6: Assessment in Positive CBT);
- Diagnosis should include an exploration of everything that works in your client's life;
- Diagnosis should not only be about the problem (problem analysis) but also about what the client wants to have instead of the problem (goal analysis);
- The problem solving structure assumes a necessary connection between a problem and its solution, as in modern medicine. This assumption underlies the field's emphasis on assessing problems before making interventions.

It is not (always) necessary to start treatment with assessing problems. Bakker and colleagues (2010) propose the use of "stepped diagnosis" (see Chapter 6);

- Diagnosis is also about the alliance with your client: is there a visitor-, complainant-, or customer-relationship (see Chapter 5);
- Functional behavior analyses can be made of problems and/or exceptions to the problems (see Chapter 6).

Question 4: *What if my client wants something that is not good for him?*

- Ask your client how this may be helpful to him;
- Ask your client what is happening in his life that tells him that continuing this behavior (for example, drinking alcohol) is good for him;
- Use the third-person perspective: "Suppose we would ask your partner (children, colleagues) about how this might be helpful to you or to them, what do you think she/they would say?";
- It is only on the rarest occasions that taking away the self-determination of your client is necessary.

Question 5: *What if my client does not want anything at all?*

- Give your client compliments for showing up and talking to you;
- Discuss with your client the disadvantages or even the dangers of change;
- Ask your client which changes his referrers identified as necessary to implement, in order for him to not return;
- Invite the client to meet with you again in the future;
- Don't give any homework suggestions;
- See Chapter 5 (mandated clients) for further suggestions.

Question 6: *What if the goal of my client is unrealistic?*

- If there is no solution, there is no problem (but a disability). A problem can be solved, a disability cannot and has to be dealt with in the best possible way;
- If your client has an unrealistic goal (winning the lottery, wanting someone who died to be alive, wishing the accident had never happened), ask what difference that would make in his life. Or ask your client what this would mean to him;
- Ask yourself whether you are dealing with not just a complaint or wish (to bring about a different feeling or a change in another person) but with an actual goal, the attainment of which lies within the client's control (a soundly and positively formulated goal).

Question 7: *What if my client cannot visualize?*

- Find out with your client what the reason might be. Sometimes visualizing the preferred future or using imagery is difficult for our clients (for example,

in the case of autism). Sometimes clients are reluctant to engage with imagery, because of fears about what the image represents;
- Define what you mean by imagery;
- Start with positive and neutral images to find out whether your client has access to visual imagery;
- Ask your client to bring photos, for example, of herself as a child, of her parents, or other relevant situations;
- Engage your client in relaxation procedures prior to imagery;
- Start with a "safe place" imagery and also end that way;
- Give your client experiences of taking control of imagery, for example being the director on the stage;
- Use auditory, kinesthetic, olfactory, or gustatory stimuli instead of visual ones.

Question 8: *What if my client answers "I don't know"?*

- Ask your client: "Suppose you did know, what would you say?" Or: "Suppose you did know, what difference will that make?";
- Ask your client: "Suppose I was to ask your partner (children, colleagues, best friend), what would they say?" "Would they be surprised?" "Which person you know would be least surprised?";
- Agree with your client and say: "Yes, I am asking you some tough questions, please take your time.";
- Ask yourself: "Is it important to my client to know?" ;
- Ask your client: "How would your life be different if you did know?" Or: "How would your life be better if you did know?" Or you may say: "Take a guess!";
- Say: "Of course you don't know yet, but what do you think?";
- Say to yourself that something important is probably going on at this point and allow your client more time.

Question 9: *What if my client does not want to talk about what is bothering him or what if there is a secret?*

- Put your client at ease and respect that he is not (yet) ready (and perhaps will never be ready) to tell you what is bothering him;
- Don't think it is necessary for your client to unveil his secret to you;
- Ask your client: "Suppose you would tell me what is bothering you, what difference will that make?";
- Ask your client: "Suppose there is a solution, what would your life look like then?"

Question 10: *What if my client is in a crisis situation?*

- Remember that clients in crisis quickly stabilize if they are invited to direct their attention to what they want to be different (goal formulation) and to make use of their past successes and their competencies;

- Ask coping questions and competence questions: "How do you manage to go on, given this difficult situation?";
- Install hope in your client: "What are your best hopes? What difference will that make?";
- Ask how you can be helpful: "How can I help you?";
- Be curious of what your client has already attempted since the start of the crisis and what has been helpful, even just a little bit;
- Ask your client what he would like to be different in his life or in his situation;
- Ask your client: "Suppose you would feel calmer and everything became a bit clearer to you. What would be different then? What is the first thing you would do?";
- Ask your client: "How were you able to get up in the morning, come here, and ask for help?";
- Ask your client: "What are you doing to take care of yourself under these circumstances?";
- Ask your client: "Who (and what) do you think would help the most at this moment?";
- Ask: "What, in your opinion, is the most useful thing that I as a therapist can do?";
- Ask if things could be worse than they are now. If so: how come things are not worse?;
- Ask your client: "What is the most important thing for you to remember in order for you to handle this situation?";
- Ask scaling questions: "On a scale of 10 to 0, where 10 means that you're dealing optimally with the situation, and 0 means that you can't deal with it at all, how well are you dealing with all of this?" "How is it that you are already at that number?" "What would a higher number on the scale look like?" "How would you be able to tell that you were one point higher?" "How would you be able to go up one point?" "How motivated are you to go up one point?" "How much confidence do you have that you will succeed in going up one point?" "What difference would it make for you if you went up one point?"

Question 11: *How many sessions are needed in Positive CBT?*

- In Solution-Focused Brief Therapy the average amount of sessions is 3–4 (with the same follow-up results as in problem-focused therapies);
- In Positive CBT the amount of sessions will be less than the average amount of sessions in traditional CBT, because if there is to be an assessment of the problem at all, it will be much briefer;
- Remember that in Positive CBT the client defines the goal in therapy (and not the therapist) and indicates when to stop therapy. Usually this occurs at an earlier stage than the therapist might anticipate;
- Remember that during the first Positive CBT session the client is already asked about when he would consider therapy to be successful and when it could end. This is indicative of the fact that therapy is limited and

goal-oriented. This is different from traditional forms of psychotherapy – including traditional CBT – in which conversations about concluding therapy are only held when therapy is almost over.

Question 12: *Can I ask my client to choose between traditional CBT and Positive CBT?*

- As a CBT therapist you should have the skills to use both forms of CBT;
- Erickson, the famous psychiatrist-hypnotherapist, often gives his client the choice of two or more alternatives. The feelings of choice and freedom are maintained better than in a situation where the client is told exactly what to do. In fact, once your client chooses a particular alternative, he is probably more committed to that choice.

Question 13: *How do I cooperate with problem-focused colleagues?*

- Remember it is very likely that your colleagues are still thinking and acting in a problem-focused way. Therefore, they place greater emphasis on problems (and are more prone to finding problems);
- Make sure you keep your client's goals in mind and that his goal is always your guide. It is easy to get distracted. Meetings with your colleagues may get bogged down in a lengthy discussion of problems or complaints about another person or other people. In a meeting, always ask what the goal of the meeting is so that you can work in a solution-focused way;
- Establish a positive framework. Making the (hidden) positive motivation of everyone involved explicit may put your colleagues at ease and allow them to work in a goal-oriented manner;
- Compliment your colleagues and always explicitly express your appreciation of the progress being made and their collaboration;
- Regularly point out the successes and strengths of your colleagues and summarize them. Be generous;
- Use positive "guerilla actions." Now and then show your colleagues, without explaining too much, what it is exactly that you do when using Positive CBT. For example, show them that you ask about exceptions to the problem and that you highlight areas of strengths and resources;
- Remember to be the change you want to see in your team/organization.

Question 14: *What if my client has not done his homework?*

- The importance of homework as seen in traditional CBT is no longer deemed useful in Positive CBT;
- Ask yourself if homework suggestions will generate more information than if the client does not perform homework (see Chapter 10);
- Accept nonperformance as a message about your client's way of doing things rather than as a sign of resistance;
- Say to your client that you are sure he must have a good reason for not doing his homework and invite him to tell you more about this reason;

- Remember to keep a cooperating relationship with your client, even without him doing any homework;
- Only provide feedback for the client to reflect on, or assign an observational homework task rather than a behavioral one. Your client may not yet, or may no longer be, in a customer-relationship (see Chapter 6);
- Do you want too much too soon? Look for smaller changes, use scaling questions regarding the goal or the exceptions, or counsel the client not to move too fast.

Question 15: *What if my client wants to find an explanation for what is wrong with him?*

- Remember we human beings are explanation seekers;
- Also remember that you as a Positive CBT therapist do not need to find an explanation in order to be able to help your client reach his goal;
- Ask your client: "Suppose you were to have an explanation, what difference would that make?";
- Ask: "How would an explanation be helpful to you?";
- Ask: "What part of the explanation do you already have?";
- Ask your client what he can do to come up with information that may be useful in finding the explanation he wants;
- Ask how you might be helpful in helping him to come up with an explanation.

Question 16: *What if my client only wants to talk about his past?*

- Ask yourself whether you are you working with someone who is willing to change. Maybe you have a complainant-relationship with your client (see Chapter 5) and should adjust your interventions accordingly (see Chapter 5);
- Ask yourself whether you are working on your client's goal. Make sure that the client wants to reach the goal more than you do;
- Ask your client: "How many sessions do you think you need to talk about your past before you are ready to talk about your future?";
- Ask him how talking about the past will help him to reach his goal;
- Ask him how he will know that he has talked enough about the past and can start looking at the future;
- The present and future determine how we look at our past: it is said that it is never too late to have a happy childhood. Ask your client three resilience questions about his past (see Chapter 7).

Question 17: *What if my client returns to "problem talk" all the time?*

- Don't get discouraged, because this happens quite often;
- Gently interrupt your client and say: "Ok, we'll come back to that." Once your client has moved on to a more clearly defined goal or can find exceptions to the problem, often there is no need or wish anymore to return to the topic;

- Ask your client how long / how many sessions he thinks are necessary before he can move on from talking about his problem to starting to talk about what he wants and his preferred future;
- Consider whether you have a customer-relationship with your client or maybe a complainant-relationship and, if so, adjust your interventions accordingly (see Chapter 5);
- Ask your client: "How do you think that talking about your problem will help you reach your goal?";
- Say to your client that he must have a good reason to keep talking about his problem and invite him to tell you about this reason;
- Ask your client: "Suppose you said everything you want to say about your problem, what would change for you then?";

Question 18: *What if there is no progress or even deterioration?*

- If you have a positive alliance: if your approach does not work, stop and do something else. Continuing with an approach that is not working and doing more of the same when there is no progress are two of the four pathways to impossibility, as described in Chapter 11;
- Remember Einstein said: "Insanity is doing the same thing over and over again, expecting different results";
- Keep in mind that therapy should not be used for the purpose of just sustaining or maintaining clients;
- Remember that we therapists are very bad at identifying deteriorating clients and routinely overestimate our effectiveness (see Chapter 10);
- Don't assume that deterioration of your client's situation comes before the situation gets better. Instead, this is an indicator that portends a final negative outcome (see Chapter 11);
- Ask your client (or supervisor or colleagues) what you should do differently;
- If you have a negative alliance, refer your client to a colleague;
- More diagnosis may be needed (see Chapter 6 for the concept of "stepped diagnosis");
- Invite others into the conversation (partner, children, friends);
- Use the ORS and SRS (see Chapter 10).

Question 19: *What if I become irritated, discouraged, or start to feel uncertain?*

- If you feel irritated, discouraged, or uncertain (so-called "countertransference"), you need to focus more on the therapeutic alliance;
- Ask yourself what you can do differently to enhance the alliance (see Chapter 5) instead of thinking what the client should do differently;
- Suppose you would be one point higher on the scale of the alliance than you are now, what would you do differently then? How would your client react differently? This is a nice question used in peer consultation;
- Give your client more compliments by focusing on his strengths, successes, and competences;
- Use the past of your client to look for exceptions to his problem;

- Ask a supervisor or colleagues in peer consultation what you can do differently to enhance the alliance;
- Use the ORS and SRS (see Chapter 10).

Question 20: *What if my client has very complex problems?*

- Remember that complex problems do not need complex solutions and that you as a therapist do not need to know as much as possible about your client's problems in order to effectively help him;
- "Occam's razor," often expressed as the "law of parsimony," is a principle that generally recommends, when faced with competing hypotheses that are equal in other respects, selecting the one that makes the fewest new assumptions;
- Use "skeleton keys," as described in Chapters 4 and 10. You don't have to analyze each lock (e.g., each problem) before you can use these keys. This is an example of the use of Occam's razor;
- Follow Einstein's Constraint: "Everything should be kept as simple as possible, but no simpler" (Einstein, 1905);
- Read the story Brilliant Insights in Chapter 10 and see how complicated theoretical formulations make things worse instead of better.

Epilog

What does it take to become a Positive CBT therapist? The answer of Steve de Shazer, one of the founders of Solution-Focused Brief Therapy, would be: "Only a small change is needed" (1985, p. 33).

And I think he is right. Because when you look at what is working, you will undoubtedly find strengths, competences, and resources that you already possess, together with Positive CBT interventions you probably already use. From there on, you may ask yourself where you already are on the scale and design what your next (small) step might be or what you would consider to be the next significant sign of progress.

With Positive CBT a lot can change for the benefit of our clients, ourselves, our colleagues, and for the world. Psychotherapy, including CBT, can become a more positive force for both our clients and – last but not least – for ourselves as therapists. Psychotherapy will as a result become more positive, more hopeful, shorter, easier, and more fun.

I hope that reading this book has been one of those steps in the right direction. Maybe you are already on the other side!

Web Sites

www.asfct.org
Association for the Quality Development of Solution Focused Consulting and Training (SFCT)

www.authentichappiness.org
Seligman with Positive Psychology questionnaires

www.brief.org.uk
BRIEF, London

www.brieftherapysydney.com.au
Brief Therapy Institute of Sydney, Australia

www.brief-therapy.org
Brief Family Therapy Center, Milwaukee: founders SFBT

www.centerforclinicalexcellence.com
International Center for Clinical Excellence (ICCE), a worldwide community dedicated to the promotion of excellence in behavioral healthcare services (Miller)

www.derby.ac.uk/mhru/whos-who/professor-paul-gilbert
Gilbert, author

www.eabct.com
European Association for Behavioural and Cognitive Therapies (EABCT)

www.ebta.nu
European Brief Therapy Association (EBTA)

Practicing Positive CBT: From Reducing Distress to Building Success, First Edition. Fredrike Bannink.
© 2012 John Wiley & Sons, Ltd. Published 2012 by John Wiley & Sons, Ltd.

www.edwdebono.com
De Bono, author

www.enpp.eu
European Network for Positive Psychology (ENPP)

http://fredrickson.socialpsychology.org/
Fredrickson (research broaden-and-build theory of positive emotions)

www.fredrikebannink.com
Author of this book

www.gingerich.net
Gingerich: research on SFBT

www.heartandsoulofchange.com
Duncan, author

www.institutret.com

www.ippanetwork.org
Institute Positive Psychology Association (IPPA)

www.korzybski.com
Korzybski Institute Belgium, SFBT training and research center

www.johnwheeler.co.uk
Wheeler (certificate of competence)

www.padesky.com
Padesky, author

www.positivemeetings-app.com
Bannink about positive meetings app

www.positivepsychology.org
University of Pennsylvania (Seligman)

www.posttraumatic-success.com
Bannink about posttraumatic success

www.pos-cbt.com
Bannink about Positive CBT

www.ppc.sas.upenn.edu/ppquestionnaires.htm
University of Pennsylvania with Positive Psychology questionnaires

www.reteaming.com
Furman, solution-focused team coaching

www.sfbta.org
Solution-Focused Brief Therapy Association (SFBTA)

www.sfwork.com
Centre for Solution Focus at Work (McKergow)

www.solutionsdoc.co.uk
Macdonald with Solution-Focused research

www.solutionfocused.net
Institute for Solution-Focused Therapy (Dolan)

www.solworld.org
Solutions in Organisations Link (SOL)

www.ted.com
Talks about Technology, Entertainment, Design (TED)

www.wcbct2010.org
World Congress of Behavioral and Cognitive Therapies (WCBCT)

Appendix A

Protocols for the First Session

Protocol for the First Session 1

Submit all questions to each client present.

Problem:
"What brings you here?" "How is that a problem for you?" "What have you already tried and what has been useful?"

Goal formulation:
"What would you like to be different as a result of these sessions?" Here the therapist may ask the "miracle question" (see Chapter 12) or other questions about goal formulation.

Exceptions:
"When have you caught a glimpse of this miracle?" "How did you make that happen?" Alternatively: "When is the problem absent or less noticeable?" "How do you manage that?" "Which personal strengths and resources do you use?"

Scaling:

- *Progress:* "Where are you now on a scale of 10 to 0?" "How do you manage to be at that number?"
- *Motivation:* "10 means you're willing to give it your all, and 0 means you're not willing to put in any effort."
- *Confidence:* "10 means that you are very confident, and 0 means you have no confidence at all that you can reach your goal."

Concluding the session:

- If the client gives a concrete and detailed response to the miracle question or another question about goal formulation, suggest: "Pick a day in the coming week and pretend the miracle has happened and observe what difference that makes."

Practicing Positive CBT: From Reducing Distress to Building Success, First Edition. Fredrike Bannink.
© 2012 John Wiley & Sons, Ltd. Published 2012 by John Wiley & Sons, Ltd.

- If the client does not give a concrete and detailed response to the miracle question or another question about goal formulation, suggest: "Pay attention to what happens in your life that gives you the sense that this problem can be solved." Or say: "Pay attention to what is happening in your life that you would like to keep happening because it's good (enough)."
- "Do you think that it is necessary / would be useful for you to return? If so, when would you like to return?"

Protocol for the First Session 2

Submit all questions to each client present.

1. *What are your best hopes? What else?*
2. *What difference will that make? What else?*
3. *What is already working? What else?*
4. *What would be a next sign of progress / What will be your next step? What else?*

Appendix B

Protocol for Finding Exceptions

As you look for exceptions, you may inquire about the client's observations and, using the interactional matrix (see Chapter 7), about what important others might be able to perceive. One can distinguish between exceptions pertaining to the desired outcome (the goal) and exceptions pertaining to the problem. Submit all questions to each client present.

Exceptions Pertaining to the Goal

1. *Elicit*
   "So when your goal has been reached (or the miracle has happened), you will talk to each other about how your day has been. When do you already see glimpses of that? If your husband were here and I asked him the same question, what do you think he would say?"
2. *Amplify*
   "When was the last time you and your husband talked to each other? Tell me more about that. What was it like? What did you talk about? What did you say? And what did he say? What did you do when he said that? What did he do then? What was that like for you? What else was different about that time? If he were here, what else would he say about it?"
3. *Reinforce*
   Nonverbal: Lean forward, raise your eyebrows, make notes (do what you naturally do when someone tells you something important).
   Verbal: Show interest. "Was this new for you and him? Did it surprise you that this happened?"
   Pay compliments: "It seems that it was pretty difficult and that it required courage for you to do that, given everything that's happened in your relationship. Please tell me more."
4. *Explore how the exception came to be, ask for details, and pay compliments*
   "What do you think you did to make that happen? If your husband were here and I were to ask him that, what do you think he would say you did

Practicing Positive CBT: From Reducing Distress to Building Success, First Edition. Fredrike Bannink.
© 2012 John Wiley & Sons, Ltd. Published 2012 by John Wiley & Sons, Ltd.

that helped him tell you more about his day? Where did you get the idea to do it that way? What great ideas you have! Are you someone who often comes up with the right ideas at the right time?"

5. *Project exceptions into the future*
"On a scale of 10 to 0, where 10 means a very good chance and 0 means no chance at all, how do you rate the chances of something like that happening again in the coming week (or month)? What would it take? What would help to have that happen more often in the future? Who needs to do what to make it happen again? What is the most important thing you need to keep remembering to make sure it has the best chance of happening again? What is the second most important thing to remember? What would your husband say about the chance of this happening again? What would he think you could do to increase that chance? If you decided to do that, what do you think he would do? If he were to do that, how would things be different for you (in your relationship)?"

Exceptions Pertaining to the Problem

1. *If the client cannot describe a goal (or miracle) and only talks in problem terms.* "When was there a time in the past week (or month, or year) when your problem was less severe or when the problem was absent for a short period of time?" Then continue with the five steps for exceptions pertaining to the goal (or miracle).

2. *What is better?* All subsequent sessions commence with the exploration of these exceptions. Remember to follow all five steps and to ask both individual and relational (interactional matrix) questions. After examining an exception, always ask: "What else is better?"

3. *Coping questions.* Sometimes the client is unable to find exceptions and the difficulties he faces are enormous. In that case, you may ask coping questions to find out what the client does to keep his head above water: "I'm surprised. Given everything that's happened, I don't know how you cope. How do you do that? Which of your personal strengths do you use? How do you keep your head above water?"

4. *If a client describes a prolonged unpleasant situation with ever-discouraging events.* In such a case, you might say: "I understand that you have many reasons to be down. There are so many things that turned out differently than you'd hoped. I wonder how you've kept going and how you've been able to get up every morning and start a new day. Please tell me more."

5. *If the client says he or she must go on, for example, for the children's sake.* In such a case, you might say: "Is that how you do it? You think of your children and how much they need you? You must care about them a great deal. Please tell me more about what you do to take good care of them."

Appendix C

Protocol for Subsequent Sessions

Submit all questions to each client present.

With the use of EARS: Eliciting, Amplifying, Reinforcing, and Start again (see Chapter 11).

Eliciting

"What is better (since your previous visit)?"

Amplifying (asking for details)

"How does that work? How do you do that exactly? Is that new for you? What effect does that have on . . . ? What is different then between you and . . . ?"

Reinforcing

Give the client compliments and/or ask competence questions ("How did you do that?" "How did you decide to do that?")

Start Again

"What else is better?"

Do more of it

"What would be helpful for you to do that more often?" If absolutely nothing is better: "How do you cope? How do you get through that? How come things aren't worse? If you can continue to do that, would you have accomplished what you came here for?"

Practicing Positive CBT: From Reducing Distress to Building Success, First Edition. Fredrike Bannink.
© 2012 John Wiley & Sons, Ltd. Published 2012 by John Wiley & Sons, Ltd.

Scaling progress

"Where are you now? How did you make that happen? What does a one point higher rating look like? What will be different then? How would you be able to get there? What would be helpful for you to do that? Who will be the first to notice? How would that person notice? How would he react? And what difference will that make for you? At what rating would you like to end up?"

Homework suggestions

If the client wants do some homework, give behavioral tasks for a client in a customer-relationship, observational tasks for a client in a complainant-relationship, and no tasks for a client in a visitor-relationship (see Chapter 5).

Future sessions

"Is it necessary or would it be useful for you to return?" If so: "When would you like to return?"

Appendix D

Positive FBA Interview

A Functional Behavior Analysis (FBA) can be made of problems and/or of exceptions to problems. Here you find a Positive FBA, using the "miracle question." Instead of the miracle question, you may ask other variations of goal formulation questions, for example: "What would you like to see instead of your problems?" (Also see Chapters 4 and 6.)

1. Suppose tonight while you are sleeping, a miracle happens and your problems that we talk about today are all solved. But because you are asleep, you don't know that this miracle happens. What will be the first thing you notice tomorrow morning when you are waking up that would tell you that this miracle has happened? What will be the first thing you notice yourself doing differently that will let you know that this miracle occurred? What else? And what else?
2. Please tell me about some recent times when you were doing somewhat better or (part of) the miracle was happening, even just a little bit.
3. When things are going somewhat better for you, what have you noticed that you or others do differently then? What other consequences have you noticed?
4. On a scale of 10–0 (10 being the miracle has happened and 0 being the worst), where would you say you are at today?
5. What will you be doing differently that will tell you/others that you are one point higher on the scale?
6. What will be better for you/others when you are one point higher on the scale? What other consequences will you notice?
7. What/who will help you to achieve one point higher on the scale?

Practicing Positive CBT: From Reducing Distress to Building Success, First Edition. Fredrike Bannink.
© 2012 John Wiley & Sons, Ltd. Published 2012 by John Wiley & Sons, Ltd.

Appendix E

Externalization of the Problem

Externalizing the problem is described in more detail in Chapter 7.
Name of the problem: . . . .
The problem controls me/us   I/we have control of the problem
1   2   3   4   5   6   7   8   9   10

1. Circle your current state on the above scale;
2. Where are you on the scale compared with the last time we met? If you went up on the scale, indicate how you managed that;
3. If you remained at the same level as last time, indicate how you managed to stay stable;
4. If you ended up lower on the scale, indicate what you have done before to get ahead again;
5. What did you do in the past in a comparable situation that was successful?;
6. What have important others in your life noticed about you this past week? How has that influenced their behavior toward you?

Practicing Positive CBT: From Reducing Distress to Building Success, First Edition. Fredrike Bannink.
© 2012 John Wiley & Sons, Ltd. Published 2012 by John Wiley & Sons, Ltd.

Appendix F

Interactional Matrix
(Changing Perspectives)

Changing perspectives is described in more detail in Chapter 7.

Table A.1 Interactional matrix.

Reporting position	Goal	Hypothetical solution/Mircale question	Exception
Self	What is your goal in coming here?	What will you be doing differently? What will the other person be doing differently?	What are you doing differently? What is the other person doing differently?
Other	What would the other person say is your goal in coming here?	What would the other person say you will be doing differently?	What would the other person say you are doing differently?
	What would the other person say is his goal in coming here?	What would the other person say he will be doing differently?	What would the other person say he is doing differently?
Detached	What would I say or what would the fly on the wall say is your goal in coming here?	What will I or the fly on the wall see you doing differently?	What would I or the fly on the wall see you doing differently?

Source: Bannink, F.P. (2010). 1001 Solution Focused Questions. *Handbook for Solution Focused Interviewing*. New York: Norton.

Practicing Positive CBT: From Reducing Distress to Building Success, First Edition. Fredrike Bannink.
© 2012 John Wiley & Sons, Ltd. Published 2012 by John Wiley & Sons, Ltd.

Interactional Matrix (Changing Perspectives)

Another way to practice your Positive CBT skills is to ask your clients questions from the interactional matrix. It is important to use the following sequence, starting with Question 1 and then moving on to 2 and 3, especially when clients want someone else to change.

1. When this problem will be solved, what will you notice is different about the other person? What will you see him/her doing differently? What else?
2. When this problem will be solved, what will this other person notice that is different about you? What will you see him/her doing differently? What else?
3. When this problem will be solved and you are being watched by an outside observer, what will he/she notice that is different about your relationship with the other person? What will this observer see both of you doing differently? What else?

Appendix G

Questionnaire for the Referrer

1. In your opinion, what will be the best possible outcome of collaboration among you as referrer, the client, and me/our institution?
2. What are the client's strengths and what aspects of his performance are satisfactory and should be maintained?
3. What are the limitations we need to take into account?
4. In your opinion, what resources does the client have?
5. What do you think will be the first sign that would indicate to the client that a treatment is meaningful and useful? And what would be the first sign for you?
6. When does this already happen now? Please give an example.

Practicing Positive CBT: From Reducing Distress to Building Success, First Edition. Fredrike Bannink.
© 2012 John Wiley & Sons, Ltd. Published 2012 by John Wiley & Sons, Ltd.

Appendix H

Exceptions Journal

In traditional CBT clients are asked to keep a journal recounting their thoughts, feelings, and actions when specific situations arise. This problem-focused journal helps to make the client aware of his maladaptive thoughts and show their consequences on behavior, whereas in Positive CBT a journal may be kept to find exceptions to the problem and show their consequences on behavior.

However, you don't have to be ill to get better. Everyone can look at times when they are a bit closer to where they would like to be. Following are 18 questions. You can just answer a few questions every day and vary them.

1. What is better today (even just a little bit)?
2. What else is better?
3. What did I do differently to make it better?
4. Who noticed this and how?
5. If nobody noticed it, what could they have noticed about me, had they paid more attention?
6. What do I hope important others in my life will notice that I do differently?
7. What did I think or believe about myself that was helpful to make these exceptions happen? What was different?
8. What would others say about the way I made these exceptions happen? Which of my personal strengths, qualities, and abilities would they say were helpful?
9. What do I have to do to make these exceptions happen more often?
10. What would my life look like if these exceptions were to happen more often?
11. How can important others help me to let these exceptions happen more often?
12. Who could I invite to help me?
13. What would be the best way to ask them for help?
14. When I intend to repeat what is working, what should I do?

Practicing Positive CBT: From Reducing Distress to Building Success, First Edition. Fredrike Bannink.
© 2012 John Wiley & Sons, Ltd. Published 2012 by John Wiley & Sons, Ltd.

15. What should or could I think about myself or about others to be successful?
16. What would others say I should or could think to be successful?
17. What would others answer to the question what I should or could keep on doing to be successful?
18. Which compliments can I pay myself today?

Appendix I

Session Rating Scale (SRS)

Session Rating Scale (SRS V.3.0)

Name _____Age (Yrs):____
ID# _____ Sex: M / F
Session # ____ Date: _____

Please rate today's session by placing a mark on the line nearest to the description that best fits your experience.

	Relationship	
I did not feel heard, understood, and respected.	I————————————I	I felt heard, understood, and respected.

	Goals and Topics	
We did *not* work on or talk about what I wanted to work on and talk about.	I————————————I	We worked on and talked about what I wanted to work on and talk about.

	Approach or Method	
The therapist's approach is not a good fit for me.	I————————————I	The therapist's approach is a good fit for me.

	Overall	
There was something missing in the session today.	I————————————I	Overall, today's session was right for me.

International Center for Clinical Excellence
www.centerforclinicalexcellence.com
www.scottdmiller.com (with permission)

Practicing Positive CBT: From Reducing Distress to Building Success, First Edition. Fredrike Bannink.
© 2012 John Wiley & Sons, Ltd. Published 2012 by John Wiley & Sons, Ltd.

References

Allen, R.E. and Allen, S.D. (1997) *Winnie-the-Pooh on Success: In Which You, Pooh, and Friends Learn About the Most Important Subject of All*. New York: Dutton.

American Psychological Association's Board of Professional Affairs' Advisory Committee on Colleague Assistance (ACCA) (February 2006) Report on Distress and Impairment in Psychologists.

Ankarberg, P. and Falkenstrom, F. (2008) Treatment with antidepressants is primarily a psychological treatment. *Psychotherapy Theory, Research, Practice, Training*, 45, 3, 329–339.

Anker, M.G., Duncan, B.L., and Sparks, J.A. (2009) Using client feedback to improve couples therapy outcomes; a randomized clinical trial in a naturalistic setting. *Journal of Consulting and Clinical Psychology*, 77, 4, 693–704.

Anker, M.G., Owen, J., Duncan, B.L., and Sparks, J.A. (2010) The alliance in couple therapy: partner influence, early change, and alliance patterns in a naturalistic sample. *Journal of Consulting and Clinical Psychology*, 78, 635–645.

APA Presidential Task Force on Evidence-Based Practice (2006) Evidence-based practice in psychology. *American Psychologist*, 61, 4, 271–285.

Arntz, A. and Weertman, A. (1999) Treatment of childhood memories: theory and practice. *Behaviour Research and Therapy*, 37, 715–740.

Aristotle. Nicomachean Ethics (1998) Mineola, NY: Dover Publications Inc.

Arts, W., Hoogduin, C.A.L., Keijsers, G.P.J., *et al.* (1994) A quasi-experimental study into the effect of enhancing the quality of the patient-therapist relationship in the outpatient treatment of obsessive-compulsive neurosis. In S. Brogo and L. Sibilia (eds). *The Patient-Therapist Relationship: Its Many Dimensions*, Rome: Consiglio Nazionale delle Ricerche, pp. 96–106.

Bakker, J.M., Bannink, F.P., and Macdonald, A. (2010) Solution-focused psychiatry. *The Psychiatrist*, 34, 297–300.

Bannink, F. P. (2005) De kracht van oplossingsgerichte therapie: Een vorm van gedragstherapie (The power of solution-focused therapy: A form of behavioural therapy). *Gedragstherapie*, 38, 1, 5–16.

Bannink, F.P. (2006a) De geboorte van oplossingsgerichte cognitieve gedragstherapie (The birth of solution-focused cognitive behavioural therapy). *Gedragstherapie*, 39, 3, 171–183.

Practicing Positive CBT: From Reducing Distress to Building Success, First Edition. Fredrike Bannink.
© 2012 John Wiley & Sons, Ltd. Published 2012 by John Wiley & Sons, Ltd.

References

Bannink, F.P. (2006b) *Oplossingsgerichte Mediation (Solution-Focused Mediation)*. Amsterdam: Pearson.

Bannink, F.P. (2007a) *Gelukkig Zijn en Geluk Hebben: Zelf Oplossingsgericht Werken (Being Happy and Being Lucky: Solution-Focused Self-Help)*. Amsterdam: Harcourt.

Bannink, F.P. (2007b) Solution-Focused Brief Therapy. *Journal of Contemporary Psychotherapy*, 37, 2, 87–94.

Bannink, F.P. (2008a) Oplossingsgerichte therapie als vorm van cognitieve gedragstherapie (Solution-focused brief therapy as a form of cognitive behavioral therapy). *Tijdschrift VKJP*, 35, 3, 18–29.

Bannink, F.P. (2008b) Posttraumatic Success: Solution-Focused Brief Therapy. *Brief Treatment and Crisis Intervention*, 7, 1–11.

Bannink, F.P. (2008c) Solution-focused mediation: The future with a difference. *Conflict Resolution Quarterly*, 25, 2, 163–183.

Bannink, F.P. (2009a) *Positieve Psychologie in de Praktijk (Positive Psychology in Practice)*. Amsterdam: Hogrefe.

Bannink, F.P. (2009b) *Praxis der Losungs-fokussierten Mediation (Solution-Focused Mediation in Practice)*. Stuttgart, Germany: Concadora Verlag.

Bannink, F.P. (2009c) Solution focused conflict management in teams and in organisations. *InterAction: The Journal of Solution Focus in Organisations*, 1, 2, 11–25.

Bannink, F.P. (2009d) Visitor, complainant or customer? In J. Bertschler (ed.), *Elder Mediation: A New Solution to Age-Old Problems*. Seven Hills, OH: Northcoast Conflict Solutions, pp. 77–89.

Bannink, F.P. (2009e) *Oplossingsgerichte Vragen. Handboek Oplossingsgerichte Gespreksvoering*, 2e druk. Amsterdam: Pearson.

Bannink, F.P. (2010a) *1001 Solution-Focused Questions. Handbook for Solution-Focused Interviewing*. New York: Norton.

Bannink, F.P. (2010b) *Handbook of Solution-Focused Conflict Management*. Cambridge, MA: Hogrefe Publishers.

Bannink, F.P. (2010c) *Oplossingsgericht Leidinggeven (Solution-Focused Leadership)*. Amsterdam: Pearson.

Bannink, F.P. (2012) *Praxis der Positiven Psychologie*. Gottingen: Hogrefe.

Bannink, F.P. and Jackson, P.Z. (2011) Positive Psychology and Solution Focus – looking at similarities and differences. *Interaction: The Journal of Solution Focus in Organisations*, 3, 1, 8–20.

Baumeister, R.F., Bratslavsky, E., Muraven, M., and Tice, D.M. (1998) Ego depletion: is the active self a limited resource? *Journal of Personality and Social Psychology*, 74, 1252–1265.

Baumeister, R.F., Bratlavsky, E., Finkenauer, C., and Vohs, K.D. (2001) Bad is stronger that good. *Review of General Psychology*, 5, 323–370.

Baumgartner, T., Heinrichs, M. Vonleuthen, A., *et al.* (2008) Oxytocin shapes the neural circuitry of trust and trust adaptation in humans. *Neuron*, 58, 639–650.

Bavelas, J.B., Coates, L., and Johnson, T. (2000) Listeners as co-narrators. *Journal of Personality and Social Psychology*, 79, 941–952.

Beck, A.T. (1967) *Depression: Clinical, Experimental, and Theoretical Aspects*. New York: Harper & Row.

Beck, A.T. (1988) *Love is Never Enough*. New York: Penguin.

Beck, J.S. (2011) *Cognitive Behaviour Therapy. Basics and Beyond* (second edition). New York: Guilford.

Beck, A.T., Weissman, A., Lester, D., and Trexles, L. (1974) The measurement of pessimism: The hopelessness scale. *Journal of Consulting and Clinical Psychology*, 42, 861–865.

References

Beckhard, R. and Harris, R. (1987) *Managing Organizational Transitions* (second edition). Reading, Mass.: Addison-Wesley.

Beijebach, M., Rodriguez Sanches, M.S., Arribas de Miguel, J., *et al.* (2000) Outcome of solution-focused therapy at a university family therapy center. *Journal of Systemic Therapies*, 19, 116–128.

Bennett-Levy, J., Butler, G., Fennell, M., *et al.* (2004) *Oxford Guide to Behavioural Experiments in Cognitive Therapy*. New York: Oxford University Press.

Berg, I.K., and Steiner, T. (2003) *Children's Solution Work*. New York: Norton.

Beutler, L.E., Malik, M., Alimohamed, S., *et al.* (2004) Therapist effects. In M.J. Lambert (ed.). *Bergin and Garfield's Handbook of Psychotherapy and Behavior Change* (fifth edition) (pp. 227–306). Hoboken: John Wiley & Sons, Inc.

Blackwell, S.E., and Holmes, E.A. (2010) Modifying interpretation and imagination in clinical depression: A single case series using cognitive bias modification. *Applied Cognitive Psychology*, 24, 3, 338–350.

Boer, de I., and Bannink, F.P. (article forthcoming) Solution-Focused Schema Therapy.

Bono, E. de (1985) *Conflicts, A Better Way to Resolve Them*. London: Penguin.

Brewin, C.R. (2006) Understanding cognitive behaviour therapy: a retrieval competition account. *Behaviour Research and Therapy*, 44, 765–784.

Brewin, C.R., Wheatley, J., Patel, T. *et al.* (2009) Imagery rescripting as a brief stand-alone treatment for depressed patients with intrusive memories. *Behaviour Research and Therapy*, 47, 569–576.

Bruins, B. (2008) Herstel van persoonlijk succesvol functioneren: rode draad bij gedragsactivering (Recovery of successful personal functioning: behavioural activation). *Constructional Behaviour Analysis Archives*, 4, 1–10.

Byrd-Craven, J., Geary. D.C., Rose, A.J., and Ponzi, D. (2008) Co-ruminating increases stress hormone levels in women. *Hormones and Behaviour*, 53, 489–492.

Cameron, K. (2008) *Positive Leadership*. San Francisco: Berreth Koehler.

Carver, C.S. and Scheier, M.F. (1998) *On the Self-Regulation of Behavior*. New York: Cambridge University Press.

Cialdini, R.B. (1984) *Persuasion. The Psychology of Influence*. New York: Collins.

Clement, P.W. (1994) Quantitative evaluation of 26 years of private practice. *Professional Psychology: Research and Practice*, 25, 2, 173–176.

Constantino, M.J., Castonguay, L.G., and Schut, A.J. (2002) The working alliance: a flagship for the "scientist-practitioner" model in psychotherapy. In G.S. Tryon (ed.). *Counseling Based on Process Research: Applying What we Know*, Boston: Allyn & Bacon, pp. 81–131.

Cooperrider, D.L. and Whitney, D. (2005) *Appreciative Inquiry: A Positive Revolution to Change*. San Francisco: Berett-Koehler.

Danner, D.D., Snowdon, D.A., and Friesen, W.V. (2001) Positive emotions in early life and longevity: findings from the nun study. *Journal of Personality and Social Psychology*, 80, 5, 804–813.

David, D. (2007) Quo vadis CBT? Transcultural perspectives on the past, present and future of CBT: interviews with the current leadership in CBT. *Journal of Cognitive and Behavioural Psychotherapies*, 7, 2, 171–217.

Davidson, R.J., Kabat-Zinn, J., Schumacher, J., *et al.* (2003) Alterations in brain and immune function produced by mindfulness meditation. *Psychosomatic Medicine*, 65, 564–570.

De Jong, P. and Berg, I.K. (2002) *Interviewing for Solutions*. Belmont: Thomson.

Deming, W.E. (1986) *Out of the Crisis*. Cambrigde MA: MIT Center for Advanced Engineering Study.

References

DeRubeis, R.J., Brotman, M.A., and Gibbons, C.J. (2005) A conceptual and methodological analysis of the nonspecific argument. *Clinical Psychology: Science and Practice*, 12, 174–183.

de Saint-Exupery, A. (1979) *The Wisdom of the Sands*. Chicago: University of Chicago Press.

De Shazer, S. (1984) The death of resistance. *Family Process*, 23, 79–93.

De Shazer, S. (1985) *Keys to Solution in Brief Therapy*. New York: Norton.

De Shazer, S. (1988) *Clues: Investigation Solutions in Brief Therapy*. New York: Norton.

De Shazer, S. (1991) *Putting Difference to Work*. New York: Norton.

De Shazer, S. (1994) *Words Were Originally Magic*. New York: Norton.

Diener, E. and Seligman, M.E.P. (2002) Very happy people. *Psychological Science*, 13, 1, 81–84.

Dolan, Y. (1998) *One Small Step*. Watsonville, CA: Papier-Mache.

Drugan, R.C. (2000) The neurochemistry of stress resilience and coping: a quest for nature's own antidote to illness. In J.E. Gillham (ed.) *The Science of Optimism and Hope. Research Essays in Honor of Martin E. Seligman*, Pennsylvania: Templeton, pp. 57–71.

Dugas, M.J., Freeson, M.H., and Ladouceur, R. (1997) Intolerance of uncertainty and problem orientation in worry. *Cognitive Therapy and Research*, 21, 593–606.

Dunbar, R.I.M., Baron, R., Frangou, A., *et al.* (2011) Social laughter is correlated with an elevated pain threshold. *Proceedings of the Royal Society B: Biological Science*, published online before print September 14, 2011.

Duncan, B.L. (2005) *What's Right With You: Debunking Dysfunction and Changing Your Life*. Deerfield Beach, FL: Health Communications.

Duncan, B.L. (2010) *On Becoming a Better Therapist*. Washington DC: American Psychological Association.

Duncan, B.L. (2011) What therapists want: it's certainly not money or fame. *Psychotherapy Networker*, 47, 62, 40–43.

Duncan, B.L., Hubble, M.A., and Miller, S.D. (1997) *Psychotherapy with "Impossible" Cases: The Efficient Treatment of Therapy Veterans*. New York: Norton.

Duncan, B.L., Miller, S.D., and Sparks, A. (2004) *The Heroic Client: a Revolutionary Way to Improve Effectiveness Through Client-directed, Outcome-informed Therapy*. San Francisco: Jossey-Bass.

Duncan, B.L., Miller, S.D., Wampold, B.E., and Hubble, M.A. (2010) *The Heart and Soul of Change: Delivering What Works in Therapy* (second edition). Washington, DC: American Psychological Association.

Dweck, C.S. (2006) *Mindset: The New Psychology of Success*. New York: Random House.

Einstein, A. (1905) Does the inertia of a body depend upon its energy content? (in German). *Annalen der Physik*. pp. 639–641.

Einstein, A. (1954) *Ideas and Opinions*. New York: Crown.

Elliot, A.J. (ed.) (2008) *Handbook of Approach and Avoidance Motivation*. New York: Psychology Press.

Elliot, A.J. and Church, M.A. (1997) Approach-avoidance motivation in personality: approach and avoidance temperaments and goals. *Journal of Personality and Social Psychology*, 82, 5, 804–818.

Elliot, A.J. and Sheldon, K.M. (1998) Avoidance personal goals and the personality–illness relationship. *Journal of Personality and Social Psychology*, 75, 1282–1299.

Elliot, A.J., Sheldon, K.M., and Church, M.A. (1997) Avoidance personal goals and subjective well-being. *Personality and Social Psychology Bulletin*, 51, 1058–1068.

References

Estrada, C.A., Isen, A.M., and Young, M.J. (1994) Positive affect improves creative problem solving and influences reported source of practice satisfaction in physicians. *Motivation and Emotion*, 18, 4, 285–299.

Flora, S.R. (2000) Praise's magic reinforcement ratio: five to one gets the job done. *The Behaviour Analyst Today*, 1, 64–69.

Fowler, J.H. and Christakis, N.A. (2008) Dynamic spread of happiness in a large social network: longitudinal analysis over 20 years in the Framingham Heart Study. *British Medical Journal*, 337, a2338.

Frank, J.D. (1974) Psychotherapy: The restauration of morale. *The American Journal of Psychiatry*, 131, 271–274.

Franklin, C., Trepper, T.S., Gingerich, W.J. and McCollum, E.E. (2012) *Solution-Focused Brief Therapy. A Handbook of Evidence Based Practice*. New York: Oxford University Press.

Fredrickson, B.L. (1998) What good are positive emotions? *Review of General Psychology*, 2, 300–319.

Fredrickson, B.L. (2000) Cultivating positive emotions to optimize health and well-being. *Prevention & Treatment*, 3, 0001a.

Fredrickson, B.L. (2003) The value of positive emotions. *American Scientist*, 91, 330–335.

Fredrickson, B.L. (2009) *Positivity*. New York: Crown.

Fredrickson, B.L. and Losada, M.F. (2005) Positive affect and the complex dynamics of human flourishing. *American Psychologist*, 60, 678–686.

Frost, R. (1920) *Mountain Interval*. New York: Holt and Company.

Furman, B. (1998) *It is Never Too Late to Have a Happy Childhood*. London: BT Press.

Furman, B. and Ahola, T. (2007) *Change Through Cooperation. Handbook of Reteaming*. Helsinki: Helsinki Brief Therapy Institute.

Gable, S.L. (2006) Approach and avoidance social motives and goals. *Journal of Personality*, 71, 175–222.

Gable, S.L., Reis, H.T., Impett, E.A. and Asher, E.R. (2004) What do you do when things go right? The intrapersonal and interpersonal benefits of sharing positive events. *Journal of Personality and Social Psychology*, 87, 2, 228–245.

Gilbert, P. (2010) *Compassion Focused Therapy*. The CBT Distinctive Features Series. New York: Routledge.

Gladwell, M. (2005) *Blink*. London: Penguin.

Glass, C. (2009) Exploring What Works: is SF the best way of harnessing the impact of positive psychology in the workplace? *Interaction: The Journal of Solution Focus in Organisations*, 1, 1, 26–41.

Gollwitzer, P.M. (1999) Implementation intentions: strong effects of simple plans. *American Psychologist*, 54, 7, 493–503.

Gordon, K.C., Baucom, D.H., Epstein, N., *et al.* (1999) The interaction between marital standards and communication patterns. *Journal of Marital and Family Therapy*, 25, 211–223.

Goldstein, N.J., Martin, S.J. and Cialdini, R.B. (2007) *Yes! 50 secrets from the science of prsuasion*. London: Profile Books.

Gottman, J.M. (1994) *What Predicts Divorce? The Relationship Between Marital Processes and Marital Outcomes*. New York: Erlbaum.

Grant, A.M. and O'Connor, S.A. (2010) The differential effects of solution-focused and problem-focused coaching questions: a pilot study with implications for practice. *Industrial and Commercial Training*, 42, 4, 102–111.

References

Green, L.S., Oades, L.G., and Grant, A.M. (2006) Cognitive-behavioural, solution-focused life coaching: Enhancing goal striving, well-being, and hope. *The Journal of Positive Psychology*, 1, 3, 142–149.

Grotberg, E.H. (1995) *A Guide to Promoting Resilience in Children: Strengthening the Human Spirit*. The Hague: The Bernard van Leer Foundation.

Grotberg, E.H. (2003) *Resilience for Today: Gaining Strength from Adversity*. Westport, CT: Praeger.

Hackmann, A., Bennett-Levy, J., and Holmes, E.A. (2011) *Oxford Guide to Imagery in Cognitive Therapy*. New York: Oxford University Press.

Haidt, J. (2006) *The Happiness Hypothesis: Finding Modern Truth in Ancient Wisdom*. New York: Basic Books.

Hannan, C., Lambert, M.J., Harmon, C., *et al.* (2005) A lab test and algorithms for identifying clients at risk for treatment failure. *Journal of Clinical Psychology*, 61, 2, 155–163.

Hawton, K., Salkovskis, P.M., Kirk, J., and Clark, D.M. (1995) *Cognitive Behaviour Therapy for Psychiatric Problems: a Practical Guide*. Oxford: Oxford University Press.

Hayes, S.C., Strosahl, K.D., and Wilson, K.G. (2003) *Acceptance and Commitment Therapy: An Experiential Approach to Behaviour Change*. New York: Guilford.

Heath, C. and Heath, D. (2010) *Switch. How to Change Things When Change is Hard*. London: Random House.

Heiden, C. van der (2011) On the Diagnosis, Assessment, and Treatment of Generalized Anxiety Disorder. Rotterdam: Thesis Erasmus University.

Hershberger, P.J. (2005) Prescribing happiness: positive psychology and family medicine. *Family Medicine*, 37, 9, 630–634.

Hiatt, D. and Hargrave, G.E. (1995) The characteristics of highly effective therapists in managed behavioral providers networks. *Behavioral Healthcare Tomorrow*, 4, 19–22.

Histed, M.H., Pasupathy, A., and Miller, E.K. (2009) Learning substrates in the primary prefrontal cortex and striatum: sustained activity related to successful actions. *Neuron*, 63, 244–253.

Hoebel, B.G., Avena, N.M., and Rada, P. (2008) An accumbens dopamine-acetylcholine system for approach and avoidance. In A.J. Elliot (ed.) *Handbook of Approach and Avoidance Motivation*, New York: Psychology Press, pp. 89–107.

Holmes, E.A., Lang, T.A., and Deeprose, C. (2009) Mental imagery and emotion in treatments across disorders: Using the example of depression. *Cognitive Behaviour Therapy*, 38, 21–28.

Impett, E., Gable, S.L., and Peplau, L.A. (2005) Giving up and giving in; the costs and benefits of daily sacrifice in intimate relationships. *Journal of Personality and Social Psychology*, 89, 327–344.

International Cognitive Therapy Newsletter (1991), 6, 6–7.

Isaacowitz, D.M., Vaillant, G.E., and Seligman, M.E.P. (2003) Strengths and satisfaction across the adult lifespan. *International Journal of Ageing and Human Development*, 57, 181–201.

Isen, A.M. (2005) A role for neuropsychology in understanding the facilitating influence of positive affect on social behaviour and cognitive processes. In C.R. Snyder and S.J. Lopez, *Handbook of Positive Psychology*, New York: Oxford University Press, pp. 528–540.

Isen, A.M. and Reeve, J. (2005) The influence of positive affect on intrinsic and extrinsic motivation: facilitating enjoyment of play, responsible work behaviour, and self-control. *Motivation and Emotion*, 29, 4, 297–325.

References

Isen, A.M., Rosenzweig, A.S., and Young, M.J. (1991) The influence of positive affect on clinical problem solving. *Medical Decision Making*, 11, 221–227.

Kabat-Zinn, J. (1994) *Wherever You Go, There You Are: Mindfulness Meditation in Everyday Life*. New York: Hyperion.

Keyes, C.L.M. and Lopez, S.J. (2005) Toward a science of mental health. In C.R. Snyder and S.J. Lopez, *Handbook of Positive Psychology*, New York: Oxford University Press.

King, L.A. (2001) The health benefits of writing about life goals, *Personality and Social Psychology Bulletin*, 27, 798–807.

Klaver, M. and Bannink, F.P. (2010) Oplossingsgerichte therapie bij patienten met niet-aangeboren hersenletsel (Solution-focused therapy with patients with brain injury). *Tijdschrift voor Neuropsychologie*, 5, 2, 11–19.

Kopelman, S., Rosette, A.S., and Thompson, L. (2006) The three faces of Eve: strategic displays of positive, negative, and neutral emotions in negotiations. *Organizational Behaviour and Human Decision Processes*, 99, 81–101.

Korrelboom, C.W., Jong, M. de, Huijbrechts I., and Daansen P. (2009) Competitive Memory Training (COMET) for treating low self-esteem in patients with eating disorders: a randomized clinical trial. *Journal of Consulting and Clinical Psychology*, 77, 974–980.

Krakow, B. (2004) Imagery rehearsal therapy for chronic posttraumatic nightmares: a mind's eye view. In R.I. Rosner, W.J. Lyddon, and A. Freeman (eds), *Cognitive Therapy and Dreams*, New York: Springer, pp. 89–109.

Kranz, D., Bollinger, A., and Nilges, P. (2010) Chronic pain acceptance and affective well-being: a coping perspective. *European Journal of Pain*, 14, 10, 1021–1025.

Kuiper, E.C. and Bannink, F.P. (2012) Veerkracht, een pleidooi voor het bevorderen van veerkracht in de jeugdhulpverlening (Resilience, a plea for enhancing resilience in youth care). Kind en Adolescent Praktijk, 3/2012.

Kuyken, W., Padesky, C.A., and Dudley, R. (2009) *Collaborative Case Conceptualization*. New York: Guilford.

Lally, P., Jaarsveld, C. van, Potts, H., and Wardle, J. (2010) How are habits formed: modelling habit formation in the real world. *European Journal of Social Psychology*, 40, 998–1009.

Lamarre, J. and Gregoire, A. (1999) Competence transfer in solution-focused therapy: Harnessing a natural resource. *Journal of Systemic Therapies*, 18, 1, 43–57.

Lambert, M.J. and Ogles, B.M. (2004) The efficacy and effectiveness of psychotherapy. In M.L. Lambert (ed.), *Bergin and Garfield's Handbook of Psychotherapy and Behaviour Change* (fifth edition), Hoboken: John Wiley & Sons, Inc, pp. 139–193.

Lambert, M.J., Whipple, J.L., Vermeersch, D.A., et al. (2002) Enhancing psychotherapy outcomes via providing feedback on patient progress: a replication. *Clinical Psychology and Psychotherapy*, 9, 91–103.

Leary, T. (1957) *Interpersonal Diagnosis of Personality*. New York: Ronald.

Lefcourt, H.M. (2005) Humor. In C.R. Snyder and S.J. Lopez, *Handbook of Positive Psychology*, New York: Oxford University Press, pp. 619–631.

Libby, L.K., Eibach, R.P., and Gilovich, R. (2005) Here's looking at me: the effect of memory perspective on assessments of personal change. *Journal of Personality and Social Psychology*, 88, 1, 50–62.

Lieberman, M.D., Eisenberger, N.I., Crockett, M.J., et al. (2007) Putting feelings into words. *Psychological Science*, 18, 5, 421–428.

Lindaman, E. and Lippitt, R. (1979) *Choosing the Future You Prefer*. Ann Arbor, MI: HRDA Press.

References

Linehan, M.M. (1993). *Cognitive Behavioural Treatment of Borderline Personality disorder.* New York: Guilford.

Litt, A. (2010) Lusting while loathing: parallel counterdriving of wanting and liking. *Psychological Science,* 21, 1, 118–125.

Losada, M.F. and Heaphy, E. (2004) The role of positivity and connectivity in the performance of business teams: a nonlinear dynamics model. *American Behavioral Scientist,* 47, 6, 740–765.

Lyubomirsky, S. (2008) *The How of Happiness.* New York: Penguin.

Macdonald, A.J. (2011) *Solution-Focused Therapy. Theory, Research & Practice* (second edition). London: Sage.

Masten, A.S. (2001) Ordinary magic: resilience processes in development. *American Psychologist,* 56, 227–238.

McKay, K.M., Imel, Z.E., and Wampold, B.E. (2006) Psychiatrist effect in the psychopharmacological treatment of depression. *Journal of Affective Disorders,* 92, 2–3, 287–290.

McKergow, M. (2009) Leader as host, host as leader; towards a new yet ancient metaphor. *International Journal for Leadership in Public Services,* 5, 1, 19–24.

Menninger, K. (1959) The academic lecture: Hope. *The American Journal of Psychiatry,* 12, 481–491.

Metcalf, L. (1998) *Solution Focused Group Therapy.* New York: Free Press.

Miller, W.R. and Rollnick, S. (2002) *Motivational Interviewing: Preparing People to Change* (second edition). New York: Guilford.

Miller, S.D., Duncan, B., and Hubble, M.A. (1997) *Escape from Babel: Toward a Unifying Language for Psychotherapy Practice.* New York: Norton.

Miller, S.D., Hubble, M. A., and Duncan, B. L. (eds). (1996) *The Handbook of Solution-Focused Brief Therapy: Foundations, Applications and Research.* San Francisco: Jossey-Bass.

Miller, S.D., Hubble, M.A., and Duncan, B.L. (2007) Supershrinks: learning from the field's most effective practitioners. *The Psychotherapy Networker,* 31, 6, 26–35.

Mischel, W. and Ayduk, O. (2004) Willpower in a cognitive-affective processing system: the dynamics of delay of gratification. In R.F. Baumeister and K.D. Vohs (eds), *Handbook of Self-Regulation: Research, Theory, and Applications,* New York: Guilford, pp. 99–129.

Mischel, W., Shoda, Y., and Rodriguez, M.L. (1989) Delay of Gratification in Children. *Science,* 244, 933–938.

Moskowitz, J.T. and Epel, E.S. (2006) Benefit Finding and Diurnal Cortisol Slope in Maternal Caregivers: A Moderating Role for Positive Emotion. *Journal of Positive Psychology,* 1, 83–92.

Moskowitz, G.B. and Grant, H. (eds) (2009) *The Psychology of Goals.* New York: Guilford.

Murray, S.L., Holmes, J.G., and Griffin, D.W. (2003) Reflections on the self-fulfilling effects of positive illusions. *Psychological Inquiry,* 14, 289–295.

Myers, D.G. (2000) The funds, friends and faith of happy people. *American Psychologist,* 55, 56–67.

Nolen-Hoeksema, S. (2000) Growth and resilience among bereaved people. In J.E. Gillham (ed.), *The Science of Optimism & Hope. Research Essays in Honor of Martin E.P. Seligman* (pp. 107–127). Philadelphia: Templeton Foundation Press.

Nolen-Hoeksema, S. and Davis, C.G. (2005) Positive responses to loss. In C.R. Snyder and S.J. Lopez, *Handbook of Positive Psychology,* New York: Oxford University Press, pp. 598–607.

References

Norcross, J.C. (2002) Empirically supported therapy relationships. In J.C. Norcross (ed.), *Psychotherapy Relationships That Work: Therapist Contributions and Responsiveness to Patients*. New York: Oxford University Press.

Oettingen, G. (1999) Free fantasies about the future and the emergence of developmental goals. In J. Brandtstadter and R.M. Lerner (eds), *Action & Self-Development: Theory and Research Through the Life Span*, Thousand Oaks, CA: Sage, pp. 315–342.

Oettingen, G. and Stephens, E.J. (2009) Fantasies and Motivationally Intelligent Goal Setting. In G.B. Moskowitz and H. Grant, *The Psychology of Goals*, New York: Guilford, pp. 153–178.

Oettingen, G., Hönig, G., and Gollwitzer, P. M. (2000) Effective Self-Regulation of Goal Attainment. *International Journal of Educational Research*, 33, 705–732.

Oettingen, G., Pak, H., and Schnetter, K. (2001) Self-regulation of goal setting: turning free fantasies about the future into binding goals. *Journal of Personality and Social Psychology*, 80, 5, 736–753.

O'Hanlon, B. (1999) *Evolving Possibilities*. Philadelphia: Brunner/Mazel.

O'Hanlon, B. (2000) *Do One Thing Different*. New York: Harper Collins.

O'Hanlon, B. and Rowan, R. (2003) *Solution Oriented Therapy for Chronic and Severe Mental Illness*. New York: Norton.

Ong, A.D., Bergeman, C.S., Bisconti, T.L., and Wallace, K.A. (2006) Psychological resilience, positive emotions, and successful adaptation to stress in later life. *Journal of Personality and Social Psychology*, 91, 730–749.

Orlinsky, D. and Ronnestad, M.H. (2005) *How Psychotherapists Develop: A Study of Therapeutic Work and Professional Growth*. Washington DC: American Psychological Association.

Oyserman, D., Bybee, D., & Terry, K. (2006) Possible selves and academic outcomes: how and when possible selves impel action. *Journal of Personality and Social Psychology*, 91, 1, 188–204.

Panksepp, J. (1998) *Affective Neuroscience*. New York: Oxford University Press.

Papp, P. (1983) *The Process of Change*. New York: Guilford.

Peacock, F. (2001) *Water the Flowers, Not the Weeds*. Montreal: Open Heart.

Peterson, C. (2006) The Values in Action (VIA) Classification of Strengths: The un-DSM and the real DSM. In M. Csikszentmihalyi and I. Csikszentmihalyi (eds), *A Life Worth Living: Contributions to Positive Psychology*, New York: Oxford University Press, pp. 29–48.

Piper, W.E., Ogrodniczuk, J.S., Joyce, A.S. *et al.* (1999) Prediction of dropping out in time-limited, interpretive individual psychotherapy. *Psychotherapy: Theory, Research, Practice, Training*, 36, 2, 114–122.

Plaud, J.J. (2001) *Positive reinforcement*. Living & Learning, 1, 3.

Pope, K.S. and Tabachnick, B.G. (1994) Therapists as patients: a national survey of psychologists' experiences, problems, and beliefs. *Professional Psychology: Research and Practice*, 25, 247–258.

Prochaska, J.O., Norcross, J.C., and DiClemente, C.C. (1994) *Changing for Good*. New York: Morrow.

Raue, P.J. and Goldfried, M.R. (1994) The therapeutic alliance in cognitive behavioural therapy. In A.O. Horvath and L.S. Greenberg (eds), *The Working Alliance: Theory, Research and Practice*, Hoboken: John Wiley & Sons, Inc, pp. 131–152.

Rock, D. (2009) *Your Brain at Work*. New York: HarperCollins.

Roeden, J.M., and Bannink, F.P. (2007a) *Handboek Oplossingsgericht Werken Met Licht Verstandelijk Beperkte Clienten* (Handbook for Solution-Focused Interviewing With Clients With Mild Intellectual Disabilities). Amsterdam: Pearson.

References

Roeden, J.M., and Bannink, F.P. (2007b) *Hoe organiseer ik een etentje? Oplossingsgerichte gedragstherapie met een verstandelijk beperkte vrouw* (How do I organize a dinner? Solution-focused behavioral therapy with a woman with an intellectual disability). *Gedragstherapie*, 40, 4, 251–268.

Roeden, J.M., and Bannink, F.P. (2009) Solution focused brief therapy with persons with intellectual disabilities. *Journal of Policy and Practice in Intellectual Disabilities*, 6, 4, 253–259.

Rosenhan, J. (1973) On being sane in insane places. *Science*, 179, 250–258.

Ross, M., and Wilson, A.E. (2002) It feels like yesterday: self-esteem, valence of personal past experiences, and judgements of subjective distance. *Journal of Personality and Social Psychology*, 82, 792–803.

Rossi, E.L. (eds) (1980) *The Nature of Hypnosis and Suggestion by Milton Erickson* (collected papers). New York: Irvington.

Rothman, A.J. (2000) Toward a theory-based analysis of behavioural maintenance. *Health Psychology*, 19, 64–69.

Rowe, G., Hirsh, J.B., and Anderson, A.K. (2007) Positive affect increases the breadth of attentional selection. *Proceedings of the National Academy of Sciences of the United States of America*, 104, 383–388.

Ruini, C., and Fava, G.A. (2004) Clinical applications of well-being therapy. In P. A. Linley and S. Joseph (eds), *Positive psychology in practice*, Hoboken: John Wiley & Sons, Inc, pp. 371–387.

Saleebey, D. (ed.) (2007) *The Strengths Perspective in Social Work Practice*. Boston: Allyn & Bacon.

Sapyta, J., Riemer, M., and Bickman, L. (2005) Feedback to Clinicians: Theory, Research and Practice. *Journal of Clinical Psychology*, 61, 2, 145–153.

Selekman, M.D. (1993) *Pathways to Change: Brief Therapy Solutions with Difficult Adolescents*. New York: Guilford.

Selekman, M. D. (1997) *Solution-Focused Therapy With Children: Harnessing Family Strengths for Systemic Change*. New York: Guilford.

Seligman, M.E.P. (2002) *Authentic Happiness*. London: Brealey.

Seligman, M.E.P. (2005) Positive Psychology, Positive Prevention, and Positive Therapy. In C.R. Snyder & S.J. Lopez (eds), *Handbook of Positive Psychology*, London: Oxford University Press, pp. 3–9.

Seligman, M.E.P. (2011) *Flourish*. New York: Free Press.

Seligman, M.E.P., and Csikszentmihalyi, M. (2000) Positive psychology: an introduction. *American Psychologist*, 55, 5–14.

Seligman, M.E.P., Reivich, K., Jaycox, L., and Gilham, J. (1995) *The Optimistic Child*. Boston: Joughton Mifflin.

Seligman, M.E.P., Steen, T.A., Park, N., and Peterson, C. (2005) Positive Psychology progress. Empirical validation of interventions. *American Psychologist*, 60, 5, 410–421.

Shapiro, F. (2001) *EMDR: Eye Movement Desensitization and Reprocessing: Basic Principles, Protocols and Procedures* (second edition). New York: Guilford.

Sharot, T. (2011) *The Optimism Bias*. New York: Random House.

Siegel, D.J. (1999) *The Developing Mind*. New York: Guilford.

Siegel, D.J. (2001) Toward an interpersonal neurobiology of the developing mind: attachment relationships, 'mindsight' and neural integration. *Infant Mental Health Journal*, 22, 67–94.

Siegel, D.J. (2010) *Mindsight. The New Science of Personal Transformation*. New York: Bantam Books.

References

Smock, S., Froerer, A., and Bavelas, J.B. (article forthcoming) Microanalysis of positive and negative content in solution focused brief therapy and cognitive behavioral therapy expert sessions.

Snyder, C.R. (1994) *The Psychology of Hope:You Can Get There From Here*. New York: Free Press.

Snyder, C.R. (2002) Hope theory: Rainbows in the mind. *Psychological Inquiry*, 13, 249–275.

Snyder, C.R. and Lopez, S.J. (2005) *Handbook of Positive Psychology*. New York: Oxford Univeristy Press.

Snyder, C.R., Lapointe, A.B., Crowson, J.J., and Early, S. (1998) Preferences of high- and low-hope people for self-referential input. *Cognition and Emotion*, 12, 807–823.

Snyder, C.R., Michael, S.T., and Cheavens, J. (1999) Hope as a psychotherapeutic foundation of common factors, placebos, and expectancies. In M.A. Hubble, B. Duncan, and S. Miller (eds), *The Heart and Soul of Change*, Washington DC: American Psychological Association, pp. 179–200.

Snyder, C.R., Rand, K.L., and Sigmon, D.R. (2005) Hope theory: A member of the positive psychology family. In C.R. Snyder and S.J. Lopez (eds), *Handbook of Positive Psychology*, London: Oxford University Press, pp. 257–276.

Stam, P., and Bannink, F.P. (2008) De oplossingsgerichte organisatie (The solution-focused organization). *Tijdschrift VKJP*, 35, 2, 62–72.

Stams, G.J., Dekovic, M., Buist, K., and Vries, L. de (2006) Effectiviteit van oplossings-gerichte korte therapie: een meta-analyse (The efficacy of solution-focused brief therapy; a meta-analysis). *Gedragstherapie*, 39, 2, 81–94.

Steptoe, A., Wardle, J., and Marmot, M. (2005) Positive affect and health-related neuroendocrine, cardiovascular, and inflammatory responses. *Proceedings of the National Academy of Sciences*, 102, 6508–6512.

Tamir, M. and Diener, E. (2008) Approach-avoidance goals and well-being: one size does not fit all. In A.J. Elliot (ed.), *Handbook of Approach and Avoidance Motivation*. New York: Psychology Press, pp. 415–428.

Tamir, M., Mitchell, C., and Gross, J. J. (2008) Hedonic and instrumental motives in anger regulation. *Psychological Science*, 19, 324–328.

Tedeschi, R.G. and Calhoun, L. (2004) Posttraumatic growth: a new perspective on psychotraumatology. *Psychiatric Times*, 21, 4.

The British Psychological Society (2011) Response to the American Psychiatric Association: DSM-5 development. http://apps.bps.org.uk/_publicationfiles/consultation-responses/DSM-5%202011%20-%20BPS%20response.pdf

Tomori, C. and Bavelas, J.B. (2007) Using microanalysis of communication to compare solution-focused and client centered therapies. *Journal of Family Psychotherapy*, 18, 3, 25–43.

Tompkins, P. and Lawley, J. (2003) *Metaphors in Mind*. London: Developing Company Press.

Turner, C., Spencer, M.B., and Stone, B.M. (2005) Effect of working patterns of UK train drivers on fatigue—a diary study. *Shiftwork International Newsletter*, 22, 150.

Vaillant, G.E. (1995) *Adaptation to Life*. Cambridge MA: Harvard University Press.

Vasquez, N.A. and Buehler, R. (2007) Seeing future success: Does imagery perspective influence achievement motivation? *Personality and Social Psychology Bulletin*, 33, 10, 1392–1405.

Walter, J.L. and Peller, J. E. (1992) *Becoming Solution-Focused in Brief Therapy*. New York: Brunner/Mazel.

References

Walter, J.L., and Peller, J.E. (2000) *Recreating Brief Therapy: Preferences and Possibilities*. New York: Norton.

Wampold, B.E. (2001) *The Great Psychotherapy Debate: Models, Methods and Findings*. Hillsdale NJ: Erlbaum.

Wampold, B.E. and Bhati, K.S. (2004) Attending to the omissions: a historical examination of evidence-based practice movements. *Professional Psychology: Research and Practice*, 35, 6, 563–570.

Watzlawick, P. (1976) *How Real is Real?* New York: Random House.

Watzlawick, P., Weakland, J.H., and Fisch, R. (1974) *Change: Principles of Problem Formation and Problem Resolution*. New York: Norton.

Weiner-Davis, M., De Sahzer, S., and Gingerich, W.J. (1987). Building on pretreatment change to construct the therapeutic solution: an exploratory study. *Journal of Marital and Family Therapy*, 13, 4, 359–363.

Wells, A. (1995) Metacognition and worry: a cognitive model of generalized anxiety disorder. *Behavioural and Cognitive Psychotherapy*, 23, 301–320.

Wells, A. (1997) *Cognitive Therapy of Anxiety Disorders: A Practical Manual and Cconceptual Guide*. Chichester, John Wiley & Sons, Ltd.

Westra, J. and Bannink, F.P. (2006a) 'Simpele' oplossingen! Oplossingsgericht werken bij mensen met een lichte verstandelijke beperking, deel 1 ('Simple' solutions! Solution-focused interviewing with people with mild intellectual disabilities, part 1). *PsychoPraxis*, 8, 4, 158–162.

Westra, J. and Bannink, F.P. (2006b) 'Simpele' oplossingen! Oplossingsgericht werken bij mensen met een lichte verstandelijke beperking, deel 2 ('Simple' solutions! Solution-focused interviewing with people with mild intellectual disabilities, part 2). *PsychoPraxis* 8, 5, 213–218.

White, M. and Epston, D. (1990) *Narrative means to therapeutic ends*. New York: Norton.

Wilson, T.D., Centerbar, D.B., Kermer, D.A., and Gilbert, D.T. (2005) The pleasures of uncertainty: prolonging positive moods in ways people do not anticipate. *Journal of Personality and Social Psychology*, 88, 1, 5–21.

Wittgenstein, L. (1968) *Philosophical Investigations* (G.E.M. Anscombe, Trans., third edition). New York: Macmillan. (Originally published in 1953)

Yalom, I.D. (2008) *The Gift of Therapy*. New York: HarperCollins.

Young, J.E., Klosko, J.S., and Beck, A.T. (1994) *Reinventing Your Life: How to Break Free from Negative Life Patterns and Feel Good Again*. New York: Penguin.

Youssef, C.M. and Luthans, F. (2007) Positive organizational behaviour in the workplace: the impact of hope, optimism, and resiliency. *Journal of Management*, 33, 774–800.

Zimmerman, M., McGlinchey, J.B., Posternak, M.A., *et al.* (2006) How should remission from depression be defined? The depressed patient's perspective. *American Journal of Psychiatry*, 163, 148–150.

Author Index

Subject Index

ABC model
  Ellis 37, 225
  of psychological disturbance and change
    118–119
acceptance and commitment therapy
  (ACT) 24, 28–29
  and mindfulness 110
acetylcholine 56
acknowledgement of problems 65–66
act of kindness 164
action triggers 130–131
ADHD 26
affect labeling 139
agency thinking 43, 69, 80
alliances *see* therapeutic alliances
amygdala 54, 57, 58, 139
amygdala whisperers 54
anger 146
APA Presidential Task Force on Evidence-
  Based Practice 165
applied relaxation 26
appreciation wall exercise 245
appreciative inquiry 244–245
approach emotions 83, 210, 220
approach goals 56, 82–87, 115, 146,
  209–210
assessment 77–98
  case conceptualization 77–78
  goals 79–87
  of motivation to change 93
  positive functional behavior analysis
    95–98
  positive self-monitoring 93–95

of problems, complaints and constraints
  87–88
of progress, motivation, hope and
  confidence 90–92
of strengths and resources 88–90
authentic happiness theory 36
Authentic Happiness web site 37, 88,
  164, 224
avoidance goals 56, 82–87, 115, 146,
  209–210

behavior change 72
behavior maintenance 180–185
behavioral experiments 136–137,
  160–165, 228
  discovery-oriented experiments
    136–137
  experimental manipulation of the
    environment 136, 137
  observational experiments 136, 137
behavioral tasks 155, 162, 177, 273
beliefs 21
  unhelpful beliefs 115–124
benzodiazepines 59
blame stories 100
borderline personality disorder 26, 29
brain, the 51–52
  plasticity of 52–53
bright spots 101–102
British Psychological Society 8
broaden-and-build theory of positive
  emotions 40, 140, 142–143, 147,
  241, 247

Practicing Positive CBT: From Reducing Distress to Building Success, First Edition. Fredrike Bannink.
© 2012 John Wiley & Sons, Ltd. Published 2012 by John Wiley & Sons, Ltd.